The Pulse of Creation

The Pulse of Creation
God and the Transformation of the World

PAUL R. SPONHEIM

FORTRESS PRESS
Minneapolis

THE PULSE OF CREATION
God and the Transformation of the World

Cover design: Craig Claeys; cover photo © 1999 Photodisc, Inc.
Interior design: Beth Wright

Unless otherwise noted, Scripture quotations are from the New Revised Standard Version of the Bible, copyright © 1989 by the Division of Christian Education of the National Council of Churches of Christ in the United States of America, and are used by permission.

The publisher gratefully acknowledges permission to reprint the following material:
"Fire and Ice" by Robert Frost, p. 220 in *The Poetry of Robert Frost*, ed. Edward Connery Lathem, copyright © 1951 Robert Frost, © 1923, 1969 Henry Holt and Company.
Text from "Denegating God," by Mark C. Taylor, in *Critical Inquiry*, Summer 1994 (pp. 592–610), copyright © 1994 University of Chicago Press.
Text from p. 2 of *Ceremony* by Leslie Silko, copyright © 1977 Leslie Silko; used by permission of Viking Penguin, a division of Penguin Putnam, Inc.
"Bi-Focal" from *The Way It Is: New and Selected Poems* by William Stafford, copyright © 1960, 1998 Estate of William Stafford; used by permission of Graywolf Press.
Text from "Agnus Dei" from "Mass for the Day of St. Thomas Didymus," pp. 114–15, and from "Many Mansions," p. 116, in *Candles in Babylon* by Denise Levertov, copyright © 1982 Denise Levertov; used by permission of New Directions Publishing Corp. and Gerald Pollinger, Ltd.
Text from "Answer to Our Leftist Friends Who Ask Us Why We Pray," p. 24, in *Revolutionary Patience* by Dorothee Soelle, translated by Rita and Robert Kimber, copyright © 1974 Wolfgang Fietkau Verlag, translation copyright © 1977 Orbis Books.
Poem on p. 38 from *New and Selected Poems*, by Mary Oliver copyright © 1992 Beacon Press.

Library of Congress Cataloging-in-Publication Data

Sponheim, Paul R.
    The pulse of creation : God and the transformation of the world /
Paul R. Sponheim.
        p.   cm.
    Includes bibliographical references and index.
    ISBN 0-8006-3188-9 (pbk. : alk. paper)
    1. Creation.   I. Title.
BT695.S68   1999
231.7'65—dc21   99-16998
                                                                      CIP

The paper used in this publication meets the minimum requirements of American National Standard for Information Sciences—Permanence of Paper for Printed Library Materials, ANSI Z329.48-1984.

Manufactured in the U.S.A.   AF 1-3188
03   02   01   00   99   1   2   3   4   5   6   7   8   9   10

Contents

Foreword

"Things happen," says Paul Sponheim. "So what?" you ask. I reply: "Plenty." As a starting point for theology, "things happen" locates us smack in the middle, and while *The Pulse of Creation: God and the Transformation of the World* takes us to the edges—to Genesis at the beginning, Revelation at the end—Paul keeps the center of gravity where and when it should be, the place and time of our life: here and now. Things happen.

Not so long ago if you picked up a theology book with "creation" in the title, you would expect to read about the orderliness of everything, arguments from design, all ducks in a row. It comes as a surprise, then, to find Paul making an "argument from interruption," with ducks flying all over the place. The God he knows is full of surprises, an imaginer more than an engineer. But this God is also faithful, trustworthy, though not to be taken for granted. As Paul says, "There are interruptions and then there are interruptions," and there is no guarantee that every one of them will be an occasion for transformation. "To be a human being is to be a candidate for interruption." This can be great, or things can get messed up, really messed up.

As I said, Paul Sponheim's theology locates us at the center, but, blessedly, we're not all he sees at the center. His book is part of a larger, and welcome, movement in theology these days: the recovery of the excitement and breadth and openness of a genuinely trinitarian point of view, one that resonates with Niels Bohr's response when Wolfgang Pauli, following a lecture on particle physics, said, "You probably think these ideas are crazy." "I do," responded Bohr, "but unfortunately they are not crazy enough." If we start with the Creator, without jumping too quickly to Christ (or, when we get to Christ, remembering "through whom all things were made"), and if we give the Spirit her due, the sharp distinction we too often make between "us" and "them"—"they" being all the other animal, vegetable, and mineral denizens of the cosmos—seems foolish. "Christian faith connects God with the other, and so with the new."

"The new." It's because he finds in Christian theology the God who is making all things new that Paul Sponheim preaches and teaches and writes the gospel. He knows that the new is coming to be in every corner—this book is about nothing short of the transformation of the world—whether the God of Christian theology is perceived there or not, but he believes that Christian theology is sufficiently supple and tensile to learn from and energize a whole universe's worth of change.

Paul presents careful, steady arguments, and he has many conversation partners, poets as well as theologians, and pre-eminently that endless source of fresh, ironic insight, Søren Kierkegaard. The scope of this book is impressive; we are clearly in the presence of someone who, with humility and tenacity, has learned the tradition thoroughly in order to add to it. But theology, like God, is in the details too, and I have enormous confidence in a theologian who puts silence and laughter together on the same page, prescribing "silence for the infernally chatty among us" and "laughter for the deadly serious." Every theological discussion needs less talk and more humor.

This book is full of motion. We hear of a God who moves outward, toward, and forward. We are on the way, not there yet. But we are not paralyzed. "It is the Creator of heaven and earth who calls people into service in the church council and the city council." How do we come to know? Paul quotes the great line from poet Theodore Roethke, "I learn by going where I have to go." "The Christian as Christian does know something," Paul says. But: "Christians do not honor Christ if they fail to distinguish between what is finished and what is not." And in the increasingly insistent encounter with other religious traditions, "It helps to know that Christians need not expect to have the answers in place before the conversation. To be that amply equipped might be to miss the living speaking of God."

Paul Sponheim has written a book that expands horizons and loosens up stiff spiritual joints. He says we are all immigrants, dislodged from foundations but with a "sense of possibility and movement." He is a reliable and companionable guide.

Patrick Henry
Institute for Ecumenical and Cultural Research
Collegeville, Minnesota

 Preface

I have written this book for two reasons: (1) I join many human beings in claiming that transformation is needed. We would be other than we are. We make this claim in words and in deeds, howsoever fragile and flawed, that would make a difference. The difficulties in delivery suggest we might be able to use whatever help a book can offer. (2) I join most Christians in believing that God wills and works to change things for the better and that the lives of Christians are to contribute to that change. This common Christian conviction needs to be argued the more strongly in the face of theological tendencies that discourage and demean human striving.

Thus both reasons have uphill going ahead of them. Marx's familiar identification of a Christian theology of the oppressed creature as opium carries forward in sharper form his judgment that "the philosophers have only *interpreted* the world in various ways; the point is, to *change* it."[1] That this is the point need not be held only by those dwindling numbers for whom Karl Marx still speaks with authority. Therefore in this book's first chapter I look about in this land to demonstrate the need and quest for transformation and ponder the ambiguity of American religion, its agony and ecstasy.

These reasons have moved me to write, and these two, the human and the Christian, have come together in the writing. I do write as a Christian and of the Christian. One of my concerns has been to lift up that "second kind of righteousness" of which Martin Luther preached—not the righteousness "that swallows up all our sins in a moment" but that alien righteousness that "begins, makes progress, and is finally perfected at the end through death."[2] But as I wrote in these last years of the twentieth century, it eventually became clear also to me that exhortations for the Christian colony were insufficient. Necessary, but insufficient. Predicament and resource were wider, far too wide to focus on the remnants of Christendom or even on the primitive outcroppings of something radically new in Christian existence. Moreover, as I reflected on "the Christian thing," it dawned on me that the logic of Christian faith itself pointed believers out beyond the walls of the sanctuary.[3] I might have expected as much. In earlier books I had urged Christians to consider the *conceptual* challenge of "the other."[4] Now I came to see the *moral* call Christians face to serve what is truly life-giving. The second chapter develops this point, that Christian obedience is to serve the Creator's will for life. Christian faith knows this: it is by the will of God that life is gift and task. For all. To be eligible for participation in God's transformation of the world one credential is required: to be a creature.

With the doctrine of creation, then, the needed scope is set. But what is "set" turns out to be a dynamic process, for, as Jesus said, the Creator is "working still" (John 5:17). Creation is living; it has a pulse. Creation continues. We could have learned this from contemporary science's privileging of energy over substance, or from the biblical writers in their praise of the living wisdom of creation. In any case, here the book finds its title and its heart, as chapters 3 through 5 set forth the pulse beat of interruption and calling in relationship. In each chapter the human and the Christian come together in the rhythm of creation. The book then closes by bringing this analysis back home to the Christian community to consider how servants of the Word may locate worlds in which to learn and serve.

The scope of my intent settled that this would be at best a sketch, given limitations of time and capacity. There can be special clarity in a sketch, and I hope that this book will serve in such a way. I realize, however, that the rather stark lines seen here may soften somewhat as other artists add body to what I seek to picture. Whitehead wisely said, "Seek simplicity, and distrust it!"[5] Even simply to sketch the shape of what God the Creator is up to requires a potentially confusing sampling, or better a weaving together, of many voices. The range of the participants in this conversation is essential, while the selection of speakers has some arbitrariness about it. Some missing voices can at least be mentioned here.

My colleague, Lee Snook, has contributed an important study of God's power, *What in the World Is God Doing?* This book was published in the summer of 1999 and hence is not cited in my text, though I gladly claim Lee's influence in my writing. I came upon Tyron L. Inbody's *The Transforming God: An Interpretation of Suffering and Evil* too late to let it be heard in the back-and-forth of the book.[6] He has most helpfully drawn the resource of process relational thought into conversation with biblical and trinitarian themes. I applaud the seriousness with which he confronts the problem of evil. I set that seriousness within a sense of the momentousness of "time with the other," even for God. Accordingly, I do not think a theistic account of original creation threatens the creature's freedom by offering the Creator an escape clause that can be exercised now or then.[7] I stand with Inbody in the call "to modify our triumphalism or theology of glory with some of Luther's theology of the cross."[8] Among the many other voices to be consulted are those of the scientists and theologians Nancey Murphy and her colleagues at Fuller Seminary gathered to ask *Whatever Happened to the Soul? Scientific and Theological Portraits of Human Nature.*[9] This book appeared too late for me to draw directly on its many insights, but I want here to signal the value of the "non-reductive physicalism" understanding emphasized in this volume by authors from a helpfully broad range of disciplines. I mention these three texts merely as a paltry sample of studies that have much to say in the ongoing conversation.

There are other voices that have made a difference directly in shaping this book's sketch. Along the way the following persons read and offered comment on all or part of the manuscript: Susan Black, John B. Cobb Jr., Terence Fretheim, Patrick Henry, Paul Martinson, Kirsten Ann Scribner Mebust, Kirsten Mickelson, Linda Nelson, Ann Pederson, Marjorie Suchocki, and Curtis Thompson. Ms. Mebust, a poet and theologian, was my student assistant during the last years of this project and contributed generously through her research and writing skills. I wish to thank the board of Luther Seminary and its president, Dr. David Tiede, for granting me sabbatical leave study time and for continuing support. Many staff colleagues at the seminary have contributed to my work on this manuscript. Some of them are named in notes. One who is not named there is Ms. Alice Loddigs, the faculty secretary, who has helped me in many ways. I spent a sabbatical semester at the Institute for Ecumenical and Cultural Research at St. John's University in Collegeville, Minnesota. I am grateful to the staff at the Institute and particularly to Dr. Patrick Henry, its director, for his support and guidance and for providing the generous foreword that greets the reader with the hospitable welcome visitors at St. John's know well. My colleagues there that semester contributed to a lively and nurturing matrix: Frances Adeney, Kari Borresen, Thomas Hand, Paul Johnson, Terry Muck, John Painter, Christine Pohl, and Jay Rock. My wife, Nell, has been a lifelong believer in the concept of transformation, and I thank her for the support and encouragement she has offered. Last but emphatically not least, I thank Henry French, editorial director at Fortress, for his support and guidance in bringing this book into print, and Beth Wright for her effectiveness as production editor.

I complete this preface in the term I finish my thirtieth year at Luther Seminary. I dedicate this volume to my students in my near-ly four decades in the classroom. In an early book I spoke of my debt to my teachers, and mentioned such men as Reidar Thomte and Jaroslav Pelikan. I remain grateful to such folks for their tutelage, even as I now would honor my students who have become my teach-ers. These two groups join others (some named above) in a commu-nity of colleagues who, clustered together in this little volume, speak a word that would be flesh, transformatively.

1. The Creation Groaning for Transformation

We know that the whole creation has been groaning in labor pains until now; and not only the creation, but we ourselves, who have the first fruits of the Spirit, groan inwardly while we wait for adoption, the redemption of our bodies.

—Romans 8:22-23

Groans get our attention, but we wonder what is going on. Groans do not seem clear or simple. Perhaps that is part of their inarticulateness: many things may lie behind or crowd together in such voicing. But experience has given us some context in which to hear the groaning meaningfully.[1] Creatures in pain often groan. Just so: one who sets out in end-of-twentieth-century America to write of transformation hears sounds that convey pain. We groan because we need transformation.

We Need Transformation

People living in the United States will likely not deny that the pervasive presence of violence and the threat of violence call out for change. A decade ago Cornel West sounded the alarm:

> . . . The most striking feature of contemporary American society is its sheer violence and brutality. Civic terrorism pervades the streets of our cities. Sexual violation and abuse are commonplace in our personal relationships. And many of our urban schools have become policed combat zones. By the year 2000, much of America may become uninhabitable—that is, it may be impossible to live here without daily fear for one's life.[2]

This is not a uniquely American problem, of course. In his bombshell article in the February 1994 *Atlantic*, Robert Kaplan began by remarking:

> Crime is what makes West Africa a natural point of departure for my report on what the political character of our planet is likely to be in the twenty-first century.[3]

We take little real comfort from the company of the many who are also experiencing this worldwide epidemic. Indeed it seems the

1

United States still might justly claim pride of place. We welcome with some skepticism the occasional news report indicating that the incidence of violent crimes in some cities has declined somewhat. Such news makes little impact upon the pervasive fear of becoming a victim. Some citizens have barricaded themselves in gated communities or voted for zoning restrictions on low-cost housing, only to find that violence does not respect the boundaries of class and income, age or gender. The specter of children shooting children in school cafeterias and on playgrounds returns us rather quickly to press the questions of the what and the how of such violence. We do not doubt that our society needs transformation.

Violence threatens us by its breadth, but perhaps even more by its depth. As we come to the end of this century of holocausts and ethnic cleansings, the camouflage of euphemism does not manage to cover what glares at us as clear-eyed evil. Nazis at mid-century and neo-Nazis now cannot be squeezed into some normalizing classification as overly enthusiastic patriots. The man who terrorizes his wife is not a helpless victim of explosive anger.[4]

Other elements seem quite objectively to cry out for transformation, almost as a groan's very inarticulateness witnesses to the brute presence of something that the propositions and perspectives of our minds could never produce. Citing the political and strategic impact of surging populations, deforestation, soil erosion, water depletion, and air pollution, Kaplan wrote that "it was time to understand 'the environment' for what it is: the national security issue of the early twenty-first century."[5] These problems are not something he or we made up. They may be of our making and how we think surely figures into the making, but the problems now bear their own efficacy as they return home to their makers, even as they reach out to threaten the innocent.[6] The hole in the ozone layer and the reduction of the rain forest are not matters confined to human consciousness. St. Paul seems newly right; the groaning comes not only from human creatures, but from creation itself.

How shall we understand this situation? What is at work here? The information age offers glimpses of a more complex world, a more diverse humanity. Does the reality of difference suggest that the presence and threat of violence find their source in the sheer fact of pluralism? Surely difference offers the potential for conflict, perhaps even providing the occasion for violence. What we meet out-side—the disturbing presence of the other—makes a difference inside us. Our own sense of reality is no longer available to us as a secure possession. We no longer feel settled at home in our percep-tions or our convictions. We may wonder how to protect ourselves, or even how to gain control over the relationships with others and dominion over the ground where the other meets us. "To be pure, one must act—so runs the logic of anxiety."[7] Clearly one must ask, what gives that logic life? Why in anxiety do I raise my fist against my neighbor? Why *this* act? Perhaps that question will still stand unanswered at the end of the day, but we make some headway by asking how human identity is understood within the operating logic of violence. To get at that, we must ponder the reality of individual-ism in Western culture.

Charles Taylor notes that "the very term 'identity' is somewhat anachronistic for premodern cultures . . . [since] the issue cannot arise in the reflexive, person-related terms that it does for us."[8] Indi-vidual selfhood emerged with the modern world and has become its significant image, the mark of our Western heritage. This sense of individual identity surely is not automatically the fit subject of repentance. Taylor points out that the notion of self is one of a devel-oping awareness among other beings such "that we cannot do with-out some orientation to the good, that we each essentially are (i.e., define ourselves at least inter alia by) where we stand on this."[9] He sharply criticizes those "modes of thought" that "tend to think we have selves the way we have hearts and livers."[10]

We are wisely warned against defining the individual in isolation, whether in celebration or lament. But while Taylor may be right that "one is only a self among other selves,"[11] we must also face up to the pernicious individualism that Robert Bellah and colleagues analyzed in *Habits of the Heart*. Their work gave attention to the fruit of a self normed and constituted by nothing beyond one's own skin:

> If the self is defined by its ability to choose its own values, on
> what grounds are those choices themselves based? For . . . many
> . . . there is simply no objectifiable criterion for choosing one value
> or course of action over another. One's own idiosyncratic prefer-
> ences are their own justification, because they define the true self.
> . . . The right act is simply the one that yields the agent the most
> exciting challenge or the most good feeling about itself.[12]

Defining myself by myself may not strictly require that I dominate the other, but this slope is surely a slippery one. The self-normed self stands at the end of a long historical development reaching back to René Descartes. Descartes could not doubt his own existence, but he needed an appeal to a non-deceiving God to assure himself of the existence of the world.[13] He found clarity and certainty in his own conscious self-knowledge, even to the point of measuring the world by the criteria of his own ideas. Later, in a strangely similar way, David Hume insisted that trustworthy knowing must begin with the raw data of the senses, which the subjective self actively orders, creating a reality for itself from what can be seen, touched, tasted, and felt. In both cases, the testimony or even the existence of another is suspect unless it can be verified or manipulated by the subjective self.

Another way to speak of our extreme contemporary individualism is to speak of the collapse of the world into the self. How would that be the "end" of the modern world? Stephen Toulmin has spoken of the self-world distinction/relation as the "chief girder in the framework of modernity."[14] He calls the world where Descartes and Hume both lived "cosmopolis," the place where self and world are in synch. In that place subjective perceptions could be trusted to correspond to reality that was reliably mechanistic, predictable in its yielding to our understanding and control. We do not live there anymore, if it is the case that the world has collapsed into the self.[15]

Judith Jordan identifies four formative influences in the modern world that have contributed to the sovereignty of the self. Newtonian physics defined a world with separate entities acting on one another in ways that can be measured. This physics then became the model for psychology, a modern science of the self. Western democracy with its reverence for the individual and personal freedoms began to rule more and more of the political world. Western culture conceived child-rearing as the task of pushing a helpless, dependent infant toward self-sufficiency and independence from the primary relationships of parents, grandparents, and siblings. This new culture and new science began to speak in new ways of the individual mind and self. Human development came to be understood as a process of fencing off the self from the other, shoring up the defenses of the person's ego, fulfilling the need of the individual self for freedom and protection from assault by both internal and external demands.[16] Down the road leading out from a self so understood lie gated communities and zoning restrictions. These complex developments, inner and outer, have some appeal. But the gains come at a cost.

Jean Baker Miller offers this interpretation of Erik Erikson's influential understanding of self-development, one of the crowning achievements of twentieth century behavioral science:

> . . . After the first stage, in which the aim is the development of basic trust, the aim of every other stage, until young adulthood, is some form of increased separation or self-development. . . . When the individual arrives at the stage called "intimacy," he is supposed to be able to be intimate with another person—having spent all of his prior development striving for something very different.[17]

Therefore, according to Erikson's model, the stream of human development must direct the self away from identification with and dependence on the other. Perhaps the modern spirit moved us toward self-possession and self-control. History has shown that such self-possession has often led in the direction of an imperial sense of possession and control of the other. But toward what are such modern currents moving us now? One could say that in "postmodern" developments the modern world is at an end. Or one might say that in the deconstructive postmodern collapse modernism reaches its end. When the individual increasingly withdraws into a self-defined reality, which no other can share, what can the objective "world" reliably mean? Similarly, modern "man" rose up against entrenched superstition and privilege. This has reached its full circle as well. Where are we now? John B. Cobb Jr. has put the matter so:

> Modernity has been a long series of critiques of reason, at least of the full-orbed reason of medieval thinkers. Deconstruction carries this critique to its logical conclusion. It uses the methods of modernity to undercut all the positive content of modernity.[18]

The academy has not been much help in stemming this tide. At the university we find the self of a scientist eschewing the vaunted objectivity of a "scientific method" and coming very clean about her social location in setting a research program. Acknowledgment that scientific data are theory-laden is certainly appropriate, but in steering away so vigorously from the mirage of objectivism, might one not end up in the ditch on the other side of the road? In the laboratory (or at least in the Philosophy of Science seminar) real world truth claims seem strangely out of fashion. And down the hall a philosopher tells us that the proper role of philosophy is not to "mirror" some supposed real world but to edify the self.[19]

Of course, when the world collapses into the self, the self does not remain unchanged. Without external referents, the self also wavers and collapses, as when a tent's stakes are pulled out of the ground, and then its walls and poles give way. One might speak of the self "imploding." On the other hand, we seem left with a scattered self as if we are dealing with the debris of an explosion. Jean Bethke Elshtain speaks of "families imploding and crime exploding."[20] Hardly a "trace" of the Cartesian ego remains.[21] The bars intended as defenses for the ego become a kind of isolation cell from which we observe but cannot partake in space-time. The self cut off from its constitutive relationships occupies a lonely world. That loneliness may take a temporal form, as we have come to think of the past as simply and thus irrelevantly past, and of the future, not yet palpable, as unreal. The self, compressed into the present moment, doubts the sustenance of the past or even the possibility of a future. Our communication choices are revealing. It shouldn't surprise us that the self, once nurtured by narratives of a past whose efficacy is not spent, is now being replaced by the viewer assaulted by the thirty-second sound byte.[22]

We Seek Transformation

Perhaps this line of analysis is too severe. Perhaps the groaning we hear is not simply a cry of pain, but also a cry of labor; the voicing of the strenuous struggle toward transformation. We who live in these United States know at least in some raw physical sense that we need transformation. But cannot more be credibly claimed? We actively seek transformation; we work at it.

Take, for example, the popular target of individualism. In 1995 political scientist Robert Putnam added momentum to the lament over the decline of American civic order with the provocatively titled article, "Bowling Alone."[23] Attending to a decline in U.S. political participation and a drop in membership and participation in certain voluntary organizations (for example, the League of Women Voters, the PTA), Putnam found symbolic force in the fact that "more Americans are bowling today than ever before, but bowling in organized leagues has plummeted in the last decade or so."[24] Many voices joined in his chorus of concern about eroding social capital, and I still believe there is merit in his contention.[25] But Nancy Ammerman reminds us: "Knowing that people are not bowling in leagues does not tell us that they are necessarily bowling alone." Through her study of nine rapidly changing communities, she came to the conviction that "the American civic order has remarkable recuperative powers" and "congregations are a significant part of that story."[26] Others have made similar points; Princeton sociologist Robert Wuthnow argues that Americans are redefining the forms and nature of their engagement by opting for smaller and more flexible commitments.[27] The matter is not simple. Clearly our context is characterized by a strong tendency toward involvement in particular groups or communities. People tend to come to political involvement not so much as individuals but as members of groups. What is one to make of this?

I view this as an indication of the active quest for transformation; American political involvement presses for a changed future. Yet I find the underlying need for transformation to be inadequately met in this phenomenon. Parties, action groups, and associations move us beyond the isolated individual self on whom the environing world has no constitutive bearing. Membership in the group gives the individual a sense of belonging, a feeling of being anchored. Nevertheless, I worry about a perduring and even escalating element of isolation in the group's self-definition in relationship to "outsiders." A cool indifference, which may masquerade under the current liturgy of "civility" or "just getting along," "being nice," may prevent us from effectively recognizing the truly significant differences that divide us. Robert Frost's poem "Fire and Ice," published well before the Third Reich reached tentacles across the map of Europe, seems both prophetic and apocalyptic then and now:

> Some say the world will end in fire,
> Some say in ice.
> From what I've tasted of desire
> I hold with those who favor fire.

> But if I had to perish twice,
> I think I know enough of hate
> To say that for destruction ice
> Is also great
> And would suffice.[28]

Contemporary North Americans know that ice *does* suffice, and fire is not far away. The coolness that lies cloaked in apparent civility may usher in a killing frost in which we demonize the other, turning the other into the enemy and letting negation dictate definition. This demonizing dynamic itself takes various forms, as in the "revolt of the elite" or in claiming universality for the dominant tradition.[29] Whether subtly or forcefully, something good is spoiled in the failure to truly engage the other. Both dynamics can be defended. The call to civility can be a call to productive conversation and nurturing creative activity, and some differences do reveal defining moments requiring the clear vision and moral courage to stand one's ground. But the transformation we hope for in the celebration of community will take place only when diverse individuals and communities come together in a public square they truly share. Not all group activities meet that standard. The fact that individuals come together to form a group does not mean that what is thus created genuinely works for human flourishing. The members of a gang of thieves are still thieves. The moral content of the values espoused and the ends chosen still require evaluation.

Such evaluation is readily avoided. Deep in the ditch of the denial of genuine difference lies the anesthesia of homogenization.[30] In this development of the lowest common denominator the depth of evil (and of good) is often obscured. Against this tide solitary voices speak. One such is surely Elie Wiesel, who in more than thirty books has called on us to remember what "civilized" folk are capable of doing.[31] It seems that there are some who do remember, who do know how high the moral stakes are at the end of this turbulent century. In any case, there are people deeply involved in work that I can only call transformative. When citizens league together to address needs in housing, health, and transportation, transformation takes place. When corporate lawyers and business executives team up to advocate for human rights, and when foundations come forward to support inner city agencies working the turf of "at-risk" youth, then the groans to be heard come from the struggle to make a material difference for the better in actual human lives.[32]

So, how does the balance sheet look? Where shall one come down on the continuum of optimism and pessimism? I will not yield to the temptation to pronounce a definitive grand judgment. For my purposes in this book it is sufficient to suggest two things: (1) there is a need for communities of faith to join in the work of transforma tion, and (2) as they take up such work, communities will find allies outside their own borders.

Consider the role of science and technology in our situation. Did the Apollo mission provide an escape from, or a clearer vision of, this aching earth? Much can be made of the transformative promise of science and technology on either side of the familiar nature/nurture debate. The remarkable studies of identical twins raised apart suggest that much of our *nature* seems "given" in our genetic inheritance.[33] But even this given is not rigidly fixed. The rapid development of recombinant DNA research over this last half century has made this clear; so has the ambitious Human Genome project.[34] With the recent discovery of the genes predisposing to Huntington's Disease, Cystic Fibrosis, Alzheimers, and inherited breast cancer, will thousands of people come to be classified as uninsurable and unemployable? Will selective abortions increase? Will genetic engineering be undertaken in the hope to influence the future evolution of humanity? The questions crowd in on us. Certainly one thing the science of genetics offers us is a challenge to engage in a thoroughgoing process of reflection—to seek, to find, and to apply agreed upon values.

On the *nurture* side, the road into the future seems particularly well paved by the prodigious possibilities characterizing the Age of Information. Are the Internet and all of the "interactivity" generated by digital communication the logical historical consequence of the outspoken democratic journalism of the likes of Thomas Paine and Thomas Jefferson?[35] Who would not celebrate that consequence? After all:

> In computer networks the global village has found its public square (the analogy to London's Hyde Park may be apt), whereby media users are transformed from vegetative "couch potatoes" to active participants in dialogues performed before potentially vast publics, linked not by geography but by technology and interests alone.[36]

One would have to join the Luddites not to recognize that science and technology have given people potentially powerful means and, indeed, allies in the work of transformation. But when one inquires into how things actually happen to be working, the first point returns: in the work of transformation, there is a need for faith to fill.

I wrote earlier of the compressed character of the contemporary self, caught in the high-speed electronic moment. Rather similarly, technology seems to provide a "lightness of being" such that the question of the purpose of human life is not fully engaged.[37] Our machines contribute to our isolation at the same time they "free" us from our classrooms and workplaces and other shared public spaces. We become disengaged from daily relationships with others and from the need for cooperation in order to do our work and meet our needs.[38] Once again, despite the evident potential of technology's offerings, the field's inequity of access itself demonstrates our society's failure to address such difficult issues as that of the widening income gap between the rich and the poor.[39] One may anticipate other deep divisions in our culture, which are likely to find expression and perhaps to be exacerbated in the "coverage" and communication occurring in the culture. Racism and sexism come quickly to mind.[40] How can technology and science transform the minds, the hearts, of their makers?

So, it would seem, we move toward the realm of religion. The complex reality of religion in our context calls for comment, but moving "toward" that, one may note the contemporary appeals to something like religion. What of the dynamics driving the expansion in recent decades of the therapeutic movement? Epidemics of depression sweeping the nation reveal selves crying out for healing. People purchasing a book titled *What You Can Change and What You Can't* (with the subtitle, *The Complete Guide to Self-Improvement*) seem unwilling to stay within the parameters of change provided by labor-saving devices.[41] Yet will exhortation and self-discipline alone effect the needed cure of the ailing human spirit? Hardly a week's mail arrives without receiving word of conferences devoted to some form of "spiritual transformation." Sponsors include such wild revolutionaries as the Harvard Medical School (Department of Continuing Education) and the Immaculate Heart College Center of Los Angeles together with the University of Santa Monica.[42] The human members of creation seem to be groaning for a redemption that will not reduce reality to what can be measured by the senses. The explosion of talk of soul and spirituality in the workplace and of ethics' initiatives in the business world gives voice to this lament. In matters political we hear similar cries, well typified by Vaclav Havel's call for sacrifice:

> My concern is that the West come to understand that the great task of self-defense against the communist menace has been supplanted today by an even more difficult task: to assume courageously, in its own interests and in the general interest, its share of responsibility for the new organization of things in the entire Northern Hemisphere.[43]

Are we not on religious, if not holy, ground when David Whyte speaks of the preservation of the soul in corporate America and defines soul as "the palpable presence of some sacred otherness in our labors, whatever language we may use for that otherness: God, the universe, destiny, life, or love?"[44] Or when Havel grounds the summons to responsibility in a "Turning Toward Being"? Perhaps we have come upon new ground, but the groaning has not stopped.

The Agony and the Ecstasy of American Religion

The groaning continues and continues to be ambiguous. If one could hear both need and quest in the sounds surfacing in the culture, one should not be surprised to hear something similarly mixed in the religion in that culture. Perhaps there is this difference: the need and the quest, the correlating elements, are intensified. In the experience of American religion, human beings groan in agony and ecstasy. That will be my focus as I set the stage for the real life drama of transformation into which I believe we are called.

The subject and study of religion in America are vast.[45] The task here is not to analyze it fully, but to understand better the problem and the promise of American religion regarding transformation in life and thought. I write as an advocate of the Christian religion, believing that the Christian faith holds out great promise for participation in the transforming work God wills. But I cannot honestly claim that religious folk in this land, including those of us claiming the name Christian, effectively serve that will and work. What accounts for the discrepancy?

With that question in mind, let us turn our attention to American religion. It may be difficult to mark definitively the boundaries of this thing called religion, but clearly they will include the churches. We call some of them "mainline," as if they dominate the horizon of American religion. Once they did. How do matters now stand with them? They are in decline. If as human beings we seek transformation, fewer Americans are seeking and finding it in the established churches of Christendom. Not that the citizenry has become less religious. Harvey Cox wrote his controversial *The Secular City* in the 1960s as part of the death of God movement, but in the 1990s he has come forward to acknowledge in *Fire from Heaven* that religion could well appropriate Mark Twain's line, "The rumor of my death is vastly exaggerated."[46] Harold Bloom has collected some of the numbers:

> The United States of America is a religion-mad country. . . .
> *The People's Religion* by George Gallup, Jr. and Jim Castelli
> (1989) polls the nation and discovers that 88 percent among us
> believe that God loves them, 9 percent are uncertain, while
> only 3 percent say that the Lord's affection for them is non-
> existent. But then 94 percent of us believe in God and 90 per-
> cent pray. These astonishing figures contrast remarkably to
> Western European convictions. . . .[47]

So, whence comes the decline of the mainline? Perhaps those who are voting with their feet can tell us. Mary Farrell Bednarowski has studied the rise of six new religions (Mormonism, Christian Science, Theosophy, The Unification Church, Scientology, and the New Age movement) and has heard a groaning over the old:

> As the new religions understood the situation, the established
> traditions were lacking in their abilities to hold together tradi-
> tional theological tensions in ways that responded to human
> experience or even acknowledged common sense—the inconsis-
> tencies of a God depicted as both loving and angry or the lack
> of a reasonably articulated relationship between human effort
> and the achievement of salvation or enlightenment. The estab-
> lished religions were likewise judged wanting in their respons-
> es to contemporary intellectual currents in the culture—the
> rise in prestige of the sciences, for example, or psychology. And
> they were assessed as particularly unable to formulate doctrines
> of human nature that acknowledge the reality of sin without
> insisting on the moral helplessness of mankind.[48]

Is that too severe? Her reading of perceived mainline deficiencies is supported by people who are leaving mainline churches, folk who have traveled not to these new religions but perhaps a lesser distance to various forms of evangelicalism. Elements of what Bednarowski's new believers were missing seem to be found here, where there is clearly a strong emphasis on personal religious experience and an emphasis on actual changes that Christian faith can work. One can be "born again," and that is hardly a matter of business as usual. According to Samuel S. Hill, being born again can be defined as:

> . . . the direct experience of a person in a notable single event or a specifiable period when that person shifts his or her life focus from any other center to Jesus Christ. It is as if that person had undergone a personal microchronic passage from B.C. to A.D. Whenever used, it bespeaks an earnest, outspoken and transformed Christian and refers to churches that preach that message.[49]

Those of us still rooted in the mainstream may find ourselves inquiring, like Nicodemus, "How can anyone be born after having grown old?" (John 3:4a). In any case, what we see in evangelicalism is not decline. Erling Jorstad has chronicled the dazzling array of popular religious periodicals, the music of evangelicalism from new gospel to Christian rock, and the dominance of evangelicalism in media treatment of religion, and he has offered the understated judgment that "the evangelical voice . . . stands as a dominant force throughout the last twenty-five years."[50] There seems at the very least to be here the voice of a questing, a seeking for transformation. Jorstad identifies three self-established criteria for "evangelical popular religion":

> . . . whether it [the faith] would help win the world for Christ, whether it would help recharge the sources of daily renewal within the believer, and whether it would provide the whole armor to withstand through doctrine, ethics, and discipleship a confused and sinful world.[51]

Is there not only a seeking but a finding? Those in the evangelical churches are thriving at least. Marty and Appleby suggest that "fundamentalism may be a reaction to secular modernity, but it is not necessarily reactionary." It is in its own way a very modern force. The people of whom they write are not "losing their established place in society," but rather "often are *newly* empowered people."[52] In their evangelical faith they seek and find some kind of power. Does this seeking and finding offer authentic transformation?

Two factors give rise to doubt. First, the record of fundamentalism is not such that all those who seek transformation there are finding it. The religious quest in the United States remains on the move, not just onward to the new religions, or back to those movements on the way to religion that employ some traditional religious appeals, such as Alcoholics Anonymous' reference to a higher power. No: in traditional Christian terms this travel through fundamentalism and popular religion often slips across the border to forms of popular sacrilege. The entire winter 1996 issue of the predictably stodgy and comfortably abstract *Journal of the American Academy of Religion* was devoted to "Religion and Popular Culture." It featured wildly diverse articles: David Chidester on the church of baseball (offering continuity, belonging, memory, rules, sacred space and time), Carolyn Marvin and David Ingle on the blood sacrifice of nationalism as our civil religion, and Stephen O'Leary on neopagan rituals in cyberspace ("attempts to fulfill authentic spiritual needs now unmet by the major institutions of religious tradition").

Second, religion in American culture seems not so much to transform the strains of the culture, as to reflect them. When we look at fundamentalism, its relationship with modern culture appears more mutually reinforcing than critical. Martin E. Marty has suggested, for example, that fundamentalism has a symbiotic relationship with modernity. He notes the irony of how reactive Protestants in finding a narrowing focus in premillenialism "themselves contributed to the kind of chopping up of life, the specialization that was itself an aspect of modernization."[53] That mirror image effect could be seen elsewhere, in the literalism of doctrine, in the high technology of market strategy.[54]

This hurried glance at the mainline, the new religions, and evangelicalism might foster the impression that much of American religion is at best irrelevant if we are looking for a genuinely transformative force. But that would be a partial judgment. The character of our cultural situation is highly pluralistic. Religion in this land is no less varied. Accordingly, those dangers described earlier do not suddenly melt away as we turn religious. The otiose civility toward difference that is comfortably linked with individualistic religion chills the atmosphere of religion as well as culture.[55] Or the violent domination of the other that civility cloaks may flare up out of control in both realms.

Religion and culture share the need for transformation. The long history of religion's links with violence must be faced anew. That history is not private property for Americans, of course. But we have had not a little of "The Noise of Conflict" in our story.[56] One community of faith takes up at least verbal arms against another, or some members do so against other members of the community.[57] Such violence is not ended, as is evident in the churches' struggles over sexual orientation issues in the 1990s.[58] Indifferentism and religious domination do indeed keep company with one another, strange as it might seem. Both tendencies seem to define the self or familiar group without reference to the engagement with other, different creatures. That definition links such apparently opposing tendencies as an internally granted warrant for the normativity of personal choices and the legalistic scrutiny of the mores of the behavior of other selves.[59] Religion is no stranger to either the isolation or the imperialism of the self.

So in looking at the reality of religion in this culture, the simple sentence with which we began this chapter stands: we need transformation. Yet is this judgment not also to be challenged? Take Christianity: when one looks at the propositions of the faith, is it not clear that this community gathers around one who said he came to bring life abundantly (John 10:10), and who began his ministry by bringing good news for the poor and release for the captives, sight for the blind and freedom for the oppressed (Luke 4:18)? That ministry moves forward still. When one looks at the practices of the community, what is one to make of the grassroots explosion in Bible study or of the worldwide activity of the churches in relief efforts? When one looks at the people of this religion, does one not have to interrupt any liturgy of condemnation to pause over a Martin Luther King or a Sister Helen Prejean? There seems to be power in this religion, power for transformation.

How shall one account for these wild extremes, for the agony and the ecstasy of the Christian religion? More pointedly, since I claim that Christian faith promises the power for transformation, how do I account for the fact that we so regularly "get it wrong"? A

conventional sociological or psychological explanation would suggest to us that "the forming of identities and the drawing of boundaries are inevitable, and they do always require a definition of who I
am or my group is and a discrimination relative to what I or my
group are not."[60] That is a helpful perspective. But I want to add a
more specifically theological element by considering the term *ecstasy*.
In ecstasy, etymologically, one "stands outside of oneself."[61] But
there is ecstasy and then there is ecstasy. We tend to leave our true
selves behind as we set out to do battle for God:

> Human beings are not very good at being God. If, in their zeal
> to act for God, Christians slip into supposing they act as God,
> they may, not surprisingly, bluster against other human beings
> whose presence may threaten to remind them that they are
> creatures. When they try to be God, they get the God thing
> wrong and so they turn against the other.[62]

This is not altogether adequate as an explanatory thesis. It is not
as helpful in understanding the indifferentist face of American religion. Yet a connection can be discerned. In ecstasy, I stand outside
myself. I may do that by claiming to become one with God with the
effect that I can act with what I (wrongly) suppose to be divine
power and intention against my enemies. But actually, as I draw
closer to becoming God in power and judgment, I lose God. Or, I
may stand outside my self by submerging myself in "my" God with
the result that I lose my concrete connection with other human creatures on ground where mutually contradictory claims cannot both be
true. Those other folks do not matter to me; God speaks to me alone,
within the garden of my individual soul. Again I have lost the real
God who will not be found but with the others. Both maneuvers
seem to be present in what Harold Bloom has provocatively called
"The American Religion":

> Freedom, in the context of the American Religion, means
> being alone with God or with Jesus, the American God or the
> American Christ. In social reality, this translates as solitude, at
> least in the inmost sense. The soul stands apart, and something
> deeper than the soul, the Real Me or self or spark, thus is made
> free to be utterly alone with a God who is also quite separate
> and solitary.[63]

Bloom writes that "what makes it possible for the self and God to
commune so freely is that the self already is of God; unlike body and

even soul, the American self is not part of the Creation. . . ."[64] There lies, I propose, the corrective: to reclaim the truth that we are creatures together. In this there is a genuine connection between the truly human and that which is qualitatively other. And within creation there is ecstatic power for transformation.

2. Creation Comprehending the Whole Work
of God: A View from the Middle

The Christian lives in this context as part of the groaning creation
and reaches out to another context. She turns to faith to focus
and direct her thinking and living. Needing and seeking transformation, puzzled by and participating in the agony and ecstasy of
American religion, the Christian seeks direction from the faith
bequeathed to the saints (Jude 1:3). In turning to faith he does not
abandon the concrete realities of life. The point in turning to faith is
not escape but engagement. For the Christian, faith provides perspective for transformation through the doctrine of creation. Indeed,
I will argue that what this doctrine provides is not a first act or first
chapter soon to be superceded by assertions that go "beyond" creation talk. Rather, creation comprehends the whole work of God. H.
H. Schmid speaks in this way of biblical theology:

> All theology is creation theology, even when it does not speak
> expressly of creation but speaks of faith, justification, the
> reign of God, or whatever, if it does so in relation to the world.
> And it must do that as long as it makes any claim of being
> responsible.[1]

"Comprehends"—isn't that a strange choice of words? The dictionary indicates that "to comprehend" can mean "to contain or hold
within a total scope" or it can mean "to see the nature, significance
or meaning" of something.[2] Exactly so. Applied to creation, "comprehend" must mean both. Being and knowing belong together in
this. Because the God who works to transform and to call us to such
work is the Creator, we can come to understand transformation as we
lay claim to the resources found in the doctrine of creation. There is
a danger that in so moving to comprehend we are welcoming a doctrinal monster who will devour all concrete reality in an abstraction
far removed from the throbbing groans uttered by others and ourselves. That is why I pledge to think and write "from the middle,"
the indubitably messy middle, in which we do exist. Faith's creation
talk is comprehensive; here words like *alpha* and *omega* occur. But we

will speak from the middle and seek to say what we can and need to say to grasp the transformation fitting such a location. That will make a difference even as we begin with beginnings.

Life's Beginnings: The New and the Good

And the one who was seated on the throne said, "See I am making all things new." Also he said, "Write this, for these words are trustworthy and true." (Rev. 21:5)

God saw everything that he had made, and indeed, it was very good; and there was evening and there was morning, the sixth day. (Gen. 1:31)

The Bible's last book in writing of last things testifies to a God who is doing new things. This omega bears the mark and promise of alpha. The one who brings new beginnings is the one who in *the* beginning "created the heavens and the earth" (Gen. 1:1). Such a span is unsurpassable. To speak of God is to speak of One who transcends us in both being and character. Such talk stretches our imaginations to the breaking point. It is, verily, God talk—talk of one who is truly other. Faith connects the experience of the new and of the good with such God talk. We can begin with being, with God's ontological superiority. We know of this even where we are, in the middle. Perhaps it is that vast differences of degree hint to us of a difference in kind. We cannot see back to the beginning of things. Indeed, it staggers us to realize that human beings arrived in the universe barely before midnight on the evolutionary clock. We may live with a sense of ending, but we realize that *the* end is beyond our fathoming.[3]

In the midst of life we do ourselves have some sense of an Other who has to do with beginnings and endings. Qualitatively. Each moment comes to us, fresh and fragile. And it passes. It is clear to us that we are not in charge of this coming and going. Harold Bloom, or rather the "American religion" of which he writes, is wrong.[4] The "real Me" is not free to be alone with God. We know we do not in our being belong with anyone who is alpha and omega for each moment and spans them all. We are located somewhere, sometime, and shaped out of the humus of those dimensions. Our proper classification and fitting company is the creaturely. In knowing this difference, we do not denigrate the human. As we claim the resources of the doctrine of creation, we will find ourselves speaking of human responsibility. I will write of how human beings are called to make a difference. But the surprise with which each moment meets us and the suddenness of its passing, long or short, resonates with faith's testimony that it is God who is the Creator. This is a different difference. To speak of the Creator is to speak of someone who is qualitatively other than we are. The difference from the creaturely is not one of degree; the difference between being and non-being is absolute. We may alter life and even end life, but we do not give life. This difference is sensed also by some people who do not use the language of explicit faith, but still experience that "life" is given and threatened. Perhaps there is some sensing that "our children come *through* us, but they do not belong *to* us."[5]

How has faith spoken of alpha, of God the Creator and the beginning of things? Christians have done so by speaking of God creating "out of nothing," *ex nihilo*.[6] We recognize this as strange talk, for Aristotle speaks for us in saying that out of nothing comes nothing (*ex nihilo nihil fit*). So, how shall one speak intelligibly of creation out of nothing? Well, theologians rush in to try. There is some variety in that speaking. Some theologians work with a distinction between absolute non-being and relative non-being. Thus Paul Tillich, while recognizing that the creature dialectically participates in both relative non-being (potentiality) and absolute non-being (finitude), will speak of "the *nihil* out of which God creates" as "the undialectical negation of being."[7] Does that help? One senses that Tillich is negating a claim, but is he implying some kind of being effecting a negation before and beyond his speaking? Walking further down that shadowy path, others speculate about the divine *zimsum*, the concentration or contraction by which God acts toward God to create an inward nothingness out of which the non-divine can be created.[8] But doesn't such a move merely manage to add another layer of mystery to the matter?

I share the desire evident in such efforts to convey the sense of the other by articulating the conviction that our very existence is dependent on the will of our maker. Such talk can seem so to focus on the absolute beginning as to not address us who live in the middle.[9] The qualitative sense of otherness is there to be known in our present experience in the middle of things. Pedro Trigo has expressed this well:

The language of creation is not protology, then. It is not a discourse on beginnings as such, as some particularly pregnant, archetypal time divided from all other times. The language of creation is historical. It refers to yesterday, today, and tomorrow. Our beginnings have no special privilege, no special revelatory power. To understand them, we need not undertake some ritualistic or mystical journey. They are within our reach today, if we dare to live by faith.[10]

Perhaps in making that claim about history, we are not really removing ourselves from all biblical creation talk. Dennis Olson offers this reading:

> . . . Creation in the Bible is not about the very beginnings of the appearance of matter or the cosmos. In Genesis 1, the narrative begins with God's spirit or wind sweeping over already existing waters of chaos (Gen. 1:2). We are not told how these waters came to be or what God was doing before this moment. In Gen. 2:4, the second creation story begins with an already pre-existing desert that is lifeless. Water begins to flow, and only then does God begin to form and create. . . . In other words, the two primary creation stories in the Bible begin at some point *after* the very beginnings of the cosmos.[11]

In this witness the church's own book may be joined by the book of nature. If the person of faith looks to claim whatever resource is to be found in the wider world, he may come upon discussions in the science and religion conversation that suggest "a universe with a finite past but *no* initial singularity."[12] The Christian may even thank the skeptical scientist who, in giving up a beginning to the universe (and so any God who could only act there), prods the Christian to recognize the Creator who does new things here in the middle.[13]

So we would err were we to insist that this different difference or original being of God pointed to in the *ex nihilo* can only apply to that singular, ultimate beginning. God's ontological superiority is experienced in the midst of the middle, in our here-and-now lives. Yet perhaps even more troublesome is the tendency to talk in this strange way of *the* beginning, and then to carry over that talk to speak of God's work in the middle in essentially the same way. This may have a pleasingly pious ring, but I must dissent. The continuity we experience from moment to moment and day to day suggests that what God the Creator now works with is not nothing. Is there not something, indeed are there not many things, that limit God's work in the middle? Langdon Gilkey, who in his 1959 work *Maker of Heaven and Earth* offered the definitive statement of a "strong" view of creation *ex nihilo,* doubled back in 1976 in *Reaping the Whirlwind* to recognize the reality of limitation:

> . . . we experience ultimacy not as the all-powerful, extrinsic and necessitating ordainer of what we are and do, but precisely as the condition and possibility, the ground, of our contingent existence, our creativity, our eros and meaning, our intellectual judgments, our free moral decisions and our intentional actions.[14]

If we are not prepared to recognize that the non-divine is something, are we prepared to assign a universe no better than this to a God of unconstrained freedom? Some theologians swallow hard and do just that. Here is Philip Hefner's formulation:

> There is scarcely a more offensive idea for the Christian than one that holds God in some way responsible for evil. Perhaps the only idea more repugnant is the alternative . . . that God is limited in power over anything, including evil.[15]

The Christian has good reasons to speak of ultimate origins, reasons deriving from the faith delivered and reasons arising from the experience of the new in present beginnings. But as we bring that speech of ultimate origins to bear on life in the middle we need to attend with integrity to the testimony of the present efficacy of evil. We come back to mentioning the missing moral twin in God's superiority. Would we worship a God who brought beginnings that were not both new and good? Well, *should* we?

The notion of "divine self-limitation," often used in the so-called "free will defense," provides a way, if awkward, to bring these two streams of witness together.[16] The witness is to the good of genuine relationship for the creatures and for the Creator. Self-limitation in origin, recognizing God's *ontological* superiority, yields real limitation in effect. In the notion of this limitation in effect we recognize God's *moral* superiority. God's will to create, celebrated in the *ex nihilo* image, is so decisive that God cannot or will not "call it off." Believers who say "cannot" emphasize the assurance of God's ultimate commitment in the very being of a self-binding God. To me this puts the point most strongly. There are also believers who prefer to say "will not," recognizing that the divine creative will for relationship would suffer at least a measure of defeat in any retreat to the splendor of self-imposed isolation. Similarly, for God to switch to sheer coercion would mean defeat for that same will. To say only "will not" does seem to leave the believer with an element of uncertainty in the very life of God, though some would say that is just what faith as trust is about.[17] In either formulation—that God cannot or will not abandon the creational plan, what is secured is the goodness of the God who wills and works for relationship. That good God is not a deist God, isolated from and immune to life's chances and changes. God continues to work "in, with, and under" (as Lutherans like to say of the Lord's Supper) that which is not God. But in this understanding God is not saddled with undifferentiated responsibility as in appeals to absolute control and singular causality. This is not a God who chose not to overrule Auschwitz or who was the real actor in the exploits of a Jeffrey Dahmer or an Andrew Cunanan. The qualitative transcendence of God is seen precisely in bringing about that which is new and good in the very middle of things. In the next section I will draw upon Christian faith in a God incarnate in the middle of history to make this point that genuine transcendence in relationship is not something to be protected from the stain of temporality.

This second claim, arguing for the goodness of the God of beginnings, again draws upon both faith and experience. The drumbeat of the Bible's first chapter is "good" (1:4, 10, 12, 18, 21, 25), and at the end of the sixth day, "God saw everything that he had made, and indeed, it was very good." (1:31). The creation of life is gift; it is an act not merely of power but of grace, as Gustaf Wingren reminds us:

> The very fact of life proves that God has begun to give. The
> "opus proprium" of God, which is to give and which is seen most
> clearly in the Gospel, is already operative in Creation and is
> expressed in the primary fact of life.[18]

Without denying that evil is real and that there is a time when death is indeed a gift, the Christian's fundamental experience of life's beginnings is of a gift from One whose true and "proper" work is grace.

There is more to be said about how creation is good. On the one hand, a claim arises from the experience of order. There is the order given by moral law, as written into creation under the rubric, Do this and live! (Deut. 5:33). And there is a broader kind of indicative order given graciously by the Creator. J. Richard Middleton lists coherence, reliability, and graciousness as familiar claims and adds:

> . . . creation theology provides a sense of connectedness and mutual dependence among all creatures (as depicted, for example, in Psalm 104). Such an orienting vision not only establishes and roots a person—this world becomes home—but it also provides a basis for care for the natural world and confident participation in ordinary social life and everyday tasks.[19]

One thinks as well of the incentive to science that the notion of creation has provided. If the regularities in the universe issue from the constancy of divine will, empirical scrutiny is supported and rewarded.[20] These deliverances of order, moral and cosmological, are together the good gift of the Creator. Hans-Jürgen Hermisson has pointed out how biblical thinking about the world does not obey the rules of the modern world's "fact-value split":

> This world, however, is *unitary.* Although for us it may customarily divide into nature, regulated by (seemingly firm) natural laws, and history, which is more or less contingent, ancient wisdom starts from the conviction that the regularities within the human and the historical-social realm are not in principle different from the ones within the realm of non-human phenomena.[21]

Theology has usually not neglected this theme of order, at least formally. But we have been slower to recognize the Creator's hand in change, indeed in the chaos we experience. While I do not want to argue that all change and chaos are divine works, an essential element of the Creator's work is missed if we limit ourselves to the pole of order.[22] After all, we are speaking of a God of beginnings, a God who does new things. With such a God order may serve rather than suppress change. In turning to this dynamic element we come to speak of a drama in which God acts and others act.

Life's Drama: Ambiguity, Contradiction, and Advance

> God blessed them, and God said to them, "Be fruitful and multiply, and fill the earth and subdue it; and have dominion over the fish of the sea and over the birds of the air and over every living thing that moves upon the earth." (Gen. 1:28)

> Adah bore Jabal; he was the ancestor of those who live in tents and have livestock. His brother's name was Jubal; he was the ancestor of all those who play the lyre and pipe. Zillah bore Tubal-cain, who made all kinds of bronze and iron tools. . . . Adam knew his wife again, and she bore a son and named him Seth, for she said, "God has appointed for me another child instead of Abel, because Cain killed him " (Gen. 4:20-22, 25)

> Indeed, even though there may be so-called gods in heaven or on earth—as in fact there are many gods and many lords—yet for us there is one God, the Father, from whom are all things and for whom we exist, and one Lord Jesus Christ, through whom are all things and through whom we exist. (1 Cor. 8:5-6)

We find that our experience has a narrative quality. Things happen: life and death *occur*. Christians attending to the biblical witness are not surprised by the eventful character of life. That witness indicates that the Creator from the beginning intended that it be so—that there be change, development, drama. In the previous section I spoke of the drumbeat of creation—"good . . . good . . . good," and of the climax—"very good." But this is a penultimate climax, for the very good is not the perfect. The Latin root for "perfect" suggests completion, but at the end of the sixth day God's life with the other is not finished. It is well begun . . . indeed, very well begun. But something more is intended, as Colin Gunton sees:

> . . . We need to understand it [creation] as something God creates not as a timelessly perfect whole, but as an order of things that is planned to go somewhere, to be completed or perfected, and so *projected* into time.[23]

Thus if we speak of God the creator as a God of order, we will need to speak of mutable order, indeed of change within the order. Certainly, this association of order with the creator God has been appealed to by persons intent on resisting change. Religious apologists have made this move even for the Third Reich and for apartheid, as well as for less outrageous elements of what is or what is claimed to be the status quo. Such use of a doctrine of creation surely does need to be opposed by anyone bent on transforming work. Thus the atheist Ernst Bloch sought to serve the principle of hope, but he believed the Bible set the creator against the liberator.[24] Indeed, moving inside the circle of faith we find the eminent Old Testament scholar Walter Brueggemann often juxtaposing creation faith to the prophetic or "Mosaic" faith that he lifts up as serving human transformation:

> The social function of creation theology . . . is characteristical-
> ly to establish, legitimate, and advocate order at the cost of
> transformation. . . . The problem is that regularly (I believe
> inevitably), creation theology is allied with the king, with the
> royal liturgy, and therefore with reasons of state. The outcome
> is to coalesce the royal ordering of economic distribution and
> political power with the goodness and reliability of God's
> intended order, thereby absolutizing the present order as the
> very structure God has decreed in and for creation.[25]

To this I can only say that *mis*use of creation themes does not militate against proper use. Other biblical scholars have made this point extensively. With the book usually claimed for a false polarization of creation and salvation, the book of Exodus, Terence Fretheim has shown how the analysis of the human situation and the cosmic scope of the purpose active in the divine solution depend on a creation theology.[26] J. Richard Middleton, drawing on Fretheim and other sources, has addressed Brueggemann directly, suggesting that now may be the time for Brueggemann to develop "a biblically rooted, coherently articulated theology of creation that knows the darkness and yet hopes, beyond suspicion, in the Creator's gracious and just purposes for this world."[27] In a remarkable response Brueggemann grants that "creation theology is neither inherently nor inevitably conservative," but he holds to the judgment that it "functions most often in a conservative fashion."[28]

Very well, then, I would join those who seek to show how creation theology can function for transformation. Specifically, how does the human status as creature entail responsibility to God in the drama that creation constitutes? We begin with the notion of the image of God. Claus Westermann stresses the dynamic character of what is involved:

> What God has decided to create must stand in a relationship to
> him. The creation of man [*sic!*] in God's image is directed to
> something happening between God and man. The Creator cre-
> ated a creature that corresponds to him, to whom he can speak
> and who can hear him.[29]

In the human creature's hearing the word of the Creator, then, arises the controversial call to "have dominion." The fact that the call has been misread to support (shortsighted) anthropocentrism does not nullify these words.[30] The human pair is called to knowing, knowing the Creator and the created world. More fittingly one says "world *being* created," for there is power in human knowing and naming, and the Genesis text moves us on to chapter 4, where such human functions as agriculture, music, and industry are traced in the genealogy of creation. These words are less often cited in discussing the biblical doctrine of creation, but that neglect risks sacrificing human partnership in God's continuing creation.

But does not something much more sinister lie down the road as one is driven by the will to know? Westermann considers that, but of even the temptation to be like God he can say this:

> This is a temptation not because the drive towards knowledge, towards all-embracing knowledge, was of itself opposed to God; it is not, because man [*sic!*] is created with it. But the possibility is there of a disturbance and a destruction of the proper relationship between God and man, when man in his drive after knowledge oversteps or tries to overstep his limits.[31]

Indeed, one can speak of how God draws the human creature into the creative process, as in the naming of the animals. To have a creative role does not isolate the human, for as Michael Welker points out, "not only God brings forth, but also creature brings forth creatures—animals of all species and plants (Gen. 1:12, but also 1:11, 20, 24)."[32]

The unique status of being created in the image of God does not lift human beings out of the condition of being creatures. But there is a distinctive responsibility here, and it roots in the character of the relationship between the human creature and the Creator. Christian thinkers have struggled to make clear the Creator's claim on the human creature. Thus Søren Kierkegaard, while still using the language of omnipotence of God, does not back away from human responsibility:

> O wonderful omnipotence and love! A man [*sic!*] cannot bear that his "creations" should be something directly over against him; they should be nothing, and therefore he calls them "creations" with contempt. But God, who creates out of nothing, who almightily takes from nothing and says "Be!", lovingly adds "Be something even over against me." Wonderful love, even his omnipotence is under the power of love! . . . Thus

love, which made a man to be something (for omnipotence let
him come into being, but love let him come into being over
against God), lovingly demands something of him. Now that
is the reciprocal relation.[33]

Kierkegaard serves Christian intuition in refusing to let the recognition of human responsibility compromise the fact that the Creator is
other in a categorical way. Indeed he regularly drives the two themes
toward each other, as in this passage from his journals:

It is incomprehensible that omnipotence is not only able to
create the most impressive of all things—the whole visible
world—but is able to create the most fragile of all things—a
being independent of that very omnipotence. Omnipotence,
which can handle the world so toughly and with such a heavy
hand, can also make itself so light that what it has brought
into existence receives independence.[34]

Kierkegaard can even explicitly insist in this very passage that:

Omnipotence is not ensconced in a relationship to an other, for
there is no other to which it is comparable—no, it can give
without giving up the least of its power, i.e., it can make [a
being] independent.[35]

The power of this Danish poet's prose is such that one is tempted
simply to revel in the inconceivability. But one living "in the middle" may not settle for that ecstasy.

One will go prospecting for formulations that state qualitative
transcendence in more graspable ways, such as Elizabeth Johnson's
reference to "a mutual, if asymmetrical, relation."[36] Or perhaps one
will give the qualitatively distinguishing attribute of omnipresence
the constitutive role in defining omnipotence as (some) power in
every situation. Living in the middle, one will refuse formulations
that eviscerate or even threaten the theme of human responsibility.

Kierkegaard speaks for the faith in holding high that theme, in
spite of (or precisely in the light of) references to divine omnipotence. Perhaps the test issue is whether the Creator who demands
something of the creature is actually somehow at risk in the relationship. Does God have something at stake? Here Kierkegaard does
not equivocate. In describing the incarnation he writes of the "infinite qualitative difference" between God and the human and yet
adds this:

But in this infinite love of his merciful grace he nevertheless
makes one condition: he cannot do otherwise. Precisely this is

Christ's grief that "he cannot do otherwise"; he can debase himself, take the form of a servant, suffer, die for men [sic!], invite all to come to him, offer up every day of his life, every hour of the day, and offer up his life—but he cannot remove the possibility of offense. What a rare act of love, what unfathomable grief of love, that even God cannot remove the possibility that this act of love reverses itself for a person and become the most extreme misery—something that in another sense God does not want to do, cannot want to do.[37]

Kierkegaard mentions possibility, and that is precisely the point. In this drama of creaturely life there is possibility, and so ambiguity. At times out of the matrix of possibility there arise apparently clear oppositions both in intention and result, the shining philanthropist and the malevolent despot. The person pondering those apparitions may pause over the sense that such sharp alternatives live together in the bubbling ferment of his own possibility. And there is the dawning recognition that in the middle of the moral continuum and perhaps even at the extremes matters are not quite that simple. Alfred North Whitehead's wisdom word reminds us, "Seek simplicity and distrust it."[38] Distrust recognizes that ambiguity abides.

Christian confession points to something within the ambiguous drama of life that is even more problematic. It is sin, fall from creation's promise, contradiction to creation's mandate. Genesis 4 not only recounts the ancestry of lyre and pipe, of agriculture and industry. There, crowding in on the splendor of human civilization without benefit of cosmetic adornment, is the wrong side of dominion: Cain killed Abel (4:25)! That does not seem particularly ambiguous. And at the end of this century of holocausts the Christian knows that something stands out clearly within the ambiguity of life. The Christian knows in the world and in his heart of hearts that a truthful account must speak not only of the risk of God, but of the suffering of God. Can the doctrine of creation "comprehend" even this contradiction? I say "Yes," but not in the sense that moral evil is either the Creator's intention or act.

How then? In two senses: (1) Evil parasitically draws on the very structure and energy of creation to work its will, and (2) the sinner's rebellion does not succeed in blotting out the mark of the Creator. Perhaps Augustine helps us with the first point suggesting that what sin does is to disorder human love, drawing on and distorting the drive to use and enjoy.[39] The creational structure is not withdrawn. Neither does the Creator withdraw. That is the second point. For again the Genesis text tells us that it is not pain but love that determines the heart of God:

> I will never again curse the ground because of humankind, for the inclination of the human heart is evil from youth. (Gen. 8:21b)

Thus Lutherans, who are not famous for being "soft on sin," have chosen to:

> . . . reject as a Manichaean error the teaching that original sin is strictly and without any distinction corrupted man's [sic!] substance, nature and essence, so that no distinction should be made, even in the mind, between man's nature itself after the Fall and original sin, and that the two cannot be differentiated in the mind.[40]

Clearly, I am calling for making this distinction "in the mind" and otherwise. Other Christians have found other ways of making this point, as when John Calvin insists that the defilement of sin has not altogether obliterated the gifts of creation.[41] "In the mind," and in reality, we remain creatures of God. We are beings in relationship with God, even if often unknowingly and/or unwillingly.

But I must wait no longer to write not of something remaining despite sin, but of something advancing against sin. Or some*one*, for here the Christian will speak of Jesus. The biblical witness is clear: here is the Lord of the Sabbath come to do the Creator's will. The passage cited in beginning this section, 1 Corinthians 8:6, represents others in giving this Jesus "standing" in nothing less than the work of creation. Paul writes of "one Lord Jesus Christ, through whom are all things and through whom we exist." The Christian church has striven to be clear about this as well, already as early as 144 when Marcion came to Rome and brought his message of two Gods.[42] To fathom this savior one must reach back to claim the older Testament's witness to the Creator. Theologians have let the highly particular word of Jesus illumine the God of all creation. Thus Jürgen Moltmann finds something in the original creation that parallels the mind of Christ known to the Philippians:

> This self-restricting love is the beginning of that self-emptying of God which Philippians 2 sees as the divine mystery of the Messiah.[43]

This is an important direction to move, to strain to see the face of Jesus in the mists of time's beginnings, as I have suggested in stressing how important it is to see creation as already the proper work of grace recognized so vividly in Christ. But theologians have been less complete in moving in the other direction, filling out the connection by seeing the Creator's purpose working in the story of Jesus.

Happily, there are exceptions. In writing of *Creation and Redemption* Regin Prenter could say:

> God the Creator becomes a creature himself in order to repair the damage which sin has done to created human life. The intention of the idea of the incarnation is to declare that through the event of the atonement it is none other than the Creator himself who is active in order to complete his creative work.[44]

More strongly still, decades ago Herbert Richardson devoted an essay to making this point:

> The work of Jesus Christ cannot contradict the purpose for which God created the world. To assert such a contradiction . . . . is to reiterate the old Gnostic claim that the God of the Old Testament and the God of the New Testament are two different "Gods." The scope of Christ's work must be more than redemption . . . because it must be identical with God's purpose in creating the world.[45]

Richardson did not mince words. He shared his suspicions that Reformation emphasis on human corruption so robbed human life of dignity as to undermine effective "caring about" redemption, and that Judaism's survival power arose from the sense of being "a holy people." I have noticed little written response to his work. One might argue that the explosion of empowerment in the evangelicals is an unwritten and unknowing response. In any case I believe he raised an important question about "the relative failure of Christianity to be an effective redemptive force in the world" and wisely called, with the Scotist tradition, for claiming the Creator's purpose for the work of Christ. To speak of "the sanctification of the world by His mere [!] Sabbath presence" may be too facile, but we will not want to say less than that.

Of course the fall into sin cries out for God's saving work in Christ. Richardson did not deny that. He wrote:

> To stress the priority of "God with us" over "God for us" is not, however, to deny that Jesus is our Redeemer, nor is it to

derogate from His redeeming work. Though redemption is a
subordinate purpose of His coming, it is essential to the chief
end He seeks. Moreover, it was precisely for the sake of our
redemption that Jesus Christ endured the cross.[46]

That creation "comprehends" the whole work of God does not deny
that God in Jesus is responding to something that was precisely not
intended in creation. The complaint I am lodging here is that Christians have tended to limit the work of Christ to that specific response
to the sin unintended in creation, as if God's creational purpose were
not truly served in his coming. In this tendency we have neglected
hints from people like Martin Luther, who could say this of the
words spoken in the Sacrament of the Altar:

> By these words the forgiveness of sins, life, and salvation are
> given to us in the sacrament, for where there is forgiveness of
> sins, there are also life and salvation.[47]

How truncating, those interpretations of these words that reduce
"life and salvation" to the announcement of forgiveness! Yet we have
tended to leave apart the Creator's work of blessing and the redemptive work of Christ. Such a distinction is often linked with the name
of Claus Westermann. But Westermann is very clear that Christ cannot be separated from the blessing of God. Thus he lifts up a set of
passages (Gal. 3:8-9, 14; Acts 3:25-26; and Eph. 1:3) in which
"'blessing' means explicitly and emphatically God's saving act in
Christ, or the justification wrought in this act."[48]

So the characterizations of God's creative work, the "new" and the
"good" will come back into play in speaking of this Jesus. To speak
of transformation will be to speak of how human life can be changed
because of Jesus. And we will speak of how this event makes a difference for God. There is something new here for God in the relationship with creation. I earlier raised some questions about whether
Kierkegaard recognizes adequately that creaturely responsibility
matters to God. But he is not shy in stating the decisive significance
of the incarnation for God. In a famous parable in *Philosophical Fragments* he rejects the manipulating condescension of a King who *pre-
tends* to be a servant boy in order to win a maiden's love:

> God's servant-form is not a disguise, but is actual; and from
> the hour when he with the omnipotent resolve of his omnipo-
> tent love became a servant God has so to speak imprisoned
> himself in his resolve, and now must go on (to speak foolishly)

whether he wills to or not. He cannot then betray himself; he does not have the possibility which is open to the noble king, suddenly to show that he is after all the king—which, however, is no perfection with the king (to have this possibility), but shows merely his impotence and the impotence of his resolve, that he does not actually have the power to become what he wills.[49]

What difference will this decisiveness make for the human role in God's creative project? Will that which is new for God bring something truly new for us? My response offered in hope is "Yes." It is not new to be called, and the content of the call is comprehended in the doctrine of creation. Yet to speak with Irenaeus of Christ's work as *re*capitulation is necessary but insufficient.[50] In the chapters that lie ahead I will write of empowerment in relation and of how the new-for-God works freshly there for the creation's good toward the end the Creator envisions. Now it remains to inquire how this understanding of creation shapes the Christian's approach to transformation in life and in thought even here "in the middle."

Life's Issue: Back to the Middle from the Future

. . . they cast their crowns before the throne, singing, "You are worthy, our Lord and God, to receive glory and honor and power, for you created all things, and by your will they existed and were created." (Rev. 4:10b-11)

Love never ends. But as for prophecies, they will come to an end; as for tongues, they will cease; as for knowledge, it will come to an end. For we know only in part, and we prophesy only in part; but when the complete comes, the partial will come to an end. When I was a child, I spoke like a child, I thought like a child, I reasoned like a child; when I became an adult, I put an end to childish ways. For now we see in a mirror, dimly, but then we will see face to face. Now I know only in part; then I will know fully, even as I have been fully known. And now faith, hope, and love abide, these three; and the greatest of these is love. (1 Cor. 13:8-13)

Is this enough? Can a groaning creation be addressed adequately within the bounds of a doctrine of creation? I have emphasized the dynamic character of creation, that by the Creator's will a telos is intended that lies "beyond Eden." I have suggested that the story of

Jesus is about something more than the bestowal of forgiveness or even the restoration, the repair, of an original creational state. The Christmas story is not over until history reaches its end. Given these positions, would not an adequate response to creation's groaning have to speak of that end? We ask, in what will this life issue? But can reflection on creation reach beyond creation? Incompleteness and ambiguity seem built into the very structure of creation. Can we claim some sure word about the end to nerve the creature's will for transformation?

As creatures we yearn for something that is so truly new and so truly good that it will bring life's drama to a fitting end. We do look to the future with hope. Ernst Bloch uncovered that yearning decades ago in the more than 1,400 pages comprising *The Principle of Hope*. The scope of Bloch's vision was truly staggering, drawing on music, religion, and philosophy, among other fields. In this hunger for the future one may see a searching for something that will satisfy the questions and quest that characterize human life. In our questioning we look to a time when we will not know only in part, but will know fully (1 Cor. 13:12). And we are looking for something that will not only make life clear. Much that we now suffer in the turbulence of time needs to be made right. What sort of end would do? If that end is to be decisively new, it cannot be merely more of the same, marked still by the struggle we know now. If that newness is to be the fitting end for what we know now, it must in its goodness connect with who and how we are. That is why at the end those who gather around the throne will sing praises to the one who created all things (Rev. 4:11). We ask again, "Can we claim some sure word about such an end?"

What are the prospects? There are Christian theologians who seem to offer a sure grasp of a decisive end. Thus Wolfhart Pannenberg will speak of how "it is *from* the future that the abiding essence of things discloses itself."[51] I do not see how such a grasp recognizes the volatile reality of the freedom of the creature. Must not our choices in some measure matter for the future, *our* future? If they do, is not ambiguity about the end inevitable? Somehow the relational character of life in the middle must be recognized even in the end. In many respects along the way Pannenberg often seems to offer such recognition, arguing—and illustrating—that the Christian theologian "deepens and expands" the understanding of human phenomena.[52] But such stubborn realities as contingency and relationality seem to lack recognition when the true and definitive manifests itself.[53]

What, then, can be said? Surely the Christian clings with hope to biblical words that speak of eternal peace (e.g., Isa. 26:12, 65:20-23), or of how we await a Savior who "will transform the body of our humiliation that it may be conformed to the body of his glory" (Phil. 3:21). What we hope for is indeed new, a genuine transformation. But the issue of continuity calls out for some connection with life here in the middle. Jürgen Moltmann seems to respond to that call by speaking of how "the world as creation can be and has to be a parable of its own future, the kingdom of God."[54] And he does not neglect the temporality of life in the middle:

> If all systems of life have a temporal structure, then they are all—each in its own way—open to the future. It is this temporal structure that gives them their characters as pointers.[55]

So we live in the present and into the future with hope. It does not violate the integrity of our life in the middle to believe that God has a purpose in mind—an end in view—or that God works at all times to fashion that future.[56] That sense of divine direction does not immobilize the Christian, but provides both incentive and shape for her action and thought. Accordingly, we return from this discourse about the final future to ask of how a theology of creation informs this present life.

That theology illumines (1) *what* we are to do as Christians and (2) *with whom* that doing is to be done. What are we to be up to? We are called to serve the Creator's will—to care for, to advance, the cause of creation. If we follow faithfully the lead of the Creator we will have to do with things such as birthing, eating, prospering, befriending, reconciling, and working.[57] The Creator's will for the human creatures is well written in the words of the second table of the law. The conditions for human "social cooperation" do seem to be written in the heart of creation, and Christians have the convenience of a printed version at hand.[58] The basic thrust is clear enough, though hard questions will arise in the fresh appropriation of Sinai's message. For example, our discussions and decisions about human life have all too often been limited to just that—*human* life, with nature drawn in late in the day as the object of our instrumental stewardship.[59]

But is there not a more specifically Christian calling, something that marks the Christian in his faith as one called out by God? If transformation is about change and indeed development, what about sanctification? I certainly do want to agree that the Christian *as Christian* is called into a life of discipleship. The biblical imperatives do apply; Christians are sent people. But sent where? The Christian answer is "to the neighbor"—that is, to one's fellow creatures. There is abundant need for the Christian to nourish the God relationship; prayer, for example, has a vital place. But the faith nurturing activities must not be an end in themselves. They strengthen the Christian for her vocation out in the world. Thus in prayer we open ourselves to God and find ourselves opened to the world in service.[60] Once again, creation "comprehends" the whole work of God.

It turns out that that is where God is—with the others. The Creator is to be found with the creatures. Here we come upon the logical independence and theological priority of the doctrine of creation. The question to be asked is, What is to be said of the creatures, *qua* creatures? Michael Root, commenting on Regin Prenter's thought, rules out a prevalent tendency:

> . . . one cannot assume that humanity as originally created was oriented toward the redemptive history. If such an orientation cannot be presumed, then an orientation toward redemption cannot be made a necessary part of a definition of human fulfillment, i.e., fulfilled human existence cannot be defined in terms of its relation to redemption.[61]

Any church in faithfulness to God hoping to reach human beings will have to be found in the world, where creatures are.

Of course the Christian as a member of the church council will be concerned with matters that do not make the agenda of the city council. Loren Mead has appropriately emphasized how crucial it is to "rebuild the wall" and "restore the temple":

> We must clarify what makes us different. . . . This requires us to establish the authenticity and distinctiveness of our congregations so that we live visibly in our faith, shaped by the biblical heritage, not by the least common denominator of local values and morality.[62]

But Mead is clear that this inward work is in the service of outreach, "so that we can undertake our vocation as apostles." It is the mission of God that the Christian is called to join. When Christians speak of God they make Trinity talk, and they will not cease to do that in describing the God whom they follow and join out in the world. Here the Christian is not limited to a "first article" theology, saying with Gerard Manley Hopkins:

> The world is charged with the grandeur of God. . . .
>
> . . . nature is never spent;
>
> There lives the dearest freshness deep down things; . . .[63]

Jesus is "out there," whether explicitly in the music of Bach, "the fifth evangelist," or as the *logos* of creation in whom all things hold together (Col. 1:17).[64] Similarly Christians taught by their scriptures will read the world knowing that the Spirit is the cosmic "power in-between-all-things." As Geiko Muller-Fahrenholz puts it:

> . . . The Spirit is much more than the heart and soul of Pentecostal awakenings and sanctified living. It is the core-energy of creation itself. The Hebrew Bible calls it the *ruach,* the female-motherly power alive in wild storms and gentle breezes and therefore—incarnated in Jesus—the true image of creative, unremitting love.[65]

So, what is the Christian, joining the mission of the triune God, to do? She is to care for creation. Does not Christ have a new command to give? Well, perhaps, since to care for one's child may not yet be to love one's enemies. But Gustaf Wingren well makes the point that the direction is the same:

> External creation, which is always pouring out its gifts upon men [*sic!*], speaks the same word to man as Christ, in whom God gives not only His gifts but also Himself. There is a force prompting man in his external relationships in the same direction as the command of love.[66]

What criteria are to apply for the Christian? George Lindbeck has helpfully specified three "intratextual" regulative principles:

> First, there is the monotheistic principle: there is only one God, the God of Abraham, Isaac, Jacob and Jesus. Second, there is the principle of historical specificity: the stories of Jesus refer to a genuine human being who was born, lived, and died in a particular time and place. Third, there is the principle of what may be infelicitously called Christological maximalism: every possible importance is to be ascribed to Jesus that is not inconsistent with the first rules.[67]

Such rules necessarily speak of and for continuity within the Christian community.[68]

I propose an additional criterion. Let the church be asked from within and without whether or not its specific identity is serving the care of creation. Let the pastor ask, Is life better for human beings, for nature, because the church is in this place? There will be times when what is needed is an almost single-minded focus on the inward-looking criteria. But the church is regularly tempted to settle simply for that focus, neglecting our witness and work in the world. My argument here is that the church cannot really be God's church without accepting for its evaluation the question of how the good of creatures is served through its ministry.

Who is to answer this question? Who is to identify criteria for the care of creation and then apply them to the church and any other social reality? This raises the second question, regarding *with whom* the work of caring for creation is to be done. The Christian will share with others not only the doing of the work, but the very discernment of what needs to be done. Which others? All others, in principle. If it is as Creator that God seeks and works transformation, then creaturliness becomes the primary qualifying credential for participation in this work of God. That is true of transformation in life and in thought. Of course discernment is needed. Finitude's twin, fallibility, is not to be forgotten. Moreover, God may have come decisively in the Christ, but human beings do not live and think sinlessly. Christians know that, not least about themselves.

Nonetheless, the direction in which I would err would be to emphasize that our grasping and heeding the Creator's call to transformation is to be done with the others, all the others. Thus Claus Westermann is right in observing that we should not require the language of faith and revelation in speaking of receiving the blessings the Creator bestows:

> The grateful acceptance of these blessings is not called faith and is not placed in any relationship with faith. . . . God's bestowal of blessing—growth, success, increase, provision—comes as continuing processes and has not need of the extraordinary occurrences that we mean by "revelations."[69]

God's blessings, including the understanding and care of the world, are freely given, as the rain falling on the just and the unjust. Contributions will come from surprising sources. This is easily forgotten inside the sanctuary. Indeed, the zeal of the convert may carry us to regard "the others" not merely as "outside" (as they are), but indeed as simply our enemies. But the doctrine of creation should particularly protect us from the temptation of demonizing our enemies. Pedro Trigo, a Venezuelan liberation theologian, makes the point well:

> Faith in the creator-with-us, then, ought to lead us to moderation in our *pathos* and in our conceptualization of our historical struggle for liberation. . . . When a project is being implemented, the temptation to sacralize it, and to demonize what opposes or resists it, is all but irresistible.[70]

Trigo argues that such faith in the creator:

> ought to incline us to do justice to every aspect of reality. . . . it ought to incline us to seek out channels of openness instead of entrenching ourselves in sealed blocs.[71]

And he wisely adds "it is easier to do this in the open air than in the tower of Babel."

So the Christian is called into conversation in knowing and partnership in doing the transforming will of the Creator. The Christian does not require Christian faith as a condition for such conversation or partnership, for the Christian knows that "God's relationship to the world is not limited to . . . the people who have been involved in faith by him."[72] Along the way there will indeed be God-talk and the Christian will have a witness to bring. But the Christian knows that the only God there is, the Creator, is not locked up in his dogmatics. In his influential critique, *The Gospel in a Pluralist* [not merely factually *pluralistic*] *Society,* Lesslie Newbigin drew on his forty years as a missionary to show the inadequacies of the usual alternatives: exclusivism, inclusivism, and pluralism. He saw that he could claim all three positions, even pluralism:

> The position I have outlined is . . . pluralist in the sense of acknowledging the gracious work of God in the lives of all human beings, but it rejects a pluralism which denies the uniqueness and decisiveness of what God has done in Jesus Christ.[73]

Again, it is the *missio Dei* the Christian joins. Interfaith conversations of whatever intensity are to serve the One who sends, not the one who is sent. The God who owns the mission is at work transformatively to bring the creation to completion. And the Christian who holds to the doctrine of creation developed in this chapter knows that God not only authorizes the conversation, but indeed acts in it. Thus in formulating "Commitments for Mission in the 1990s" the

Division for Global Mission of the Evangelical Lutheran Church in America said this:

> We are committed to inter-faith conversations and dialogue and through these encounters we will seek to understand persons of other faiths; *we will listen to what God has to say to us through these conversations* and through them we will witness to the crucified and risen Christ.[74]

And these mission-minded folks could go on to say this:

> We will work with the entire global community for justice, peace and the renewal of all creation.[75]

People of Christian faith know that the Creator of all cannot be evicted from any corner of the universe. God may work through diverse faiths and beyond the world of faith.[76] For example, how is the Christian to assess Hannah Arendt's testimony to "natality"?

> The miracle that saves the world, the realm of human affairs, from its normal, "natural" ruin is ultimately the fact of natality, in which the faculty of action is ontologically rooted. . . . Only the full experience of this capacity can bestow upon human affairs faith and hope, those two essential characteristics of human existence which Greek antiquity ignored altogether.[77]

So, I shall cast the net widely in the pages that follow, as I seek to bring to view the creational structure by which God wills and works transformation.[78] The mix may seem confusing, even chaotic. It is faith in the Creator that sustains and directs us, as we seek to be attentive to a wide range of reality. The challenge of such wide casting cannot be wisely avoided.

Will a doctrine of creation, bold to comprehend the whole work of God, be adequate for the task at hand? In our humanity we are merely creatures. In our sin we are not less than creatures. In our redemption we are still creatures. We are only and always creatures, because God is always Creator. Can faith in the Creator fuel and form transformative action among the creatures? That is the issue before us and the answer remains to be seen. But can we not say that it is good to be here, in the middle? Would we wisely want now another universe—say, one in which neither creature nor Creator knew limitation or risk? Martha Nussbaum does not think so:

> In raising a child, in cherishing a lover, in performing a demanding task of work or thought or artistic creation, we are aware, at some level, of the thought that each of these efforts is

structured and constrained by finite time. And the removal of that awareness would surely change the pursuits and their meaning for us in ways that we can scarcely imagine—making them, perhaps, more easy, more optional, with less of striving and effort in them, less of a particular sort of gallantry and courage. [Olympian] Gods are, as Heraclitus observed, in a paradoxical way finite; for they are dead to, closed off from, the value that we see, the beauty that delights us. . . . There would be other sources of value, no doubt, within such an existence. But its constitutive conditions would be so entirely different from ours that we cannot really imagine what they would be.[79]

Well, Christians might in faith join James Baldwin in asking after another country (Heb. 11:16).[80] We can imagine changes that are not Olympian. In the middle we are not at the end, but we do look to it. Indeed, we would move toward it in transformation. And for now it is very good to be here, in the middle, looking to and moving toward something eminently new and good. To begin or to continue, it is enough to be here. But even as we complete our orientation setting a steady compass, we may find that we are interrupted.

3. To Be Interrupted: This May Be the Beginning

To interrupt is to bring to a halt; to bring about a break in continuity or uniformity. Such talk suggests that something is already going on. Something is given. "Interrupt" is not the first word. And yet in this stopping there may be a beginning. Transformation may begin in the turbulence of interruption. Or it may not, for there are interruptions and then again there are interruptions. Perhaps the difference lies in what comes next, for "interrupt" is also not the last word. But in the middle, between the first and the last, we live where we know interruption. Does writing or speaking of this break end the interruption, thereby reestablishing the continuity of human language?[1] Interruption depends on something other than itself. We make here some effort to describe the differences known in the experience of interruption, remaining hopeful that this is not all there is.

No Abiding City: The Pulse of Life

> For here we have no lasting city. . . .
>
> (Heb. 13:14)

The notion of enduring substance has fallen on hard times. For much of the twentieth century physicists tried to wean us away by degrees from the very notion of "thing" by permitting us temporarily to fall back to some increasingly elementary particles. But the end of this development was stated forthrightly enough by Alfred North Whitehead already in 1929:

> . . . How an actual entity becomes constitutes what that actual entity is; so that the two descriptions of an actual entity are not independent. Its "being" is constituted by its "becoming." This is the "principle of process."[2]

For some Whitehead may even seem rather too calm about the pulse of life, too ready to take afternoon tea on schedule after all. How regular is that pulse, that drumbeat of becoming? What qualitative differences can we discern in the constant of change? For example, how are we to understand not the evolution of change within species, but the formation of new species? Noting the paucity of transitional fossils, recent theorists have come to speak of "punctuated equilibrium":[3]

> The fossil record shows long periods of stasis—millions of years with very little change—interspersed with bursts of rapid speciation in relatively short periods. . . . Whole developmental sequences changed at once, leading to major structural changes.[4]

Stephen Jay Gould has persistently observed that the rhythm of these alternations is not that relaxing: terror keeps company with boredom.[5]

And what of the individual human being? What is the relevance of such "big pictures" drawn by and from the selected natural sciences? Well, we live here. At the Smithsonian Institution's five-hundredth-birthday party for Copernicus, John Wheeler, the physical cosmologist and theoretical astronomer, took as his title, "The Universe as a Home for Man" (sic!).[6] Moreover, it seems that it is true not only that we are in time, but that time is in us.[7] We are inescapably temporal beings. We live from the past through the present into the future. Frank Kermode has suggested that we live with a "sense of an ending."[8] We look for the end of the story; we find suspense in incompleteness. A closer look at the human pulse of life is warranted.

Søren Kierkegaard describes the character of human temporality. In his view, each person is an unstable synthesis, a holding together in freedom of necessity and possibility.[9] Kierkegaard writes that "the possibility is to be able." When a person ponders such a possibility concretely (What am I able to do?), she becomes dizzy in anxiety. This is true of us simply as creatures:

> Anxiety may be compared with dizziness. He whose eye happens to look down into the yawning abyss becomes dizzy. But what is the reason for this? It is just as much in his own eye as in the abyss, for suppose he had not looked down. Hence anxiety is the dizziness of freedom, which emerges when the spirit wants to posit the synthesis and freedom looks down into its own possibility.[10]

The human being does not know what will happen to/through this dizzy self. But Kierkegaard is clear about how a definite result will come about—through freedom, through a decision. The human synthesis is actually established only in an act of will. It is by will that human becoming happens. We mistakenly look to reason to explain such becoming. Thus Kierkegaard was fond of making the point against Hegel that movement had no place in logic, which merely unpacks premises.[11]

Are we to juxtapose flatly the reason and the will? Do we not arrive somewhere new through our use of our rational faculties? Does not thought also throb with the pulse of life? After all, Kierkegaard himself could write this:

> Thus, consciousness is decisive. Generally speaking, conscious-
> ness—that is self-consciousness—is decisive with regard to the
> self. The more consciousness, the more self; the more con-
> sciousness, the more will; the more will, the more self.[12]

In such a way Mihalyi Csikszentmihalyi, a University of Chicago psychologist, can speak of the self as a synthesis of "two sets of instructions, one coded chemically in genes, the other coded in memes learned from the social and cultural milieu." He joins Kierkegaard in rejecting the determinism of the sociobiologists, and once again locates the critical intersection in consciousness. The self becomes conscious of the external circumstances that call for action and more fully aware of choices for response. This intervention of consciousness confers a freedom to choose and act that, despite its limitations, is real freedom.[13]

Why do we desire to know anyway? Michel Foucault asks that question and answers it:

> After all, what would be the value of the passion for knowledge
> if it resulted only in a certain knowingness . . . and not, in one
> way or another, . . . in the knower's straying afield from him-
> self? There are times in life when the question of knowing if
> one can think differently than one thinks, and perceive differ-
> ently than one sees, is absolutely necessary if one is to go on
> thinking and reflecting at all.[14]

May not such "straying afield" from oneself serve transformation? Perhaps we see that in some of the most common activities of thought. Consider the active "doubling" done in the service of thought. Paul Ricoeur has helped us recognize the "semantic imper-tinence" of holding dissimilarities together in metaphorical state-ment.[15] What of irony, when in order to convey truth we say one thing and mean another?[16] Can we celebrate satire as "the last flicker of originality" in a decadent culture?[17] Or, consider the singularity identified by William James in speaking of the power of "attention" and the strain of keeping the consciousness clear and focused.[18] In diverse ways thought promises possibility.

We also do well to ponder the place of conflict in the development of creative thinking. In writing of *How We Think,* John Dewey stressed that thinking truly begins when a "sense of a problem" is present:

> The difficulty may be felt with sufficient definiteness as to set the mind at once speculating upon its probable solution, or an undefined uneasiness and shock may come first, leading only later to definite attempt to find out what is the matter. Whether the two steps are distinct or blended, there is the factor emphasized in our original account of reflection—viz. the perplexity or problem.[19]

James Loder has made a study of scientific, aesthetic, and therapeutic knowing and finds the same first step in what he calls "transformational logic":

> The first step begins when there is an apparent rupture in the knowing event. Conflict initiates the knowing response, and the more one cares about the conflict the more powerful will be the knowing event.[20]

One who makes conflict or contradiction the very engine of thought is none other than G. W. F. Hegel. Particularly as known through Kierkegaard, he is usually touted as the archexponent of continuity in development. But one must take account of passages like this:

> What is "familiarly known" is not properly known, just for the reason that it is "familiar." . . . Knowledge of that sort, with all its talk, never gets from the spot. . . . But the life of the mind is not one that shuns death, and keeps clear of destruction; it endures death and in death maintains its being. It only wins to its truth when it finds itself utterly torn asunder.[21]

One may be granted some skepticism at this point. Hegel's mind held together rather well, after all. But these testimonies do come together with the more explicit Kierkegaardian appeals to will to tell us that there is activity, even will, in "how we think." To be a human being is to be a candidate for interruption. As creatures, as selves, then, we seem fit to "get from the spot" (Hegel) or "stray afield" (Foucault) through will and/or reason. But of course the tale of interruption is not to be fully told if one does not look outside the self. In *The Fragility of Goodness* Martha Nussbaum leads us into the world of Greek tragedy and philosophy to ponder luck. She is speaking of "what happens to a person . . . that does not happen through his or her own agency."[22] Her inquiry is not disinterested. She feels the force of that which luck troubles, still present in the contemporary self:

> . . . the Platonic conception of a self-sufficient and purely rational being, cleansed of the "barnacles" and the "seaweed" of passion, the "many stony and wild things that have been encrusted all over it," freed from contingent limitations on its power.[23]

Yet she lifts up an alternative image of the agent, the agent as plant:

> . . . a kind of human worth that is inseparable from vulnerability, an excellence that is in its nature other-related and social, a rationality whose nature it is not to attempt to seize, hold, trap, and control, in whose values openness, receptivity, and wonder play an important part.[24]

Is that which enters the self from without best termed an "interruption"? Does the "luck" label adequately recognize the receptivity and activity of the self so entered? These questions must be asked; but both terms well convey that the pulse of life given to us includes such currents flowing into the self. Theology can fittingly claim that current as part of the goodness of creation. Thus Eberhard Jungel has written of how a human being is:

> . . . that creature whose being is not in immediate correspondence with itself, but is capable of being interrupted at any moment by other things that exist, and in fact is always being so interrupted. . . . Human life occurs, then, when the continuity of earthly life and existence is interrupted, in that something intervenes and is apprehended (and thus comes to be known). Human life, therefore, *is* the interruption of the continuity of created life by the occurrence of truth.[25]

And he writes movingly of how that which is beautiful interrupts us:

> The cry, the exclamation, the shout of ecstasy or even the (no less eloquent) stupefied speechlessness, which is clearly nothing other than an interjection, a cry turned inwards: these are all unmistakable indications of such an interruption through encounter with beauty.[26]

The pulse of life impels us into contact with that which is other than ourselves, and so we come to know truth and beauty. This is often good, part of what we spoke of in the last chapter as the grace of creation. But is it always so? I think not. Do we not also, simply as creatures, experience what Edward Farley has called "benign alienation"? He refers to the sheer fact of alterity and what comes with it:

> Thus, the other is experienced as one who is in the world alongside me but who contests my version of it and pursues his or her own aims and agendas. In other words, the other is a center of needs, aims, and practical actions that I cannot possess, occupy, or replace.[27]

The resulting incompatibilities are benign in that they do not involve evil intentions. But they bring much pain into human life. With the pain come questions. Can such painful interruptions be comprehended as part of a good creation? Can they join earthquakes and hurricanes as evil "natural" to the goodness of the world?

Students of human relationship do argue that in challenging interpersonal dynamics genuine transformation can begin. In examining the major theories of developmental psychology in the twentieth century, Carol Gilligan found that conflict is often a precursor of new development. The heightened vulnerability brought on by a crisis also signals the emergence of a potential strength and a dangerous opportunity for growth.[28] May psychotherapy, for example, provide a way in which a person who has repressed chaotic and unmanageable elements of the psyche be enabled to reincorporate such realities into awareness?[29] In a similar mode Gilligan's colleague at Harvard, Robert Kegan, can speak positively of the "irritability" of the self as part of the capacity for growth.[30]

Human experience bears witness to the possibility of transformative growth beginning in painful interruption. Yet the outcome is not always so happy. Something will happen: breakdown or breakthrough or some mixture of the two.[31] We know this contingency and ambiguity in the middle of life where we are interrupted. There is a discord between our expectations and life as it actually occurs to us; as if an "against the grainness" is built into life itself, yielding a fundamental unpredictability. Some element of surprise seems to cut across life from the cosmic to the personal. Hannah Arendt wrote of this:

> It is in the nature of beginning that something new is started which cannot be expected from whatever may have happened before. This character of startling unexpectedness is inherent in all beginning and all origins. Thus the origin of life from

inorganic matter is an infinite improbability of inorganic
processes, as is the coming into being of the earth viewed from
the standpoint of processes in the universe, or the evolution of
human out of animal life. The new always happens against the
overwhelming odds of statistical laws and their probability,
which for all practical, everyday purposes amounts to certainty; the new therefore always appears in the guise of a miracle.[32]

Or in the guise of an interruption. Arendt wrote these words in
the 1950s. But Ian Barbour, physicist theologian writing more than
three decades later, offers corroborating testimony:

For every billion anti-protons in the early universe, there were
one-billion-and-one protons. The billion pairs annihilated one
another to produce radiation, with just one proton left over. A
greater or smaller number of survivors—or not survivors at all
if they have been evenly matched—would have made our kind
of material world impossible. The laws of physics seem to be
symmetrical between particles and antiparticles; why was
there a tiny asymmetry?[33]

Barbour's essay was published in 1989, that miraculous year of global
political transformation. At the end of this turbulent century we do
not need laboratory instruments to agree with Arendt that transformative, "against the odds," changes do occur. And Arendt, a German
Jew who fled to France in 1933 and to the United States in 1941,
would not deny that such change can come in crisis and with pain.[34]

We are no longer dealing merely with creational interruption,
with the fact that as finite creatures we find that we have no abiding
city. We turn next to speak of interruption in relation to the violation of creation. But what is given in the asymmetry of reality that
leads us onto the ontological ground of such violation? Whence
comes interruption in creation? In a word, from the *other*. The self
dizzy over possibility is drawn and repelled by the possibility of
moving "from the spot" to something, something other as actual and
therefore new. The French Jewish philosopher Emmanuel Levinas
has written in particularly powerful ways of this alienation through
benign alterity:

The absolutely other is the Other. He and I do not form a number. The collectivity in which I say "you" or "we" is not a plural of the "I." I, you—these are not individuals of a common
concept. Neither possession, nor the unity of number nor the
unity of concepts link me to the Stranger, the Stranger who

disturbs the being at home with oneself. But Stranger also
means free one. Over him I have no *power*. He escapes my grasp
by an essential dimension, even if I have him at my disposal.
He is not wholly in my site.[35]

David Tracy measures the matter:

> The real face of our period, as Emmanuel Levinas saw with
> such clarity, is the face of the other: the face that commands,
> "Do not kill me." The face insists: do not reduce me or anyone
> else to your narrative.[36]

Is this word of the other the whole truth of creation? I think it is
not; but this word speaks a fundamental truth and, indeed, a truth
often forgotten, neglected, or suppressed. This word speaks truthfully about creation but is not the whole truth—because God the creator is One whose very being and becoming are in relationship. In
relationship there is difference, and there is connection. Difference is
an essential component of relationship. Thence come interruptions.
It is for this reason that Arnold Boisen was right that the human
body is such that growth seeks a jagged edge of tissue.[37] And the
cosmos we creatures have been given seems more than willing to
provide jagged edges through the convergence of randomness, law-
likeness, and plurality.[38]

From difference it follows that we dwell in ambiguity, as surely as
our knowing traverses the individuality of our being.[39] This is true
of creation. The full and final certainty lies beyond us. But Simone
de Beauvoir would still remind us that this is not the whole truth,
for ambiguity is not absurdity. A half century ago she wrote this:

> To declare that existence is absurd is to deny that it can ever be
> given a meaning; to say that it is ambiguous is to assert that its
> meaning is never fixed, that it must be constantly won.[40]

To struggle to win meaning, to risk the loss of life itself—this is the
stuff of freedom. On such turf of struggle, freedom, and risk, the
hope of transformation resides. Interruption seems grounded deep in
the sheer structure of creation, as surely as the other is essentially
given in the pulse of life. Interruption is not the last word. With the
other comes connection as well. But we have not yet plumbed the
depths of interruption. We cannot rest back comfortably with the
assurance that the interruptions in our lives are well-grounded. We
cannot, for we find that what we feel is nothing less than a shaking
of the foundations.

The Shaking of the Foundations: The Destruction of Evil

> ". . . The foundations of the earth tremble. The earth is utterly
> broken, the earth is torn asunder, the earth is violently shaken."
> (Isa. 24:18b-19)

It may seem an overstatement to apply the strong word interruption
to what we have thus far considered. Time's flying arrow, the daily
round of decisions, the meanderings of our minds, the life with others—even the inevitability of our passing—what is this but the sheer
structure of our creatureliness? Well, perhaps that is so; perhaps we
would settle for saying only that, if it were not for something else
that has entered this fair creation, something that has interrupted
life and mocks any attempt to speak serenely of "going with the
flow." Is it a problem that our human habitations fade from view,
that we have no abiding city? While we debate that question something enters to shake the very foundations of what we have built
here. I speak of evil, as we must. The heart of the matter for any
Christian talk of transformation is not hurricanes but holocausts, not
the rough edges of benign alienation but the perversity of violation.[41] The Judeo-Christian tradition knows the difference. It sings
of creation, but it also cries out a second word: fall. That this is a second word, an interruption, is crucial in what Paul Ricoeur has called
the Adamic myth:

> In telling of the fall as an event, springing up from an
> unknown source, it [the myth] furnishes anthropology with a
> key concept; the *contingency* of that radical evil which the peni-
> tent is always on the point of calling his evil nature. Thereby
> the myth proclaims the purely "historical" character of that
> radical evil; it prevents it from being regarded as primordial
> evil. Sin may be "older" than sins, but innocence is still
> "older."[42]

Surely any attempt to describe the dynamics of transformation is
doomed if evil is not recognized. Of course there is the risk that we
would settle for talk, for tidily locating the intruder in our theological system. Karl Marx can still serve us with the stern reminder:
"The point is to change it." But if one of the powers of evil lies in its
gift of disguise, we are not apt to do much changing without explicit efforts at identification. If we look evil in the eye, there is some
chance that we can see how transformation can take place over

against—and even through—the interruptive destruction of evil. But how shall we employ the connective function of language to illumine the destructive severing of evil? Is not evil precisely the unspeakable? Susan Shapiro writes of the holocaust:

> . . . To speak and to write at all is necessarily to project a future and thus to order and distance oneself from the event by making it past. The other side of the risk, however, is the betrayal implicit in forever keeping silent about the event of the Holocaust, not telling, not witnessing, not testifying.[43]

She chose and I choose to risk the way of the word, seeking to illumine the dark light that evil casts.

Let us start with what may be both easiest to see and hardest to understand, the clear-eyed intent to act against the Creator and the creation. Human beings do will to harm for harm's sake. Søren Kierkegaard critiques what he terms the "Socratic definition"—that "when someone does not do what is right, then neither has he understood what is right":

> But wherein is the definition defective? . . . It lacks a dialectical determinant appropriate to the transition from having understood something to doing it. In this transition Christianity begins; by taking this path, it shows that sin is rooted in willing and arrives at the concept of defiance. . . .[44]

In such defiance the self wills to be itself, "severing itself from any relation to a power that has established it." He adds:

> . . . The self in despair wants to be master of itself or to create itself, to make his self into the self he wants to be, to determine what he will have or not have in his concrete self.[45]

Here, then, we are speaking of that sin which Reinhold Niebuhr was so trenchant in exposing, the sin of pride.[46] Here the human fist in the face of God is clearly exposed. Niebuhr held that "the Pauline exposition of man's self-glorification . . . is really an admirable summary of the whole Biblical doctrine of sin."[47] We do not lack examples of such sin; indeed, they hardly seem to interrupt business as usual. Niebuhr points to moral and spiritual pride as perhaps subtler forms. A sense of insecurity plays a role in this fall. More recently Edward Farley has elaborated on that connection:

> What happens when we anxiously experience our vulnerability as our ultimate condition? . . . What kind of resistance is possible when the world order itself is the problem? . . . When

human agents transform inescapable vulnerability into something contingent and manageable, they refuse the structure
and situation of their finitude. . . . The perennial candidates for
things that remove our vulnerability and provide a securing
foundation are religions, sciences, nations, social movements,
comprehensive interpretive schemes, methods that enable criticism of or interpret the world, value preserving institutions,
and even revolutions to procure freedom and justice.[48]

We could add to this sad and familiar bill of particulars. One thinks
of how liberation theologians have persistently called our attention
to the claiming of universal authority for a specific way of thinking.[49] The point needs to be made, and not the least with reference
to fundamental world views. Thus Robert Solomon speaks of the
Kantian "transcendental pretense":

The self is not just another entity in the world, but in an
important sense it creates the world, and the reflecting self
does not just know itself, but in knowing itself knows all
selves, and the structure of any and every possible self. . . .The
underlying presumption is that in all essential matters everyone, everywhere, is the same.

Solomon notes that this pretense "is no innocent philosophical thesis, but a political weapon of enormous power." With this weapon in
hand:

Philosophers who never left their home towns [Kant: Koenigs-
berg] declared themselves experts on "human nature," and
weighed the morals of civilizations and "savages" thousands of
miles beyond their ken.[50]

And mid-range between the individual's domineering behavior and
the grand sweep of a particular school's metaphysical vision, Michel
Foucault has shown us how the quest to gain and maintain power
lies behind and within the prevailing social conceptions of insanity,
medicine, the prison, and sexuality.[51]

We know this evil. No full listing of instances is needed and Farley's logic about the resistance to recognizing vulnerability is appeal-
ing. But neither the quantity of examples nor the quality of his
explanation remove the mystery of this heart of darkness.[52] Who can
understand the holocaust? Who can fathom Cambodia? How is such
purposeful destruction finally to be comprehended? Must we not
speak with Arthur Cohen of a "caesura," a cutting, of such human

organs of understanding as history and language?[53] As we face the purging death camps of mid-century or the ethnic cleansing of century's end, are we not exiled from the interpretive schemes our traditions reliably provide?[54] Verily, the foundations of our understanding, even our perception, are shaken to the point of destruction. What is clear in the very extreme of incomprehensibility is that human existence is interrupted by willful evil. We return from the historical journey to the point Kierkegaard made of the individual: reason does not rule the human heart. Thomas Merton wrote a "Devout Meditation in Memory of Adolf Eichmann" in which he said this:

> We rely on the sane people of the world to preserve it from barbarism, madness, destruction. And now it begins to dawn on us that it is precisely the *sane* ones who are the most dangerous.[55]

Such defiance tears the relational fabric of creation. One might speak, as Luther did, of the damage done when a self created for relationships is curved in upon itself.[56] The interruption of evil is truly destructive. That is true as well of a second face of evil, one often hidden from view. If we were to term defiance a "sin of strength," we would need a category like "sin of weakness" to speak of a softer form of destructiveness. Kierkegaard had the category in place in his understanding of the sickness unto death. He writes of the despair in which the self does not will to be itself.[57] This softer face of evil has found increasing recognition, particularly in feminist theology. Catherine Keller summarizes the distinction, pointing us in this direction:

> . . . Feminist theology has shown . . . that the traditional definitions of sin as pride, arrogance, self-interest and other forms of exaggerated self esteem miss the mark in the case of women, who in this culture suffer from too little self-esteem, indeed too little self.[58]

Here we do not speak of a fist raised against God and God's creation. Strong evil is clearly not merely a lack of the good, for it has the integrity of its own energy and efficacy.[59] Yet not all of evil's efficacy is to be found in sins of strength. But what acts against God in weakness? It is less clear just how to understand the deceptively destructive agency involved in "weakness." First of all, to speak of sins of weakness is not to deny that there are genuine victims. In our freedom, our 'strength,' we do make others victims. And at times, we may do the same in our weakness. But, secondly, even from the side of strength we can recognize some departures from a naked intent to do harm. In *The Plague* Camus wrote:

> . . . the evil that is in the world always comes of ignorance, and good intentions may do as much harm as malevolence if they lack understanding . . . the most incorrigible vice being that of an ignorance that fancies it knows everything and therefore claims for itself the right to kill.[60]

One wonders about the culpability of much of the ignorance in which we do harm, but we may need to recall how well disguised the evil may be. Karl Barth had to speak strongly to the East German pastor (who had asked whether it would be permissible to "pray away" their government) about the "Egyptian flesh pots" of the American way of life.[61] So did Alexandr Solzhenitsyn in his commencement address at Harvard two decades later, when he excoriated the American audience for *their* lack of courage and values.[62]

Robert Jay Lifton has written of how a certain numbing can take place as a protective device both for victims and victimizers.[63] That may go far to explain our behavior when we acquiesce in evil. There does seem to be a kind of banality to evil. Controversially, Hannah Arendt found that banality even in Adolf Eichmann who claimed that his role in the "Final Solution" was an accident and that almost anybody could have taken his place.[64] Perhaps she was right, and perhaps those who protest her view are right as well.[65] In the complexity of human agency in evil, may there not be *both* a will to harm and a sense of simply settling for the sinful status quo as the way things are done in the world? The second seems to minimize responsibility, as one simply accepts what is given to one. But must one follow orders?

Or to turn to the interior life of the self, do I have no responsibility with regard to, say, the depressed feelings that afflict me? Robert Solomon has argued against what he calls a "hydraulic" model of the emotions, where we are at the mercy of blind or stupid forces. His contention is that we "make ourselves depressed, think ourselves into grief, contemplate our way to joy, and litigate our way into guilt."[66] That is too much to say. I repeat: there are actual victims, and emotion is a way of connecting with a real world not subject to the dictates of the self's naked will. But may we not have some responsibility *in*, if not *for*, our emotions? We do choose how to act in our feelings. May we be back to Kierkegaard: in the self there is something that does not will to be a self?

Or at least not the self intended by the Creator. That is once again the point: the evil that interrupts in weakness works destructively. Here the destruction may be most directly the loss of possibility, but in such denigration and diminishment the self and others do actual ly suffer. The novelist William Styron, who in *Sophie's Choice* and *The Confessions of Nat Turner* wrote powerfully of the suffering initiated quite directly from without, had his own testimony to the suffering of depression within:

> Sometimes, though not very often, such a disturbed mind will turn to violent thoughts regarding others. But with their minds turned agonizingly inward, people with depression are usually dangerous only to themselves. The madness of depression is, generally speaking, the antithesis of violence. It is a storm indeed, but a storm of murk. Soon evident are the slowed-down responses, near paralysis, psychic energy throttled back close to zero. Ultimately, the body is affected and feels sapped, drained.[67]

The causes of depression may be hard to sort out, but the destructive effect is clear enough.

Is suffering the whole story? Or is there in the destruction of evil any hope for transformation? We surely need to remain vigilant against masochistic thinking at this point.[68] African American and feminist theologians warn eloquently against using the notion of redemptive suffering in such a way as to perpetuate the suffering by adding a cloak of justification.[69] Yet there may be some ways in which transformation can begin in the interruption by evil.

To be able to call evil by its real name is something. In being disillusioned something else may start. In experiencing the genuine destructiveness of evil at least the romantic dream of human progress is interrupted. In failure the taproot of evil may be exposed.[70] Perhaps that is what Franz Kafka had in mind:

> If the book we are reading does not wake us, as with a fist hammering on our skull, why then do we read it? So that it shall make us happy? Good God, we would also be happy if we had not books, and such books as make us happy we could, if need be, write ourselves. But what we must have are those books

which come upon us like ill-fortune, and distress us deeply,
like the death of one we love better than ourselves, like suicide.
A book must be an ice-axe to break the sea frozen inside us.[71]

I am convinced that something transformative can begin in such
interruption. In South Africa Nelson Mandela's government established a Truth and Reconciliation Commission. Victims told the
commission of what happened to their families, of middle-of-the-
night arrests and disappearances. And perpetrators, lured by the
promise of amnesty upon corroboration, told of what they had done.
The first received some stature in telling what they experienced and
in hearing others reveal, if not confess, their crimes. Observers close
to the scene suggested that something might be happening in the
soul of the perpetrator as well. The process was often painful. But
may the truth that interrupts us lead to reconciliation? It seems it
may.[72]

In such telling there is something more than interruption. Perhaps *what* is said interrupts, driving the speaker and the hearer back
to a painful past. But *that* it is said and heard opens out to a future.
Truth *and* reconciliation call into a new future. In interruption, even
the interruptive destruction of evil, there is relationship. We do not
interrupt ourselves. Or the self that does is not simply one with
itself. The difference of otherness acts to interrupt.

Who is that other? No single name will suffice. There are interruptions and then there are interruptions. But the Christian believes
that one other who is there is God. Even in the destruction of evil? It
is past time to own up to the ambiguity of the phrase. The genitive
is subjective: we have been speaking of the destructive interruptions
evil works, whether in strength or weakness. But before the holy
God of judgment does not evil itself face some kind of destruction?
In Isaiah's view, why do the foundations of the earth tremble? They
do so, because "the windows of heaven are opened" (Isa. 24:18b)!
What is the believer to do when driven to the "Why me?" question?
We certainly must not abandon the distinction between victim and
perpetrator. But in any given interruption, the two roles may seem
to crowd into each other.[73] And so we are led to ask another question:
may God be acting in the destruction of evil, including our evil?

Faith in the Creator provides a perspective in which the question
of God's action in the destruction of evil can be addressed. Indeed it
is the necessary perspective, if I have been correct in contending that

in all that God does we meet the creator God. In this perspective what can be said about the possibility, purpose, and method of God's action in the destruction of evil? That God continues to act toward God's creation is fundamental here. Creation does continue. Christian theologians rightly struggle to make distinctions between such notions as "preservation," "concurrence," and "government."[74] But beneath the distinctions lies the fundamental rejection of deism. As Paul made clear on Mars Hill: it is not merely our origin that is in God, for "in him we live, move, and have our being" (Acts 17:28). God continues to act in our lives, even in our acts. Hence it may well be that God is one of the actors in the interruption we experience in the destruction of evil.

Why would God act so? With what purpose? What of biblical talk of the wrath of God? Such talk cannot be dismissed, but great harm has been done by careless or calculating talk of God's wrath separated from the love of a God who in love wills to create. Abraham Heschel sets us on the right path:

> The prophets never thought that God's anger is something that cannot be accounted for, unpredictable, irrational. It is never a spontaneous outburst, but a reaction occasioned by the conduct of man. Indeed, it is the major task of the prophet to set forth the facts that account for it, to insist that the anger of God is not a blind, explosive force, operating without reference to the behavior of man, but rather voluntary and purposeful, motivated by concern for right and wrong.[75]

The choices of the creatures do matter to God. My sinful choices harm other creatures whom God loves, and indeed harm me. They harm God. Surely we must speak of the anger of God, remembering with Heschel that "the secret of anger is God's care."[76] I stand with Eberhard Jungel in this:

> The statement "God is love" must accompany all talk about God, even about the anger and judgment of God.[77]

How strange it would be if a loving God did not act to discipline the beloved, to call the beloved to repentance! The book of Hosea speaks of that disciplining love in very strong terms. In a metaphor meant to shock people who identified themselves as God's favored ones, Israel is likened to an unfaithful wife, and the husband both feels and acts: "Therefore I will hedge up her way with thorns; and I will build a wall against her, so that she cannot find her paths" (Hos.

2:6). We must be careful not to turn such metaphors around; God's pain and anger over human sin does not grant biblical permission for the domination of one spouse over another. But the prophet makes his point; God's anger is the anger of one who loves deeply and acts in hope that the beloved will repent. Of course it does not follow that what God does over against evil will feel like love to the creatures. Jungel knows that:

> To think God as love is the task of theology. And in doing so it must accomplish two things. It must, on the one hand, do justice to the essence of love, which as a predicate of God may not contradict what people experience as love. And on the other hand, it must do justice to the being of God which remains so distinctive from the event of human love that "God" does not become a superfluous word.[78]

How does this loving creator God act toward the creatures? Much could be said in response to this question, but the pertinent note to strike here is that God acts through "secondary causes," through God's creatures.[79] The Scriptures speak of this repeatedly. Any given creature may seem ill-suited to serve the Creator's will. Walter Brueggemann has called our attention to the "epistemological abrasiveness" associated with the figure of Moses.[80] It is not easy to swallow the words of this secondary cause. Indeed, James Nohrnberg has devoted nearly 400 pages to a study of the meaning of Moses in the Bible. On the last page of that study the strangeness of Moses is not overcome:

> The "symbolic" of this life is to be found in the boundaries it mediates. Putting Egypt behind him as a resource, and keeping Israel ahead of him as a reward, Moses is an honored but twice-alienated Hebrew whom God buries outside the promised land beyond Jordan, and an honorary but twice-excommunicated Egyptian who perishes in the wilderness beyond the Reed Sea. . . . Whether in Midian, Sinai, or Moab, Moses' own existence typically occupies a perilous threshold between two territories or jurisdictions, and so, perforce, defines him for either side as one coming from abroad or beyond. His was a generation that perished in the desert, yet lived in a numinous interval between worldly dispensations. He suffered a speech impediment, yet voiced the name of God. Moses' whole life—like the Passover, and the Tetragrammaton itself—is the constituting of an interruption.[81]

The sturdy figure of Moses will surely tell us that the secondary cause is no cipher. Moses looks like Moses; God is not here on display. Moses may seem—and be—a less than perfect instrument. And we have not mentioned a figure like Cyrus (Isa. 45) who—like it or not—is the Lord's "anointed." Things are not as they seem to be. Or they are not *merely* as they seem to be. When God acts to destroy evil, we may struggle to see that transformative work. And on Christian faith's reading of things those who did not see God at work in the revolutionary Jesus were not stupid.[82] This one came to bring not peace, but a sword (Matt. 10:34). Could it still be so? Could God be at work transformatively in the "dance of anger" in a relationship, in the power of internal criticism to erode the authority of an unjust government?[83] What of Luther's twenty-first thesis for the Heidelberg disputation? Could it be true that:

> It is impossible for a person not to be puffed up by his good works unless he has first been deflated and *destroyed* by suffering and evil until he know that he is worthless and that his works are not his but God's.[84]

Has God chosen to bring forth "the things that are not in order to bring to nothing things that are" (1 Cor. 1:28, RSV)? To cut to the chase: to destroy evil, may God have to destroy us?

It surely may seem so. In his much cited 1973 *Journal of Religion* article, Brian Gerrish forced the reader to confront Luther and Calvin on the hiddenness of God. Nearly a quarter century later his long time colleague at the University of Chicago, David Tracy, reached back to the distinction Gerrish stressed between God hidden under the form of the opposite in Christ and God hidden apart from Christ. Tracy particularly directs our attention to the second hiddenness, as heard in the cry of the marginalized today. He finds the sense of interruptive terror particularly present in Mark's gospel, culminating in the cry from the cross, "My God, my God why have you forsaken me?"[85]

Yet Hosea calls us back with this:

> How can I give you up, Ephraim?
> How can I hand you over, O Israel?
> How can I make you like Adam?
> How can I treat you like Zeboiim?
> My heart recoils within me;
> my compassion grows warm and tender.

I will not execute my fierce anger;
I will not again destroy Ephraim.
For I am God and no mortal
the Holy One in your midst,
and I will not come in wrath. (Hos. 11:8-9)

In another translation God's promise is "I will not come to destroy" (RSV). Faith holds to this. And to this: God will come. Indeed the Christian trusts a coming God who has come. So Gerrish can quote Luther in a way that reflects confidence that the will of that God is ultimately one:

Begin from below, from the Incarnate Son . . . Christ will bring you to the Hidden God. . . . If you take the Revealed God, he will bring you to the Hidden God at the same time.[86]

This faith struggles to believe that God would work transformatively in the interruptions that come to us, when evil bids to destroy us and when we seem about to be destroyed in our evil. When the maker of heaven and earth acts, creation is advanced, evil is undone and sins are forgiven. And we are called ahead into some new world. So would not J. B. Metz be right in his short word? "The shortest definition of religion: interruption."[87] But it is a struggle. After all there are interruptions, and then there are interruptions. In the pain of the moment, am I experiencing the creaturely gift of "discretionary shame," which guards the boundaries of personhood? Or am I experiencing the "disgrace shame" in which the worth of my person is put in question? Or am I being called to deal with my guilt as one who perpetrates and/or acquiesces in destructive evil?[88] Wise discernment is needed. So, if we find ourselves interrupted, what shall we do?

A Voice in the Wilderness: The Testimony of the Negative

In the year that King Uzziah died, I saw the Lord sitting on a throne, high and lofty. . . . Seraphs were in attendance above him. . . . And one called to another and said:
"Holy, holy, holy is the Lord of hosts;
the whole earth is full of his glory."
The pivots on the thresholds shook at the voices of those who called, and the house filled with smoke. And I said: "Woe is me! I am lost, for I am a man of unclean lips, and I live among a people of unclean lips; yet my eyes have seen the King, the Lord of hosts!" (Isa. 6:1a, 2a, 3-5)

... For my thoughts are not your thoughts,
nor are your ways my ways, says the Lord.
For as the heavens are higher than the earth
so are my ways higher than your ways
and my thoughts than your thoughts. (Isa. 55:8-9)

It's all there for Isaiah in the temple. If the whole earth is full of its Creator's glory, creatures can expect to be interrupted. But something more than creaturely finitude is being identified in the confession of unclean lips, within and without. It adds up to woe or, in another phrasing, to being lost. It is not merely that this impermanent city will pass some day or that the supports for human habitation are shaking. In this interruptive moment the prophet is lost, without the shelter of a roof over his head or the normalizing structure of a city. Such interruption pitches him into a wilderness. What is the person of faith to do? The Christian clings to a God who comes. If I should meet the coming God in a concrete moment of interruption, what might this portend for me? What might be expected for/of me?

To tremble. When interrupted, we do tremble. Derrida has it right:

I tremble at what exceeds my seeing and my knowing although it concerns the innermost parts of me, right down to my soul, down to the bone, as we say.[89]

That trembling is ambiguous:

... we tremble first of all because we don't know from which direction the shock came, whence it was given (whether a good surprise or a bad shock, sometimes a surprise received as a shock).[90]

The Christian accepts such ambiguity regarding the whence of the interruption. We have not forgotten the evil that acts against God and God's creation with a clear-eyed intensity that surely does in some sense exceed our seeing and knowing. Our own evil is that excessive. But the Christian does not think evil could evict God from the universe, or from the painful interruptions of life. If we should meet God coming concretely in such interruption, trembling does place us in the right territory. Isaiah knows this: on holy ground we tremble.

We tremble, quite simply because of who God is. It is not so much a question of what God may do. Beneath the possible behavior of God, at bottom it is before the being of God that believers tremble. For here we meet the one who as creator is truly Other, who interrupts our sense of the very limits of reality.[91] The Isaiah who speaks in the later passage has it right: there is some verticality here and the high God's thoughts are not our thoughts. What is it right to do with/before such a being? Two options make trembling sense to us: to adore or to abhor that being. Those responses have the right ontological scale. And both abhorrence and adoration remain real choices in the several ways of meeting God: first as a creature before the only one who is truly Creator, and then before the one who comes to set us free from evil, including our evil.

We might describe these options as offense or faith. Those are Kierkegaard's categories, and he makes clear that both options always apply. Thus even the "good news" of the gospel may be met with offense:

> And now, what of Christianity! Christianity teaches that this individual human being—and thus every single individual human being, no matter whether man, woman, servant girl, cabinet minister, merchant, barber, student, or whatever—this individual human being exists before God, this individual human being who perhaps would be proud of having spoken with the king once in his life, this human being who does not have the slightest illusion of being on intimate terms with this one or that one, this human being exists before God, may speak with God any time he wants to, assured of being heard by him—in short, this person is invited to live on the most intimate terms with God! Furthermore, for this person's sake, also for this very person's sake, God comes to the world, allows himself to be born, to suffer, to die, and this suffering God— he almost implores and beseeches this person to accept the help that is offered to him! Truly, if there is anything to lose one's mind over, this is it![92]

What does adoration or faith entail? What will that call forth from us? Several seemly responses exist. One is this: silence. If you should meet God in an interruption, be quiet. Again the ontological scale is right, encompassing needful extremes. Thus C. S. Lewis closed his eschatological novel *Till We Have Faces* with these words spoken by Queen Orual after experiencing a vision in the palace gardens:

> I ended my first book with the words no answer. I know now, Lord, why you utter no answer. You are yourself the answer.

> Before your face questions die away. What other answer would
> suffice? Only words, words to be let out to battle against other
> words. Long did I hate you, long did I fear you, I might—[93]

There will be a silence even in our speaking. Thus Ann and Barry
Ulanov see this in prayer:

> Language falters. . . . Language is necessarily complex. It is
> always moving from expressed meaning to unexpressed, from
> denotation to connotation. . . . We must go beyond words,
> confiding ourselves to God, letting God help us lift our hearts
> to him in silence and sometimes even without images. All of
> this is particularly clear to us when we reach the upper terraces
> of prayer. . . . We are well beyond words, yet not outside either
> thought or feeling.[94]

Perhaps Gerard Manley Hopkins had something of this in mind
when he wrote:

> My own heart let me more have pity on; let
> Me live to sad self hereafter kind,
> Charitable; not live this tormented mind
> With this tormented mind tormenting yet. . . .
> Soul, self, come poor Jack self, I do advise
> You, jaded, let be; call off thoughts awhile.[95]

And when we do call on our thoughts, there will still be some silence
in our speaking. Thus we will speak of God in metaphor, which represents a human creativity spurred precisely by the absent presence
of the One who is qualitatively other.[96]

If we think of ontological scale, talk of death will soon enough
come into our speaking. Thus in Lewis' novel the priest Arnom adds
a postscript indicating that Orual's speaking was interrupted by her
dying! We do know something when we speak of the dying one as
"meeting his maker." Silently? Well, William Styron, having made
in his melancholia "an irreversible decision" to seek the silence of
death, throws a treasured and confidential notebook of personal
reflections into the garbage ("an annihilation of self appropriate, as
always, to melancholia's fecund self-humiliation"). His decision will
find its summary in the words Italian writer Cesare Pavese wrote
before killing himself: *"No more words. An Act. I'll never write again."*[97]

But of course, these words were written by none other than Styron. And what reversed his irreversible decision? Well, words. The
sung words of Brahms's Alto Rhapsody, which brought to mind his
mother's singing of those words in his childhood. These words

interrupted him. He says, "they pierced my heart like a dagger."[98] Human beings do tremble before death and fall silent. But there are gifts of life as well that can be received in the silence of interruption. And isn't Derrida right in speaking even of the gift of death? He offers this:

> This concern for death, this awakening that keeps vigil over death, this conscience that looks death in the face is another name for freedom.[99]

Kierkegaard knew this and names the criterion for such freedom in writing of the "lilies of the field and the birds of the air":

> When all around you is solemn silence, and when there is silence within you then do you sense, and sense with the force of infinitude, the truth of the saying, "you shall love the Lord your God and him only shall you serve," and you sense that it is you, you who shall love God, you alone in the whole world.[100]

This freedom, this irreducible sense of being a creature before the Creator, is a dizzying gift that may well silence us. And yet there will be some speaking in our silence. The speaking of prayer and poetry, yes, but even that of theology. In death there is a gift, in the presence of qualitative otherness there is a knowing to which Elizabeth Johnson bears witness:

> The triune God is not simply unknown, but positively known to be unknown and unknowable—which is a dear and profound kind of knowledge.[101]

Similarly, Lewis' Orual speaks of how "Joy silenced me,"[102] and Lewis knew well what it meant to be "surprised by joy."[103] We will soon ask what to make of the fact that in this time in many spheres we seem drawn to silence.[104] But the underlying point is: when meeting God in interruption, consider silence.

Or laughter. This may seem less likely, but what if "the comic is fundamentally discrepancy, incongruity, incommensurability"?[105] Once again we would seem to be not far from holy ground. In humor something or someone enters our lives and we can be changed in such an interruption.[106] Some kind of change surely fits a God who acts in interruption to transform creatures. We were asking what might be expected for/of us who are interrupted. Some kind of change, it seems. Silence for the infernally chatty among us. Laughter for the deadly serious.

As we are interrupted, we may expect to hear a call to turn around. When the city passes, when the foundations of what we have called "civilization" or "the world" shake and crumble, and when in Isaiah's phrasing the beautiful religious spaces of our habitation are filled with smoke—then, things will change. They will change to such extent that we need to speak of something dying in us, while ever watchful for the misuse of religious appeals to sacrifice, all too readily employed to bludgeon the human.[107] We speak of this dying best when we speak quite specifically and concretely.[108] Then we will be able to speak of something being brought to life in that creature.

In such new life we are touching the very center of the reality of transformation. But the point here was merely to indicate where transformation may begin. Perhaps we may sum up by saying that where transformation always begins is in interruption, for this newness signals the work of God who is qualitatively other than we creatures. And what then is the creature's role? Perhaps it is to listen. Anselm of Canterbury understood that:

> Now then, little man, for a short while fly from your business, hide yourself for a moment from your turbulent thoughts. Break off now your troublesome cares, and think less of your laborious occupations. Make a little time for God, and rest for awhile in him. Enter into the chamber of your mind, shut out everything but God and whatever helps you to seek him, and, when you have shut the door, seek him.[109]

If we do listen, I submit that we may hear a call.

4. To Be Called: This May Be the Coming

Interruption may not be the last reality. To be brought to a halt is not necessarily to be brought to an end. Even when we try to do justice to the breaking in of interruption, we may find ourselves driven toward something other. In the last chapter I tried to face up to life's interruptions and, yet, seemed drawn to look ahead to something more. I am not alone in feeling the pull of this "yet," even in this age of interruption.[1] Mark C. Taylor, whose *Erring* description in 1984 of the death of God, self, history, and book makes my chapter seem tame and temporizing,[2] ten years later begins an article with these words:

> It calls
>> Calls daily
>>> Calls nightly
>>>> Calls (from) without
>>>>> Beginning or end
>
>>>> A whisper so feint
>>>> A rustle so slight
>>>> A murmur so weak
>
>>>> When to respond
>>> Where to respond
>> How to respond
> To a Call that approaches (from) beyond
Without ever arriving.[3]

Taylor confesses "*Erring* was to have ended it all, but it has not."[4] So it is. We are called to a new or renewed or reformed beginning. These two, interruption and calling, seem to clamor together in the rhythm of life. Some Christian theologians speak of the work of God's Spirit as "giving life by putting to death."[5] Does transformation begin in interruption? In interruption there is something other, outside of us, something nearly impossible to ignore, that halts us. In calling something new draws us. The call invites or summons us from out ahead. This *may* be the coming of transformation; that it is so is not obvious. Perhaps that is why Taylor speaks of the call as weak or slight or as a feint. We are still not beyond ambiguity, even in calling. For that reason, while process theologians John B. Cobb Jr. and Charles Birch speak of the need to "trust Life," they quickly add:

> Trust in Life is certainly not to trust that everything different is better or that the accumulation of diverse experiences in itself will enliven us.[6]

A task of discernment lies ahead. But we can begin with this: calling into transformation comes with the gift of life.

The Gift of Image: Called Together to Be Human
As Creatures Blessed on the Earth

> It is not good that the man should be alone. . . . Then the man said, "This at last is bone of my bones and flesh of my flesh. . . . Therefore a man leaves his father and his mother and clings to his wife and they become one flesh. (Gen. 2:18a, 23a)

> . . . The Lord said in his heart, "I will never again curse the ground because of humankind, for the inclination of the human heart is evil from youth . . . . As long as the earth endures, seed time and harvest, cold and heat, summer and winter, day and night, shall not cease." God blessed Noah and his sons and said to them, "Be fruitful and multiply, and fill the earth." (Gen. 8:21b, 8:22-9:1)

The Creator's gift of life is alive. The self is called to be and to become a self. The human self is not some kind of unchanging substance that remains self-identical through all the accidents of life. The self is beckoned forward into the future. The forward logic of this beckoning, this call, fits well in the theological territory of creation and fall. Claus Westermann evoked for us the image of God as something happening in the relationship between Creator and creature.[7] And I have spoken of sin in Kierkegaardian terms as either the strong choice to become another self or as the weak will not to be the self intended by the Creator.

Moreover, some of those who study human selfhood without benefit of theological frameworks do not posit a more static self. Robert Kegan can find enough of a human subject for three hundred pages, but he makes clear that "'person' is understood to refer as much to an activity to a thing—an ever progressive motion engaged in giving itself a new form."[8] Indeed, some who write of the human seem in effect to give up anything resembling substantial self-talk. Thus Richard Rorty discards "the assumption that human beings have a natural center that philosophical inquiry can locate and illuminate." "By contrast" Rorty holds:

> . . . the view that human beings are centerless networks of beliefs and desires and that their vocabularies and opinions are determined by historical circumstance.[9]

Rorty has more than a little company. Edith Wyschogrod identifies this fellowship among certain strains of postmodernism, whether in art, literature, or philosophy, as "henophobic, as repudiating the One as the foundation of thought and being." She asks, Has not the slope of the becoming self proved to be slippery here? Without some kind of coherent center in the individual, how can we speak of persons in history and their responses and responsibilities? Wyschogrod prods us to ponder the implications of henophobia for ethics by considering the category "saint":

> There can be saints only if there is singularity, if each and every time there is compassion there are more than disseminated drops of desire, if each and every time there is suffering there is more than unanchored affliction.[10]

To speak of transformation, or with Wyschogrod of saints, is to speak of a call to become a self. This self need not resemble traditional notions of substantial selfhood. Those who reinstate the substantial self are at best naïvely confident about the solidity of the subject. Ironically, even at that best they at least risk forgetting that the strong subject who sees and describes an "objective" world is significantly active, shaping the seeing and saying. At worst this reclaiming of the solid substantial self and its world is not forgetful but purposeful in the interest of particular distributions of power, as the philosophers Derrida and Foucault relentlessly reminded us.

But in our account of what it means to be human there are two margins on the page. We do well to be, as Catherine Keller puts it, "suspicious both of mere denials of 'self' and of mere assertions of it."[11] She identifies an alternative:

> Some of us will go on working and playing at an alternative sense of self, one quicksilvery enough to elude the fixed centers

of essence, one firm enough to stand its ground. Standing one's ground: this allows the persistence needed not to remain self-identical, which only blocks the flow of relation and energy; but to face difference, conflict, loss, reality, future. And a grounded self, unlike a fixed ego, thrives in its dependence on earth and only as earthling, on the matrix of relations to all the other earthlings.[12]

Keller, writing in the process tradition of Alfred North Whitehead, recognizes that a many comes together to constitute the one dynamic self.[13] But she does not stand alone on this ground. Søren Kierkegaard, not conventionally classified with process thinkers, writes of the goal and the challenge for human life:

> In the life of the individual the task is to achieve an ennoblement of the successive within the simultaneous. To have been young, and then to grow older, and finally to die, is a very mediocre form of human existence; this merit belongs to every animal. But the unification of the different stages of life in simultaneity is a task set for human beings.[14]

Despite—or even through—the interruptions that come with the pulse of life or the shaking of the foundations the self is called together by the Creator.

What more may be said in this understanding of human selfhood between the margins of unmoved substance and sheer process? Where does this story lead us? To a living self, a self facing possibility—or, more concretely, possibilities.[15] James Loder describes the step in transformative experience that follows (what I have called) interruption:

> To be temporarily baffled over a conflict in one's situation is to be drawn both consciously and unconsciously into the familiar psychological process of searching out the possible solutions, taking apart errors, keeping parts, and discarding others.[16]

A multitude of particulars lies clustered in possibility. But there is a responsible agent at hand. For example, it is possible for this becoming self to make, and to keep or break, promises. Vincent Colapietro depicts the needed agency:

> The self must be conceived as a being who is integral and centered enough to have the capacity to make promises, pledge loyalty, etc. While it may be not only fashionable, but also correct, to stress how fluid and ambiguous are the boundaries between self and other, it is nonetheless imperative to recognize there are

> limits to this fluidity and ambiguity—if there is *to be* a recog-
> nizable self capable of executing its most basic, because most
> indelibly self-defining acts. While it may also be correct to cast
> doubt on the *fixity* or even *stability* of the "I" as a center of inten-
> tion, it is nevertheless necessary to see the self as a continuous,
> even if continuously changing, center of purpose and power.[17]

It is with possibilities of that sort that the transforming call has to
do. And the doing will involve making decisions, as the self is called
to respond to the possibilities envisioned.

This becoming in possibility always takes place in relation to the
other. We can claim a second meaning for the subtitle for this section—"called together to be human." The individual ("indivisible")
self is called "together," into a dynamic process of becoming, not a
solid substance. But *selves* are called together too, for human becoming will occur in the process of partaking in relationships, which is
essential to selfhood. We have learned this in studying child development with D. W. Winnicott:

> With "the care that it receives from its mother" each infant is
> able to have a personal existence, and so begins to build up
> what might be called *a continuity of being.* . . . If the maternal
> care is not good enough then the infant does not really come
> into existence, since there is no continuity of being. . . .[18]

The risk is that the self will not be "called together" in a continuity
of being. In his discussion of "holding," physical and otherwise,
Winnicott particularly emphasized the role of key figures outside the
emerging self. But in his emphasis that the mother must be only
"good enough" (not perfect), he recognized that through the imper-
fections in the care provided, the emerging self is called to move into
the "potential space" created in the relationship.[19] More recent studies in human development have invited us to see that the relational
component does not balance individual identity but is part of its
constitution. That has been particularly noted in the study of
women's development, reaching back to Carol Gilligan's *In a Different Voice* with its witness to how women's sense of self involves issues
of responsibility for, care of, and inclusion of others.[20] More recently
a group of female faculty and therapists at the Stone Center for
Developmental Services and Studies at Wellesley College has criticized the use of terms like fusion and symbiosis for compromising
the developing combination of intimate attachment and differentiation.[21] Judith Jordan summarizes the direction of this reflection:

We are, then, beginning to construct new models of self that can encompass both the sense of coherent separateness and meaningful connection as emergent structures throughout the life span. The old lines of movement from fusion to separateness, from domination by drive to secondary process, and from undifferentiation to differentiation are presently being questioned.[22]

Perhaps we are catching on to what the ancient word in Genesis 2 tells us: it is not good for the human creature to be alone. With the gift of the image of God we are both created in and called toward relationship with the other. Robert Kegan sketches a human condition beyond both a state where the self is derived from others and one where the self is as it were an "institution" embedded in its own autonomy. He speaks of this as the "inter-individual" and of how here the two great human yearnings for differentiation and inclusion are together:

> Ego stage 5's capacity for intimacy, then, springs from its capacity to be intimate with itself, to break open the institutionality of the former balance. Locating itself now in the coordination of psychic institutions, the self surrenders its counter-dependent independence for an interdependence. Having a self. . . it now has a self to share.[23]

The human development discussed so far does not depend on religious awareness. It is not first as believers that the self-and-other dynamic arises for us, but already as creatures. The call to be human is given already in the reality of being created in the image of God.[24] But faith can make a difference in the clarity and content of the calling.

As Believers Saved for a Purpose

> "For I have seen God face to face, and yet my life is preserved." The sun rose upon [Jacob] as he passed Penuel, limping because of his hip. (Gen. 32:30b-31)

> So if anyone is in Christ, there is a new creation: everything old has passed away; see, everything has become new! (2 Cor. 5:17)

Where does the Christian find herself relative to this matter of calling? She finds herself very emphatically in creation called together with other creatures to be human. *In creation.* This much is clear in principle for Christians: faith does not transport the believer to some place other than this world, God's creation. And the Christian finds himself called *together with others* to be human. Christians know that the Creator's will for human life is given with the gift of life and are not surprised to find people apart from faith who hear that call. Indeed the Christian may be heartened by widely diverse testimonies to a common "thin" moral sense discernible within the "thickness" of particular historical and cultural understandings.[25]

So, what difference does Christian faith make? We ask this not in order to claim in the answer some presumed Christian superiority, but in order to discern what follows from faith for life. The call the Christian hears comes through interruption, not only by the pulse of life but by the destruction of evil. The Christian knows that evil— including his evil—is against God and God's creation. And the Christian knows that God is against evil, including her evil. Life is not a seamless web. And yet the Christian joins Jews and Muslims as people of the book that tells us God is "grieved to the heart" (Gen. 6:6) by evil. Even so, after the flood of judgment God can say in that same heart, "I will never again curse the ground because of humankind, for the inclination of the human heart is evil from youth" (Gen. 8: 21b). So the rainbow is set in the sky, creation's rhythms are restored, and the human beings surviving God's watery interruption are once again blessed and called.

Again, what follows from faith? Life—which is to say *new* life. Of course Christians find various ways to speak of this. With all the variety of Christian expression one central point must not be lost; this newness of life is actual. Paul the apostle doesn't seem in doubt about this: "If anyone is in Christ, there is a new creation" (2 Cor. 5:17a). How does this newness bear on the call the Christian hears to be and to become human? The most important thing to say is the shortest: it does. It hardly seems necessary to say this. Yet there are tendencies to deny that the new life is actual. A particularly vulgar and dangerous example is the formulation that because of Christ God regards the Christian graciously, but the person's actual life remains unchanged. *Simul justus et* particularly (!) *peccator.* For Christian faith such a formulation is dangerously wrong. Martin Luther, not notorious for being soft on sin, speaks luminously of two kinds of righteousness. The first righteousness through faith in Christ "swallows up all our sins in a moment," Luther says. Here we hear Paul's second word to the Corinthians: "everything old has passed away; see, everything has become new." But what follows? Because of the faith relationship with the God active in Jesus the Christ, the actual life of the believer cannot remain unchanged. This Luther calls the second righteousness:

> Therefore this alien righteousness, instilled in us without our works by grace alone—while the Father, to be sure, inwardly draws us to Christ—is set opposite original sin, likewise alien, which we acquire without our works by birth alone. Christ daily drives out the old Adam more and more in accordance with the extent to which faith and knowledge of Christ grow. For alien righteousness is not instilled all at once, but it begins, makes progress, and is finally perfected at the end through death.[26]

The Christian's new life carries a calling. A calling to what? We need to face first the fact that this new life will be one with death in it. Dietrich Bonhoeffer drove this point home in *The Cost of Discipleship:*

> When Christ calls a man [*sic!*], He bids him come and die. It may be a death like that of the first disciples who had to leave home and work to follow Him, or it may be a death like Luther's, who had to leave the monastery and go out into the world. But it is the same death every time—death in Jesus Christ, the death of the old man at His call. That is why the rich young man was so loath to follow Jesus, for the cost of following was the death of his will.[27]

There is a qualitative character to this dying. The Christian never gets finished with repentance. It is not merely that the catalogue of our acts, morally measured, is expected to show fewer failures and more successes. The sin to which we are called to die is more inward than that. Indeed, the Christian finds some genuine unity in the reality of repentance: one is always and altogether to repent. With regard to willing one thing, Søren Kierkegaard prayed for wisdom in understanding, sincerity in reception and purity, perseverance, concentration and patience in the execution of that will. That prayer well occupies the ground given in creation with the hope that "the last may be like the first, the first like the last, may be the life of a person who has willed only one thing." But then he strikes a different note:

> But, alas, this is not the way it is. Something came in between; the separation of sin lies in between; daily, day after day, something intervenes between them: delay, halting, interruption, error, perdition.

Because of the destruction of evil, the Christian's prayer must change:

> Then may you give through repentance the bold confidence
> again to will one thing. Admittedly it is an interruption of the
> usual task; admittedly it is a halting of work as if it were on a
> day of rest when the penitent . . . is alone before you in self-
> accusation. Oh, but it is indeed an interruption that seeks to
> return to its beginning so that it might rebind what is separat-
> ed, so that in sorrow it might make up for its failure, so that in
> its solicitude it might complete what lies ahead. Thus does it
> not come about that "the one distressed in repentance may suc-
> ceed in doing what the one burning in desire and the one
> determined in resolution failed to do: to will only one
> thing"?[28]

The self is called together in repentance. That is true and yet this truth has been misunderstood and/or misused in such devastating ways by folk purporting to represent Christian truth. Daphne Hampson, writing as a post-Christian theist, critiques the masochistic tendency of the Protestant theological tradition linked with Martin Luther and Reinhold Niebuhr:

> Salvation in that tradition is understood as the breaking of a
> self-enclosed self, a self which tries to become itself by itself,
> and a placing of trust in God. . . . "The sinful self, the self
> which is centred in itself must be 'crucified': . . . shattered at
> the very centre of its being." . . . If women have not on the
> whole suffered from an egotistical self, if they have not been in
> a position to dominate others, then such a prescription is
> beside the point. Rather than breaking the self, women, it may
> be suggested, need to come to themselves.[29]

This is surely a familiar criticism. But what is to be said in response? Two things, I think:

(1) Given what we face, given the reality of evil —including our own evil—against God, without death there will be no life. But it is crucial that the object of repentance be our sinfulness, not our humanity. That sinfulness includes not only sins of strength, but also those of weakness. Lois Malcolm, once again calling on Luther, now makes the point that such sins also do need to die:

> I would contend that a Lutheran dogmatics needs to recover the
> depths of the accusatory use of the law—what calls or invokes
> repentance—so that it includes all that keeps one from claim-
> ing the spiritual authority and freedom Christ gives, including,
> for example, a sense of shame and a lack of self-worth.[30]

This counsel merits acceptance with this caution: in speaking, hearing, and grasping God's call to repentance, we must refrain from assuming that we speak to a strong self within such sins of weakness. But something in the becoming self that holds one back from God's call does need to come to an end.

(2) Through this death something comes to life. In that new life it will become apparent that the weakness that sins is being overcome. It is perhaps more difficult to claim this new life for the self repenting of sins of strength. But it is crucial that we do so. What comes to life is a self willed by God the creator.[31] We come back or ahead to that. Actually, back *and* ahead. Back—for there will be creational continuity in the concrete particularity of the person. In the converted sinner we recognize the person given as creature, warts and all. But also ahead, for creation is not finished. Thus we may truly speak of a call to growth or development. Here we reconnect with a feminist concern as well articulated by Daphne Hampson:

> . . . Women naturally have a strong sense of continuity and growth. They wish to see their lives as an unfolding pattern. . . . They are interested in human lives, whether in their own person or the lives of others. Typically women have written letters, biographies, and novels. Often they have tended life. They have raised children and nursed the sick.[32]

The Christian faith surely does involve a call to "tend life," to care for growth into wholeness. Luther, Hampson's target, knew that. One no doubt can find passages that serve her critique passably well. But with his thought anchored in a strong doctrine of creation Luther was drawn to speak of growth:

> Our life is one of the beginning and of growth, not one of consummation. That person is better who has come closer to the spirit. If I have reached the moon, I must not immediately suppose that I have reached the sun as well; nor should I then despise the lesser stars. There are degrees of living and of working, then why not of understanding? . . . We are being changed from one degree of clarity to another.[33]

Of course this growth may challenge, yes even contradict, a particular cultural understanding of what growth ought to be. Once again Martin Luther:

> Christ is being preached in the gospel and is growing and increasing in the world. But this is a strange growing, one that

looks to the world like something withering and perishing. For we find the cross of Christ in it and all kinds of persecution. But we also find pure growth in it; for in the midst of death there is life, in poverty riches, in disgrace honor, and so forth—amidst evil there is sheer goodness.[34]

So, in repentance we live once again and grow more fully as God's creation. But we ask one last time, how does Christian faith figure into that call to new life? Is this life merely more of the same or is there something different here? Faith bears on the clarity and content of the call. In speaking of clarity I have in mind the motivation with which the Christian responds to the call. "We love because he first loved us" (1 John 4:19). This response is not to earn or "pay back" the love of God. The connection is far more organic or relational, as Peri Rasolondraibe makes clear in speaking of the "Way of Filiation":

> . . . When we hear the call to follow Christ, we are Word-empowered and Spirit-led to walk the way of the Son—the way of filiation—with God. I am not saying with Jon Sobrino that the way of the Son is our way *to* God. I am saying it is our way *with* God. To know Christ is to follow him. As we respond to the call "Follow Me," we learn more about the one who calls us, more about the one who is called (ourselves), and more about the journey we share together in the world.[35]

This "second use of the gospel"[36] surely does lend some clarity to the call, the clarity of a concrete person.

But what of the content of the call? For the Christian the needs of the neighbor are at the center of the call. Thus Paul Ramsey spoke of the Christian's "rights" being derived "backwards" by way of duty to the neighbor.[37] Yet we must take care not to slip back into the masochism to which Christianity seems so vulnerable. Something has gone wrong when this call is heard to require a focus upon self-sacrifice.[38] Christians might contemplate Jacob wrestling through the night at the ford of Jabbok and refusing to let the stranger go without receiving a blessing. His life is preserved and the morning sun shines on him, even if he is walking with a limp. This ancient tale does not seem to be about self-sacrifice.[39] Yet to speak, as Michael Welker does, of self-withdrawal to make space for the other, does not entail a sacrifice of self but something else:

> For the person who loves, the free self-withdrawal that characterizes the relation to the beloved persons is not perceived as a

burden or a loss. The acceptance of love is a joy for her because it makes possible the continuation and increase of love and of the freedom mediated by love.[40]

Welker's language nicely shows that the logic of this transforming call is "horizontal," not vertical.[41]

Gustaf Wingren offers this summary of what is new in the call to new life and what is not:

> There is no contradiction between this natural order and the idea that Christ has a new command to give man [sic!]. Christ's command is at one time as old as Creation and as new as salvation. . . . To care for one's children and to sacrifice oneself for one's enemies may appear to be two different things from the point of view of a barren ethical system. . . . In obeying this sharpened demand of Jesus the disciple is not breaking away from the natural law. . . . In Christ the life abundant has now appeared. This "sharpening" is the reverse side of grace and forgiveness. . . .[42]

We may have to stretch to accept Wingren's assurance of coherence, but in responding to the call, the Christian finds herself happily restored to the world of creation. Wingren has put it nicely:

> When the love of the new man [sic!] reaches down into the world of the law, it reaches down into a world already characterized by openness, a world in which there is already place for personal initiative.[43]

Surely, then, the transformation God is calling for(th) will involve a movement toward full human wholeness. This seems to be the direction in which Ted Peters wants the theological disciplines to move:

> We need to reopen discussion on the nature of salvation, especially as it concerns the relationship of the part to the whole. . . . What we need is a postmodern view which presses toward the full integration of body, soul, spirit, and context.[44]

How fine, one might say! Or how romantic. But why should we suppose we are up to what calls us? What if Walter Wink is right in arguing that "loving our enemies has become, in our time, the criterion of true Christian faith"?[45] How do we face that? Does not the cause of Christ, do not we, have real enemies? Is not L. Gregory Jones right in his severe statement of the challenge?

> Many of us tend to define our own lives more by whom we hate than by whom or what we love. This can be both because of resentment and hatred that arise from our encounters with,

and perhaps our suffering at the hands of, real enemies; but we must also confront our temptations to create enemies as a way of preserving our own distorted identities or our presumptions of power.[46]

Even if we are assured that we are not called to "forgive and forget," can we truly "will the well-being of the perpetrator"?[47] Or do we have to end up with Jonah, preferring death to facing a gracious God and the Ninevites as ones to be loved?

Hearing a call to such radical transformation, we ask "How can/does this happen?"

The Task of Imagination: Called Forward to Become Human

The Temporal and the Historical

> A river flows out of Eden to water the garden, and from there it divides and becomes four branches. . . . The Lord God took the man and put him in the garden of Eden to till it and keep it. (Gen. 2:10, 15)
>
> Just as we have borne the image of the man of dust, we will also bear the image of the man of heaven. (1 Cor. 15:49)

Genuine transformation happens as we are drawn outside of ourselves. I have stressed that in writing of the role of the other in our development. Furthermore, we are drawn "ahead" of ourselves. We participate in the fundamental temporality of reality.

This is true cosmologically before it is true anthropologically. Already as creatures, we are called to be and become human. When facing the daunting challenge to love our enemies, it is helpful to repair to the fund of possibility given in the fact Christian faith claims: most fundamentally, we are creatures in living relationship to the Creator. Yet this report from the foundation is challenged. We know that entropy is well established in the cosmos as the second law of thermodynamics, and human resistance to change is hardly a speculative proposition. So one asks, again, how can the calling into transformation be efficacious?

We are both pushed and pulled ahead, ahead of ourselves. The "push" is given by the Creator who created and continues to create with a future in mind. A future for the entire cosmos. The river that runs through Eden runs out of Eden and divides to form four great rivers, the Tigris and the Euphrates among them (Gen. 2:10). The water of life is not dammed up within Eden.[48] Of course, the force of water can be terribly destructive. Not every call is God's call. Others call and do so efficaciously. Yet when the freedom given with life turns against God, faith trusts the One who brought safety from the waters of Leviathan (Rahab) and established the dry firmament (Isa. 43:16; 51:9-11).

Human life is called ahead. C. S. Lewis wrote of literary experience, and of more:

> Here, as in worship, in love, in moral action, and in knowing, I transcend myself; and am never more myself than when I do.[49]

Kierkegaard would raise the bid here, insisting that a human being can find one's true self *only* in such self-transcendence. If the other who draws us is truly other, a new reality for us beckons.[50] Eternity lies not behind, but ahead and is only to be reached through time.[51] It seems we are made to lean into the future, to find ourselves there.

We are so *made*—yes, in this temporality of human life Christian faith sees the hand of the creator. Creatures come together to put it pointedly: life is interesting. Poets have known this. Thus Alice Walker: "Life is better than death, I believe, if only because it is less boring."[52] And philosophers have, as with Alfred North Whitehead's provocative insistence that "in the real world it is more important that a proposition be interesting than that it be true."[53] Christian faith holds that this fact, that life is interesting, is not finally a neutral matter. Simone Weil is on the mark when she writes:

> Nothing is so beautiful and wonderful, nothing is so continually fresh and surprising, so full of sweet and perpetual ecstasy, as the good. No desert is so dreary, monotonous, and boring as evil.[54]

Kierkegaard understood that by the Creator's will the link between existence and interest is not an idle one:

> For the existing person, existing is for him his highest interest, and his interestedness in existing is his actuality.[55]

In our interest God calls us forward.

Objections come quickly to mind. The Christian who grounds life and interest in the will and work of the Creator needs to face the twin facts that people are interested in evil and that worship services and theological reflection in Christendom often are incredibly boring. Perhaps we can plead that abuse (of faith) does not militate against proper use. What changes might be entailed in proper use? The community of faith must consider how the affirmation of temporality bears on the whole scope of Christian teaching and living. That consideration will both claim its beginning and come to fruition in the thoroughly relational character of Christian existence. I will say more of this further on. But some basic accents can be noted here, which bear on the temporal thrust of the calling of the human.

Christian faith connects God with the other, and so with the new. This is not a maneuver to be rushed suddenly into service in the field of ethics. Rather it roots back once again in God's will to create, or farther back still into the Trinitarian life of the One without beginning. What follows for creator and creature as we move forward, called into the drama of life? The creature is claimed, called into responsibility. Recognizing the reality of temporality, we will realize that the creator's call to the creature will itself be a timely one. Christians will speak of the "mutability" of the law given in creation.[56] Thus Gustaf Wingren speaks of how in all earthly orders "there is a strong pull . . . to serve others." But he warns against a static understanding:

> This is manifestly not a static characteristic of earthly orders; it must ever be guided forward by law. Here an active quality enters into the realm of vocations which makes unchanging conservatism impossible.[57]

As God calls, stone tablets turn into living flesh.

And human response, mixed and mysterious as it is, matters too in the very life of God. That the creature is livingly related to the Creator does mean that the Creator is genuinely related to the creature. Traditional formulations face some challenge in this reality of relationship. Increasingly, that challenge provokes significant reformulation. Consider, for example, this understanding of "sovereignty" by Clark Pinnock, a theologian writing in the Reformed tradition:

> If divine sovereignty is to be recovered as a meaningful category, we need to think of it as open and flexible. God created a universe with a degree of self-determination, a world in which things can go wrong, even terribly wrong. . . . God delights in an open creation precisely because God does not completely control it. The open model of sovereignty does not diminish but augments the glory of God's rule.[58]

This is a God who delights in creation and who weeps over Jerusalem. And over Auschwitz and Rwanda, for the holocausts of history require us to classify salvation somehow as "unfinished business." Thus Gregory Baum:

> In the face of the Holocaust Christians moved into a new sense of unredemption. They recognized the brokenness of the Church, yearned for peace and justice and put their hope in eschatological promises.[59]

The undeniable presence and efficacy of moral evil does not, however, prevent the Christian from appropriating what Walter Brueggemann has called the "liberation trajectory" in Israel's life and thought.[60] The God who brought Israel out of Egypt still wills and works against evil. This audacious insistence on the part of believers is provoked by the Fall, but it is grounded in trust in the Creator. The purpose and power known in liberation are already at work in the beginning, before evil raises a hand against God. In that trajectory the Christian will go on to speak of a new creation *begun* in the coming of the Christ.

What begins to come together in such a recital is a story. The Christian sense of calling depends not merely on metaphysical novelty, but on the gathering together of old and new in an account that begins somewhere, proceeds somehow, and ends sometime. There is that word, "ends." I said earlier that faith in the Creator finds itself both pushed and pulled ahead in calling. So far, more has been said about push. But an end could pull us toward itself. Viewing the temporal as historical, we come to sense most vividly the pull of God in our calling. For Christians there is a story to be told and heard.

Paul Ricoeur's understanding of narrative is helpful at this point. He proposes a circular thesis:

> Time becomes human time to the extent that it is organized after the manner of a narrative; narrative, in turn, is meaningful to the extent that it portrays the features of temporal experience.[61]

The circle will be healthy rather than vicious, if the interplay between time and narrative truly yields something new. Human experience does testify to the power of story. Many in the "liberation trajectory" would share the witness of Native American novelist Leslie Marmon Silko:

> I will tell you something about stories,
> > [he said]
> > They aren't just entertainment.
> > Don't be fooled.
> > They are all we have, you see,
> > > all we have to fight off
> > > > illness and death.
>
> > You don't have anything
> > if you don't have the stories.
>
> > > Their evil is mighty
> > > but it can't stand up to our stories.[62]

We human beings find ourselves employing story to speak of widely diverse aspects of reality—the universe as a whole, the social-systemic, the interpersonal.[63]

These two, time and narrative—the temporal and the historical in my phrasing, surely move toward each other, but they do not collapse into one thing. Our experience of time invites the order of narrative, but it would be wrong to deny that there are many for whom their days seem to drift away in sheer succession without adding up in any plot. Even so, one moment stands out as different in such a life: death. Death surely does in some sense "sum up" or give definition to what has preceded it. As individuals, we die as we have lived, differently. Even in our difference, we share the desire for stories that matter, a portrayal and plot in which something happens, a measuring and defining—not simply a succession, but an adding up or coming together. Together we ask what kind of story can have this ending.

Most of us probably live with some fragments of meaning in our experience of time before the end. We do not merely move as objects blown by the wind or carried by a current. We *act*. We see our acts as having some significance. In that seeing we are wagering that the reality of which we are somehow a part allows us to claim significance, for acting is not in principle senseless. In such seeing and wagering there is a kind of "inchoate narrativity" that "constitutes a genuine demand for narrative."[64] Well, an opportunity at least, if not a demand. What a text can do is to offer a plot such that the reader's temporal experience can be "refigured" or newly "emplotted." There is some disordering in this process, some "interruption" in the language of this book. But it is not so that "any dream will do," for narrative is meaningful only if it does portray actual human temporal experience in such a way as to open the future.[65] The "shock of the possible" is "no less real than that of the actual,"[66] if it so engages the reader that the fragments of meaning are gathered into a plot.

So the Christian could well testify that her life undergoes transformation as a story told takes on reality in gathering up the choices and chances of her life. Is this to be pulled into calling? Well, the story's end does lie out ahead, though the energy of life it receives and shapes is contributed by the one looking for a good story. And we are looking, for we do live with a "sense of an ending," as we tell and hear—and believe—stories.[67]

Moreover, on the grand scale, we do live "toward death" and have heard whisperings of eternity. *Something* draws us. *That* this is so is clear; *how* it is so is not. Certainty and possibility keep company in such living and hearing.[68] Does anything else have the decisiveness of the end that could pull the Christian into his calling? The Christian conviction claims that something has happened in the course of history, something that yields irreversibly a new reality for both creator and creatures. Bethlehem, Nazareth, Gethsemane, Golgotha— these name reality and so they name possibility. This happening, "once for all," lies at the center of the Christian story.[69] As Christians tell their story they speak of something that is merely begun because they trust in something that is "finished." To hold these two together, that which is finished and that which is not, represents a task for the imagination.

The True and the Possible

Do not be conformed to this world, but be transformed by the renewing of your minds, so that you may discern what is the will of God—what is good and acceptable and perfect. (Rom. 12:2)

Set your minds on the things that are above, not on things that are on the earth, for you have died and your life is hidden with Christ in God. (Col. 3:2-3)

Are we up to this? Clearly, how we think makes a difference in who we are. Some who have participated in cognitive therapy would so testify. Accordingly, God's transforming work makes a claim on our thinking. The biblical words leap out at us: "be transformed by the *renewing of your minds,* so that you may *discern* what is the will of God. . . ." and "set your *minds* on the things that are above." Is this possible?

And is imagination to serve as an instrument in the transformative task? We may agree that this renewing and setting of mind speaks to something happening to human thinking. But is not imagination as a cognitive faculty human, all too human? Questions follow from outside and inside the community of faith. How can the exercise of the imagination bring about something *real,* rather than imaginary? We know that even the past is not preserved in memory, safe from the creative power of imagination.[70] To link religion and imagination may seem suicidal for the person of faith. Is religion to be reduced to "a *life-enhancing* illusion"?[71] Is "life-enhancing" even too much to claim? Despite our bold contention that an end pulls us toward transformation has not Christian talk about *the* end had a significantly stultifying effect on moral endeavor?[72] From within the believing community one wonders if imagination is not all too earthen a vessel for the treasure of faith. What is to keep us from imagining with Alice in Wonderland six impossible things before breakfast? This latter fear is perhaps what cried out in the vociferous criticism of the Re-Imagining conferences of the 1990s. What response is to be made to these questions, to this cry?

Human imagination is a tool fit for the transformative task because through it we can (1) attend to what is true and (2) attach ourselves to what is possible.[73] These two, the true and the possible, both need to be in the work of imagination, and they need to be there together.

We may begin with this: imagination can be the servant of truth for us. Through imagination we see reality more fully. Ann and Barry Ulanov make this point very strongly:

> Imagination is tough. It is naturally open. It wants to see everything. That is a large part of its healing power. It includes the daunting negative as well as the uplifting positive. It naturally renounces denial. It looks to include the wildly spiraling off-center event as well as the grounding, centering. Imagination instructs us that seeing what is there means looking directly into off-center events and the gaps. . . . When we consent to let be, all that we screen out of our lives . . . we see the

positive and the negative collide. We recognize that they live next to each other.[74]

This enthusiastic insistence needs some quiet unpacking. First, imagination is involved even in the experience of perception. In seeing, we see something *as* this or that. We "map" reality by employing "image schemata" and metaphoric patterns. As Mark Johnson and George Lakoff put it, we "live by" metaphors that take on orientational (as, "verticality") and ontological ("substance," "field," "event") status.[75] Imagination serves as a compass and field guide for the worlds we traverse.

Very well, imagination might not be merely an optional candidate in our knowing. But recognizing the primitive role of imagination in perception may not make us less nervous. After all, this rudimentary exercise of imagination may be highly selective, reducing the challenging complexity of reality to a more comfortable set of components framed in a simplifying way. Thus come worldviews. Such "common" sense is hardly to be worshipped. Whitehead's word calls us to attention: "Seek simplicity and distrust it!" In such distrust we may see something we have missed, something new. There is more to be seen than we may suppose. Poetry springs out of such second seeing. Robert Frost writes of the experience of surprise:

Step by step the wonder of unexpected supply keeps growing. The impressions most useful to my purpose seem always those I was unaware of and so made no note of at the time when taken, and the conclusion is come to that, like giants, we are always hurling experience ahead of us to pave the future with against the day when we may want to strike a line of purpose across it for somewhere. The line will have more charm for not being mechanically straight. We enjoy the straight crookedness of a good walking stick.[76]

Or in the words of William Stafford:

So, the world happens twice—
once what we see it as;
second it legends itself
deep, the way it is.[77]

This is why we do not finally control reality by the language systems through which we surely do shape our knowing.[78] There is more to be heard than we may suppose. And there are different ways of seeing and hearing. Natural scientists join poets in witness. Thomas Kuhn's classic study of "scientific revolutions" that are occasioned by the build-up of anomalies can be considered a more theoretical account of the "surprise" to which Robert Frost refers.[79]

So, a more developed use of imagination can open us to seeing/hearing more and differently. Imagination may perform a unifying function, for example, in drawing apparent opposites into a more complex relationship.[80] Craig Dykstra writes of how transformation "comes in the form of a new patterning of the imagination":

> Often this is a pictorial image in the mind, but it may also present itself as a gesture, as a new way of saying something, or in a new pattern of action. Whatever the form of the insight, it is a creative reorganization of the imagination, in which all of the elements of the conflict are related in a new gestalt.[81]

Imagination does not create the truth that makes free (John 8:31); it grasps it. This imaginative grasp of truth can be seen quite directly in the reality of faith. Take conversion, presumably a matter of some transformation. Ekkehard Muhlenberg asserts the Lutheran insistence that this is not a human doing:

> Conversion . . . occurs when the human will follows the knowledge of God's mercy and the affection of the love of God. Human will does not materially add anything to the process, because object and objective are given in reason's knowledge and the movement or locomotion in the affection.

Or in the words of the indicative declaration of the letter to the Colossians (3:3): "you have died and your life is hid with Christ in God." Still, it does matter that we grasp the truth created by God:

> . . . The human self must *recognize* itself in the new knowledge and in the new affection and not in other affections.[82]

Muhlenberg's sense of the truth and task of conversion illustrates specifically what Martin Luther was driving at in his theses for the Heidelberg Disputation:

> A theologian of glory calls evil good and good evil. A theologian of the cross calls the thing what it actually is.[83]

Luther was lifting up the word of the cross as that which could restore the hearer to her creaturely status, calling a thing what it is in creation and in the new creation. The world seeks and needs this transformation. In his 1996 presidential address to the American Academy of Religion, Lawrence Sullivan complimented the crowd of scholars on their efforts to reach academic credibility, but then issued a moral call to "come to our senses." Of what was he speaking? Of freedom, of pain, of the arts, of neurobiology—or, one could say, of our life in creation.[84]

To come truly, to our senses . . . is that possible? There's our other word in the pair "the true and the possible." The truth can make free. In coming to see the truth of God's story the hearer does catch a glimpse of how he may have a place in that narrative. Is it too much to say that "the new seeing *is* the leap in understanding"?[85] Perhaps it is, for we seem able somehow to turn against our own best knowing. But at least we must say this, that imagination opens the way to lively possibilities for the future.[86] Those possibilities call out for actualization. That will entail disengagement from prevailing frameworks, suspension of disbelief, attention to the new that beckons, imaginative engagement in that new reality and finally surrender to the truth that calls.[87]

In these ways, to grasp the truth by an act of imagination is to be opened to new possibilities for life. This is really not an unempirical speculation. Ann and Barry Ulanov point out that violence often comes about when a person cannot "imagine" another way through a particular situation.[88] Walter Wink has suggested that we may come to see our enemy differently, when imagination leads us in fantasy to find in us the evil we have projected upon them.[89] And Walter Brueggemann has persistently pointed out the linkage between imagination and transformation in Israel's life:

> . . . prophecy is not in any overt concrete sense political or social action. It is rather *an assault on public imagination,* aimed at showing that the present presumed world is not absolute, but that a thinkable alternative can be imagined, characterized, and lived in. The destabilization is, then, not revolutionary overthrow, but it is making available an alternative imagination that makes one aware that the presumed world is imagined, not given.[90]

The true and the possible, then, *together* in imagination. We may be tempted to give up any creative use of the imagination, settling for what we think is eternal truth. Or we may drown in a sea of possibility, losing contact with reality as experienced in the present and held in memory of the past.[91] Despite the gift of image the task of imagination is no easy matter. So we pause to ask, what may sustain, even empower us in this calling?

5. To Be Related:
This Is the Empowering

Why "is" rather than "may be"? I have said only that interruption *may* be the beginning, and calling may be the coming, of transformation. Such cautious speaking recognizes that we may be interrupted and called by realities other than God. Moreover, in some moments what we see is action *against* God. But now, setting out to write of the power at work in *God's* transforming action, I am drawn to stronger speech. I write in the bold confidence that there is resource available. Thus being related is not a third moment, paralleling interruption and calling and carrying a comparable contingency. Rather relationship is the comprehensive whole in which interruptions and callings—by God and by others—occur. There is, to be sure, still a contingency having to do with how we respond to what is given. But when God interrupts and calls, God gives all there is to give. This is the Creator's doing, the work of One whose will to create depends on nothing outside itself. The creature does nothing to come into being. So what does the creature in response find lacking in what is given? Just that, nothing.

Created in and for Relationship

> So God created humankind in his image,
> in the image of God he created them;
> male and female he created them. (Gen. 1:27)

> God said: "See, I have given you every plant yielding seed that is upon the face of all the earth, and every tree with seed in its fruit; you shall have them for food. And to every beast of the earth, and to every bird of the air, and to everything that creeps on the earth, everything that has the breath of life, I have given every green plant for food." And it was so. (Gen. 1:29-30)

"The given is other."[1] In interruption, by the Creator's will the human person encounters one who is truly different, who in Levinas's language "disturbs the being at home with oneself."[2] The person is called to be human "together" with others.[3] In writing of these things, I have given much emphasis to the individual standing out over against these others, as questions of response and responsibility have held center stage. But it is time to turn the coin to ponder this: the other is given.[4]

The other is unconditionally given, so that to be is to be related to that which is other. Thus does the Creator equip the creature. The creature is not left alone. God does not create windowless monads, and God will not be evicted from God's universe. The gift, the givenness, of the other is the promise of creation. Calling offers orientation, *direction*; in relationship, we receive *directedness*, efficacy. This conviction, that the givenness of relationship is resource for transformation, is grounded for the Christian in faith's assurance of the continuing commitment of the Creator to the creation. Creation talk is faith talk. But the talk can be connected with the realities of human experience in that creation. It is with that empirical suggestion that we will begin.

In pondering this fact, that the other is given, I will focus on humankind. But the reality of human connection in relationship exists within a web of being extending far beyond and deep within homo sapiens. The cosmos itself, from quantum particles to the remote reaches of space and time, exists as a network of relationships. According to Ian Barbour, "the being of any entity is constituted by its relationships and its participation in more inclusive patterns."[5] Recounting the history of elementary particle research, he notes the "'zoo' of strange particles" emerging from experiments with high-energy accelerators. In the relative order introduced by the notion of "quarks" as the constituent element in other particles, "there seem to be only a few types of quarks . . . and a few simple rules for the ways they can combine."[6] But then he remarks:

> But quarks are a strange type of "component": free quarks have never been observed, and it appears that a quark cannot exist alone, according to the theory of quark confinement. . . . Quarks are parts that apparently cannot exist except in a larger whole.[7]

What is the nature of the whole(s)? Consider this statement by thermodynamicist Jeffrey Wicken:

> Granted, space consists of fields of force which exert regulative controls on material elements; but its "structure" is reciprocally regulated by those elements and their movements. The two

together constitute the only "whole" of which physics can speak. If all the matter were removed from the universe, there would be no field. When the ether left, so did ontological dichotomy. Space and matter have *coevolved,* and are *relationally constituted* by each other. They have no identities apart from each other.[8]

It seems, then, that as cosmological truth we have not just plurality, but relationship. Or in the word of Alfred North Whitehead, process "lies in the nature of things that the many enter into complex unity."[9] Whitehead terms this process "creativity," and the Christian theologian has reason to speak of this fundamental relational character of reality as the work of the Creator. Christian doctrine ought to include in the dogmatic discussion of creation the consideration of such basic cosmological notions as space and time.[10] Indeed, the cosmos may reflect its relation to the Creator more clearly than humanity does. As Gustaf Wingren has suggested, the presence of sin in the human heart means that Creation itself is purer than we are.[11]

Could we learn more readily of the Creator's work if we order our inquiry accordingly? Thus we approach the human realm by attending to the organic. There we find the other playing a sustaining role. As Whitehead put it:

> In museums the crystals are kept under glass cases; in zoological gardens the animals are fed.[12]

Well before Whitehead, Genesis told the tale of how the nurturing other is given: "And to every beast of the earth, and to every bird of the air, and to everything that creeps on the earth, I have given every green plant for food" (Gen.1:30).

More specifically, how is the human person relationally connected with that which is other than the self? The predisposing power of genetic inheritance is indisputable, particularly as shown by studies of identical twins raised apart.[13] But what of nurture from the environment? Clearly we do take food of several sorts from the other. Recall Donald W. Winnicott's understanding of how the mother "holds" the infant, mirroring the child back to itself and creating a "potential space" for the child's development.[14] Recent research has advanced this line of thought further and has criticized the use of concepts such as "fusion" or "merger" as inadequate to describe the complexity of the relational patterns of self to other, which even very young infants create internally and develop as they grow.[15]

From France, where social psychologists have pioneered in the field of "interindividual psychology," Jean-Michel Oughourlian has raised the question of the powerful role of the other in such a presumably personal matter as desire:

> . . .what one customarily calls the *I* or *self* in psychology is an unstable, constantly changing, and ultimately evanescent structure. . . . only *desire* brings this self into existence. Because desire is the only psychological motion; it alone, it seems to me, is capable of producing the self and breathing life into it. The first hypothesis that I would like to formulate in this regard is this; desire gives rise to the self and by its movement animates *it*. The second hypothesis . . . is that *desire is mimetic*.[16]

Could this be right—that, in the phrasing of René Girard, even our desires are not our own but are "triangular," drawn from the models we either consciously or else unwittingly admire and imitate?[17] Such an understanding surely challenges our tendency to regard relationships as accidental to selfhood. But it would make sense of studies of infant development that suggest that children as young as fourteen months are able to learn to manipulate, disassemble, and reassemble a toy they had never seen before by watching a demonstration on videotape and then repeating the action, either immediately or after an interval of up to a week.[18] Early childhood influences find a strong successor in the power of mentoring, according to the testimony of individuals who come to be involved in altruistic activities.[19]

There is considerable empirical support even for the stunning notion that in human development the relationship between persons exists prior to and functions to create the persons.[20] Could it be that the Genesis text telling us that God created humankind "male and female" (1:27) refers not only to result, but to process?[21] Human experience may suggest that, and the suggestion does not seem restricted to marriage, as some readings of Genesis would assume. In life we come to learn that we are being created in and through the relationships in which we participate. Returning to Winnicott, Michael Eigen lifts up the notion of the infant-mother dyad:

> . . . There is no such thing as an infant, but an infant-mother psychosomatic field. The quality of the surrounding and supporting milieu is the crucial medium for development of the psychosomatic life of the child.[22]

(Perhaps, too, for the continuing life of the mother.) The reference to mother and child reminds us that we are embodied creatures. So do the Hebrew Scriptures, for example, where we encounter the human person conceived of "as an animated body, not as an incarnated soul."[23] Or, looking again to child development studies, we have seen that Winnicott made much of the action and metaphor of "holding." What is it to hold?

> The main thing is the physical holding, and this is the basis of all the more complex aspects of holding, and of environmental provision in general.[24]

This recognition of physical relatedness cannot be limited to the kind of one-to-one relationship mother and infant represent. As adults we do not cease to be embodied beings. Whitehead would seem to be right in his aphorism: "No one ever says, Here I am and I have brought my body with me."[25] Or was he? Looking to the widest span, only forgetfulness or denial of our embodied condition could tempt us to ignore our dependence on the resource of nature.[26] How else shall we explain the human assault on the rain forest, the ozone layer? Yet in recent decades that dependence has been increasingly recognized (if not honored in our practice). Perhaps our recognition that nature holds us in relationship, too, can join other learnings. In between the intimacy of the interpersonal and the cosmic sweep of our dependence on nature lies the social realm. There such testimonies as that to the power of the small group movement[27] support Larry Rasmussen's summary: "Community is the concrete shape of grace."[28]

Thus experience does suggest what it cannot prove, that the fundamental nature of created being is, in the phrasing of Kyle Pasewark, "the communication of efficacy" "at the borders in the mutual, bodily presence of entities."[29] Moreover the strong role of the other(s) is to be seen even within the "borders" of the individual. In his probing book *Good and Evil: Interpreting a Human Condition*,[30] Edward Farley writes in turn of three "spheres" of human reality: the interhuman, the social, and the personal. This order of consideration is appropriate if the givenness of relationship is fundamental to personal identity. The other is present in recognition, empathy, and availability,[31] and compassion and obligation connect human beings. The passion of the interhuman is "an aspiration for acknowledgment and for others to acknowledge."[32] Perhaps most fundamentally, the human person in Farley's view is driven by "the passion for reality." That passion leads the person out beyond the borders of personal being in a desire "to be *founded*."[33]

The scope and depth of such desire or passion suggests that humankind's question and quest have to do with the very being of the other. What other? Farley makes the positive claim that "only the creative ground of things can be the meaning of the human being and its world."[34] We look to that which is not ourselves, to the other, to God. We do so in the audacious belief that, as Harold Ditmanson has put it, "reality—existence itself—is ultimately curative in all its wide forms"[35]:

> *Being-itself* is accepting. . . . Reality is not just a void. . . . Reality itself in some sense is reaching out to affirm and support the healing process.[36]

These last paragraphs with their talk of passion, desire, question, and quest speak of more than our being created *in* relationship. There is a *for* in these moments, a forward pushing that connects with the pull of call into relationship. This call is also an essential component in the logic of creation as relationship. Home may be where we "start from," in Winnicott's phrasing, but we cannot simply stay there. Creatures, "created male and female," leave father and mother to find the other (Gen. 2:23a). We are called into community in a constitutive sense, as Michael Sandel puts it:

> And what marks such a community is not merely a spirit of benevolence or the prevalence of communitarian values, or even certain "shared final ends" alone, but a common vocabulary of discourse and a background of implicit practices and understandings within which the opacity of the participants is reduced if never finally dissolved.[37]

But does not being thus created *for* relationship reintroduce the note of contingency? If this contingency is part of the created given, how certain can we be that relationship will empower us for transformation? If we interpret human experience honestly, we cannot claim that all goes swimmingly for folk moved by a passion for reality or a metaphysical desire. René Girard is well known for his theory about scapegoating, in which he proposes that a surrogate victim serves the attackers by deflecting their violence from each other onto him or her. And whence comes the violence? Girard offers the hypothesis that the birth of specifically human life had its origin in the resolution of a crisis of generalized violence. While this may be dismissed as speculative, his point is that we become most attracted to precisely those objects that are claimed and defended with the strongest violence. Whence comes the attracting, the claiming, and the defending? A theologian committed, as I am, to the distinction between creation and fall may bridle over Edward Farley's suggestion that "the intrinsic vulnerability and tragic character of the human condition" provide not only the "background" but "the *origin*" of the dynamics of evil.[38] But the pervasive evil that we cannot deny at the end of this century of holocausts and ethnic cleansings is surely served by the fabric of relationship constituting creation. Are not sadism and masochism forms of relationship? Does not the narrowing of the self through shame experiences reflect precisely the vulnerability and violation of a self in and through relationships?[39] The prescribed therapy for the shamed self is to open the boundaries of the self to include others through creativity, empathy, humor, and wisdom.[40] But what grounds do we have for being hopeful that this will in fact happen?

So, again, how is relationship empowerment for transformation? Indeed, the question goes all the way to the Creator, and to the individual in relationship to the creator. If God in creating has entered into relationship with finite forms of freedom, is not God—and with the Creator all the creatures—at risk? What is to prevent freedom from failing? I have been stressing the generosity of the Creator in giving the creature rich resource in relationship. No less a champion of the individual self than Søren Kierkegaard could say that the call to the individual is not to *choose*, but to *receive* his self.[41] But that too seems to raise a question of sorts for the individual and for God. Robert Kegan stretches his psychological study of human life to ask this question:

> The Jewish mystics say that God makes human beings because God loves stories. This is quite a modest stance to give an all-powerful, all-loving God. Even God, the mystics are saying, does not know how we are going to come out, so why should we wish for greater control or need it? Better perhaps for us to emulate this kind of God, whose pleasure in us comes not from our obedience to God's laws and regularities, however subject we may be to them, but from God's sheer fascination with how we will live.[42]

Well said and wisely seen. But perhaps for us to speak of such a God is to speak again of a relationship that is empowering.

The Creator Working Still

"Do you not believe that I am in the Father and the Father is in me? The words that I say to you I do not speak on my own; but the Father who dwells in me does his works. Believe me that I am in the Father and the Father is in me; but if you do not, then believe me because of the works themselves. Very truly, I tell you, the one who believes in me will also do the works that I do and, in fact, will do greater works than these because I am going to the Father." (John 14:10-12)

Therefore my beloved, just as you have always obeyed me, not only in my presence but much more now in my absence, work out your own salvation with fear and trembling; for it is God who is at work in you, enabling you both to will and to work for his good pleasure. (Phil. 2:12-13)

Theologian Peri Rasolondraibe speaks of the God of Christian faith as "eccentric."[43] Social scientist Michael Walzer speaks of the God of Exodus as "the crucial alternative to all mythic notions of eternal recurrence."[44] Israel crosses over the encircling sea to a new land. We may begin to perceive real empowerment for transformation in the relationship with God by pondering this strange God who moves outward, toward, and forward into that which is decisively new. Here is Rasolondraibe's formulation:

We traditionally talk about the Trinity as a community of life and love. . . . Through the history of this triune love in relation to us, however, we learn to know that God is also a community of divine sentness: The Father and the Spirit send the Son to redeem the world; the Father and the Son send the Spirit to regenerate the world; and the Son and the Spirit offer the Father so that the world might be reconciled to God. . . . This triune *God is an eccentric God,* a God who tears the Godself apart, as it were, in order to give away what God cherishes the most for the well-being of that which is other than God, even against God, namely, the world.[45]

The God of biblical faith loves the other. This claim grows out of the Christian doctrine of creation. Remember particularly Kierkegaard's beautiful testimony to how the Creator lets the creature "come into being over against God" in a reciprocal relationship.[46] In a similar way Westermann spoke of our being created in the image of God as being such that something is to happen between Creator and creature. There is an empowering decisiveness in this original relationship and, moreover, a preparation for a further continuing decisiveness. This God is eccentric in the ordinary sense of "different" or "unusual." And this difference, in the happening that is history, comes to make a difference for creatures as they are interrupted and called.

How deep does the root go for God's commitment to the other? A person aware of the creaturely resistance, indeed opposition, to God wants to know. How deep, then? Did/does God create out of necessity or in freedom? I am inclined to answer "Yes." Christian faith derives both dimensions, necessity and freedom, from the claim that God in God's own self is triune. This four-word sentence, God loves the other, speaks first of life within God. How do we get that life connected with the life that is not God's life, the life of creatures? One answer is that this connection happens only in freedom, or out of nothing even in God. That the triune love of God is without beginning thus helps us understand that God did not need the creature in order to know genuine love for the other. Robert Jenson states this well:

> As to whether the real God could have been God without any world, we can only answer . . . : The analysis of God as free event, as spirit, equally compels us to say that he would have been and forbids us to say how.[47]

So too Karl Barth, for whom "God is his own decision,"[48] pleads for a crucial distinction:

> God's loving is necessary, for it is the being, the essence, and the nature of God. But for this very reason it is also free from every necessity in respect of its object.[49]

God is truly other than we are, and our connection is rooted in the free and creative will of God. The Christian will find assurance in this. And yet our own experience of love may somehow suggest an objection, well-voiced by Paul Fiddes:

> But there seems to be something profoundly unsatisfactory about this notion of God's choosing to love the world in such a way that we can say "he need not have done so" or "he could have done otherwise." It does not seem to touch the core of the meaning of love, which must be more than willing the good of another as one alternative among other possibilities.[50]

How deep is God's love for the other? Could it be as deep as desire from eternity? Fiddes is drawn toward a view of God's good pleasure "in which there can be no otherwise" and that "provides a strong theological foundation for the idea that the material universe coexists eternally with God."[51]

How does it come about that the Creator loves the creature? Will or desire, what shall we say to this? I think, yes. A number of contemporary theologians hold together difference and connection in speaking of God in relation to creation. Thus Catherine Mowry LaCugna employs a relational ontology to restate the traditional distinction between the trinity immanent in God and the trinity working in the world:

> It would make no sense to say that God "needs" the world in order to be God, if this sets up the creature as a higher or more ultimate principle than God. . . .The reason for creation lies entirely in the unfathomable mystery of God who is self-originating and self-communicating love. While the world is the gracious result of divine freedom, God's freedom means *necessarily* being who and what God is. From this standpoint the world is not created *ex nihilo*, but *ex amore, ex condilectio,* that is, out of divine love.[52]

Or, more broadly, as he ponders "giving," Stephen Webb roots his resistance to the either/or of excess and exchange in the very nature of God:

> The Christian God squanders, but not as an exercise of blind self-affirmation or sovereign freedom; instead, God gives abundantly, in order to create more giving, the goal of which is a mutuality born of excess but directed toward equality and justice.[53]

In this squandering, creative love for the other there is freedom, for this God is alive. And there is decisiveness, for this God is truly able to will one thing in commitment. This eccentric combination is suggested by Eberhard Jungel in speaking of the Son and the Father:

> God is his own goal. And only because he is his own goal, he aims toward that being which is to be made, the creation. God by no means first becomes his goal when he aims toward man [*sic!*]. He is adequate to himself. But precisely in that he is adequate to himself, he is overflowing being, and his overflowing being is the expression of his grace, the original image of his covenant with a partner who is not God, who at first does not exist at all, but must first be created as God's partner: man. In

the eternal Son of God, who himself was not created, but comes eternally from God the Father, in this Son of God coming *eternally* from God, God aims at the man who *temporally* comes from God.[54]

Perhaps this line of thought can help the Christian grasp how it is that the other is given so decisively for us as human beings, the subject of the previous section. We are created in and for relationship, for we are created in the image of one who freely and decisively loves the other. Thus Jürgen Moltmann speaks of how "human beings are *imago Trinitatis* in their personal fellowship with one another."[55]

But image is not identity. There is this difference. We creatures are *necessarily* connected with the other in some kind of relationship. God is *freely* committed to the other in love. This is a difference that makes a difference for creatures with weak knees. Freedom forms the energy flowing in this love. That God's love for the other takes root in God's living decision to create assures the Christian that God's favor is not a response to some relative and potentially wavering accomplishment by the creature. God's will to love the other originates wholly in God. This singularity of source yields a decisiveness not to be mistaken for arbitrariness. Human sin does not sway the decisiveness and scope of this love.

Consider, for example, one of the most famous passages in the Pentateuch, Exodus 33:19: "I will be gracious to whom I will be gracious; and I will show mercy on whom I will show mercy." No doubt some have read this passage in a way that keeps the anxious soul forever in torment over possible exclusion from divine mercy. Terence Fretheim challenges that reading by showing that here what divine freedom yields is precisely decisiveness:

> God's concern is not to stake a claim for divine freedom *from* Moses or Israel, a freedom to be gracious toward some but not others if God so wills. It is a declaration *to move beyond previously stated stipulations* and reach out in mercy: "I will have mercy on you, . . . yes indeed, I will have mercy on you." This is a statement of God's graciousness *for* Moses, God's freedom *for* others, not *from* others. But it is granted only at God's initiative.[56]

That God's creative action roots in the very nature of God adds a second assurance: the love for the other in which God creates is no less than the very nature of God. There is no other God beyond or above this God who loves the other. As Jungel says: "God has him-

self only in that he gives himself away.[57] This faith does give needed
assurance. What the creature will do may indeed be in doubt. But
the love of the creator is not thus in doubt, for will God turn against
God? Clinical psychologist Moshe Halevi Spero finds, contra Freud,
that same note of assurance sounding in religious experience. Here is
his halakic reading:

> . . . "Moral motives" or religious concepts cannot be said to
> germinate from the state of helplessness *per sui*, nor even from
> the experience of *being helped* as such. Rather, they germinate in
> the experiences of a self being met and understood by the
> other, from the sense of relationship with a reliable object.[58]

That love continues.[59] New things surely do happen in the relationship with God. I have written of creation *and fall*. Sin interrupts
God's creative work and wounds the heart of God. Christian faith
finds its centering story in the Jesus who is sin's victim and victor.
But when Jesus was persecuted for healing on the sabbath (creation's
seventh day, the day of rest) he said: "My Father is still working, and
I also am working" (John 5:17). There is resource in this: the creator
is working still. Is this, though, resource for transformation? Jesus
did not claim that the Father's working and his own working are
simply one. It would no doubt be confusing to speak of them as
one.[60] To do so might suggest that God's saving act for humankind
in Jesus does not have its own decisive integrity but offers only supply for our transforming activity. Christians do not honor Christ if
they fail to distinguish between what is finished and what is not.
That nothing can separate us from the love of God in Christ Jesus
does not mean that poverty and disease are banished. But the distinction requires a connection as well. The Jesus of John's gospel
does heal. A savior who gives new life (in various forms) serves the
Creator of all life. That the Father is still working gives Jesus more
than permission, a need to work. And one notes that in this particular case Jesus seems to link staying healed with "sinning no more"
(5:14).

Moreover, Jesus responds to those who question his authority by
saying that he does not speak on his own, for "the Father who dwells
in me does his works" (John 14:10). Indeed, works he does are
offered as sufficient ground for believing that the Father is in him
and he is in the Father. Father and Son are two and not simply one,

to be sure, and to find no distinction in the "workings" of the two would likely be to err. But would it not be a greater error to drive the two apart so that no connection remains?[61]

What comes into view in such biblical passages is God's ongoing activity in enacting love for the other. Because the creator is working still, there is provision for whatever the other truly needs. Willing the other and working for the other begins "in the beginning" and does continue. God's will and work continues to yield transformation after Jesus is no longer physically present for the believing community. The one who believes in Christ "will also do the works" Jesus does. And then an even more astounding promise is given: this believer ". . . in fact, will do greater works than these because [?!] I am going to the Father" (John 14:12). Later I will consider God's transforming work "post-Jesus." In this transformation God is working at a level that does not compete with human working. Rather the Creator's deep working precisely empowers human working, as is suggested in the Philippian correspondence: "work out. . . . For it is God who is at work in you enabling. . . ." (2:12-13). But our entire talk of transformation would be trivialized if we did not speak of the very center of things. Jesus did say, "I am working." What are we to say of that?

Well, we write here of relationship. What does the story of Jesus mean with respect to transformation (1) for God and (2) for humankind? We do well to be modest in our speaking of the first. But according to Christian reading there is something new for God in this. The church struggles to put this into words with the bare abstractions of incarnation talk. Somehow in this event there is a becoming in God such that God knows the human with an unprecedented directness and intimacy. Once again, we are back to Kierkegaard's parable of the king and the maiden.[62] God's servant form was not a disguise. This is the creator God who can become what he wills. To undergo such transformation, to be so resolved, is not a weakness.[63] Does God remain a servant to us, then? Yes, and God can do no other.

And what of the transforming power of this Jesus story for humankind? Here the Christian has more to say; Melanchthon was right that to know Christ is to know his benefits.[64] And what are they? On the one hand they have to do with the theme of the previous paragraphs, the decisiveness of God's work. In the explanation to the fifth petition of the Lord's Prayer, Martin Luther answers his own question, our question: why is there "great need to call upon God and pray, 'Dear Father, forgive us our debts'"?

> Not that he does not forgive sin even without and before our prayer; and he gave us the Gospel, in which there is nothing but forgiveness, before we prayed or even thought of it.[65]

That later Lutheran, Kierkegaard, echoed this truth regarding God's definitive forgiveness:

> If by some kind of reverse adjustment the divine could be shifted over to the human, there is one way in which man [sic!] could never in all eternity come to be like God: in forgiving sins.[66]

Of course Luther went on to say that the point of the petition is "for us to recognize and accept this forgiveness." If we are talking about a relationship between God and us, human beings will somehow be involved. And Kierkegaard finds this too does not happen apart from the work of Christ:

> . . . For if the god [sic!] gave no indication, how could it occur to a man [sic!] that the blessed God could need him?[67]

Our role is to be needed and to meet the need of God. In Christ, we have more than an indication of the human role in the relationship; we have an empowering for that role. Examining this neglected dimension of Luther's thought, Simo Peura directs our attention to Luther's understanding of the Pauline dialectic of grace and gift in Romans 5:15:

> . . . Grace is God's favorable mood effecting in a sinner confidence in God's forgiveness and benevolence. . . . Gift, however, constitutes the Christian's internal good, and it opposes his internal evil, i.e., the corruption of human nature. . . . Gift effects in a sinner his real renewal. . . .[68]

Other theologians have subsequently emphasized the gift and resource of divine presence for the believer. Friedrich Schleiermacher, in his classic statement of modern systematic theology, offers us helpful distinctions between "magical," "mystical," and "empirical" understandings. He critiqued as magical "those views of Christ's reconciling activity . . . which make the impartation of His blessedness independent of assumption into vital fellowship with Him."[69] He proceeds to offer a mystical alternative by which the redeemer "assumes" the believer into the power of his God-consciousness and its blessedness. This reality of "Christ in us" is not merely empirical, as with teacher and pupil, where the relation, "like that of pattern and imitation, must always remain an external one."[70]

Schleiermacher's important effort to distinguish between Christ as external example (*"Vorbild"*) and as generative power (*"Urbild"*) may be filled out by Kierkegaard in speaking of Christ as both Redeemer and Prototype. This is an unusual prototype:

> . . . He who is truly to be the prototype and be related only to imitators must in one sense be *behind* people, propelling forward, while in another sense he stands *ahead,* beckoning. . . . Thus in one sense the prototype is *behind,* more deeply pressed down into abasement and lowliness than any human being has ever been, and in another sense, *ahead,* infinitely lifted up. But the prototype must be behind in order to be able to capture and include all. . . . The prototype must be *unconditionally* behind, behind everyone, and it must be *behind* in order to propel forward those who are to be formed according to it.[71]

Both Schleiermacher and Kierkegaard effectively convey the "forward" thrust of reality and confess a Christ who comes to the creatures as the Lord of Creation. This "reach" survives in the work of contemporary theologians keenly aware of the pluralism that assumes such a prominent role in our current postmodern or late modern consciousness. For example, John B. Cobb Jr. applies the notion of "a spiritual field of force" drawn directly from Pauline studies and more broadly from natural science:

> The real past event of the crucifixion and resurrection of Jesus, involving his total being, has objectively established a sphere of effectiveness or a field of force into which people can enter. To enter the field is to have the efficacy of the salvation event become causally determinative of increasing aspects of one's total life.[72]

But John's gospel reminds us that Jesus does go to the Father! Yet for John clearly the empowering divine presence is not diminished in this departure. To the contrary, we have already noted that John has Jesus saying that the one who believes in him "will also do the works that I do and, in fact, will do greater works than these, because I am going to the Father" (John 14:12). This surely boggles our minds, but in our stupefaction we should take care not to lose the promised reality. At the center of the promise is this, that the Spirit will come. Indeed, "it is to your advantage that I go away, for if I do not go away, the Advocate will not come to you; but if I go, I will send him to you" (John 16:7). So the Christian is promised some kind of continued, renewed, and even increased resource of divine presence. In a particularly rich exposition of *God the Spirit*, Michael Welker has once again laid claim to the notion of a "field of force"[73]:

> The persons seized, moved, and renewed by God's Spirit can know themselves placed in a force field of which they are members and bearers, but which they cannot bear, shape, be responsible for, and enliven alone.[74]

As he deploys this notion Welker makes clear that the Spirit's presence cannot be captured in some subjective frenzy. He notes that the Bible speaks of how people can "be carried by the faith of others or strengthen other people in faith, without being able at the moment to consciously appropriate this."[75] The gifts of the Spirit:

> . . . are elements of the force field of the Spirit, and at the same time they themselves constitute force fields, through which the action of the Spirit is realized and spread in the finite and shared life of human beings.[76]

Like Cobb, Welker has a keen awareness and appreciation of the challenge of pluralism and emphasizes that the force field of the Spirit "forms not a homogeneous unity, but a differentiated one."[77] Indeed, both our awareness and the force field itself are still open:

> This Spirit acts "not only on me," but on persons of all times and of all relative worlds. Nor does this Spirit act everywhere in one and the same manner, according to one "global formula." Instead this Spirit acts in diverse concrete contexts, including those that conflict with each other and those that are supposedly incompatible with each other. . . . The experience is mediated in such a way that the most determinate attestation remains open to further illumination, and the most profound disappointments do not lead to resignation.[78]

Welker's exegetical and experiential applications of this notion helpfully supplement the more direct appropriation of the scientific concept, as represented by Wolfhart Pannenberg.[79] Of course, the field of force notion may eventually end up on that large refuse pile of scientific notions eagerly adopted by enthusiastic or desperate theologians.[80] The point is somehow to identify the empowerment that

is found in the relationship with God.[81] A welcome recent development is the effort of scholars trained in the natural sciences and theology to offer formulations in which divine and human action are not
simply competitive. One of the leaders in the field, Robert John
Russell, offers this summary description:

> An appreciation for the importance of developing an objective
> noninterventionist interpretation of special providence is on
> the rise. . . . Quantum physics, if interpreted in terms of onto-
> logical indeterminism, offers the best basis for a bottom-up
> strategy. Nonlinear, nonequilibrium thermodynamics, cosmol-
> ogy, and neuroscience offer tantalizing possibilities for a top-
> down and/or a whole-part approach. A shared goal is to
> combine these approaches.[82]

If the general action of God in the universe can be conceived in ways
that do not simply compete with human agency, may we not have a
metaphysical hint about how to think about the Pauline imperative
to the Philippians—Work out, for God is at work in you? That is the
promise of efforts such as those employing field-of-force language.

Welker acknowledges, indeed insists, that the presence of the
empowering reality of the Spirit is difficult to discern and can
appear an "illusion" or "incomprehensible and inconceivable."[83] The
believer is indeed challenged by that appearance and may well ask,
"How do we know?" In response we need to speak of transforming
knowledge.

The Knowing of Freedom

> "For who has known the mind of the Lord so as to instruct
> him?" But we have the mind of Christ. (1 Cor. 2:16)

> Now the Lord is the Spirit, and where the Spirit of the Lord is,
> there is freedom. And all of us, with unveiled faces, seeing the
> glory of the Lord as though reflected in a mirror, are being trans-
> formed into the same image from one degree of glory to anoth-
> er; for this comes from the Lord, the Spirit. (2 Cor. 3: 17-18)

There is resource for transformation given in actual relationship with
the other, relationships with other created realities and relationship
with the Creator. Our knowing is not exempted from these relationships. If it were, it would be doubtful that there would be empowerment for transformation in them. What we know and how we think

do make a difference. Cognitive therapy has shown that our mental operations are part of the human problem or (and?) part of the solution. There is efficacy to ideas embraced, or even entertained.[84] Paul Ricoeur speaks for us when he says, "words may change the 'heart,' that is the refulgent core of our preferences and the position we embrace."[85]

When we turn to Christian existence, it does not cease to be true that our knowing and thinking can be a resource for transformation. After all, the Christian claims to know something. In the relationship of Christian existence there is an Other to be known—no, who *is* known, as surely as faith does not simply collapse into subjective passion. Søren Kierkegaard is popularly known for the sentence "Subjectivity is the Truth," but he would not leave the believer sunk in a relationless faith:

> Christianity exists before any Christian exists, it must exist in order that one may become a Christian, it contains the determinant by which one may test whether one has become a Christian. It retains its objective subsistence apart from all believers, while at the same time it is the inwardness of the believer. In short, here there is no identity between the subjective and the objective. Though Christianity comes into the heart of ever so many believers, every believer is conscious that it has not arisen in his heart. . . .[86]

The Other the Christian knows is eminently other; here difference is decisive. The Creator's intention is grounded nowhere else but in the divine will, as the prophet Isaiah made clear:

> Who has directed the spirit of the Lord,
> or as his counselor has instructed him?
> Whom did he consult for his enlightenment,
> and who taught him the path of justice?
> Who taught him knowledge,
> and showed him the way of understanding? (Isa. 40:13-14)

We might well speak of knowing this One as the knowing of freedom. A knowing it is, for Paul in 1 Corinthians immediately follows his quotation of Isaiah with this: "But we have the mind of Christ" (1 Cor. 2:16).[87] According to Michael Welker, the miracle of Pentecost is precisely the miracle of understanding:

> What is decisive in this story, what is "miraculous" about the Pentecost event, is not the fantastic and ominous characteris-

tics of the Pentecost story—the "sound from heaven" and the divided tongues of fire—not the "speaking in tongues" that initially evokes only incomprehension. The miracle of the baptism in the Spirit lies not in what is difficult to understand or incomprehensible, but in a totally unexpected comprehensibility and in an unbelievable, universal capacity to understand and act of understanding.[88]

And it matters. The Christian as Christian does know something. In this knowing there is power for transformation, so that one comes to know, to experience, what true freedom is even in one's own life. In Paul's second letter to the Corinthians (3:17-18), he says so: "Where the Spirit of the Lord is, there is freedom." The one who looks to God comes to look like God, "transformed into the same image." Paul emphasizes that "this comes from the Lord, the Spirit." Of course, it is possible merely to look *at* Jesus and experience no true freedom, no transformation. God will not shanghai the creature, but in love create freedom anew. But if one looks and sees the glory of the Lord, apparently mirrored in the unveiled (freed) faces of other believers, one truly experiences transforming knowledge, "from one degree of glory to another."[89] Apparently some seem not to see. For that matter, it is certainly possible to see the folks gathered in the churches in other ways (there are other things to be truthfully seen), but faith comes to another "opinion" (*"Doxa,"* in Greek, means "glory" or "opinion").[90]

What does this knowing entail? Reversal toward restoration. Something gets turned around; Paul earlier insisted that in Christ God has made foolish the wisdom of this world (1 Cor. 1:20). Our knowing in and of the world does not escape human fault. This reversal is, as it clearly must be, a gift. Old Testament professor Diane Jacobson is not in the business of undervaluing wisdom, but she recognizes reversal when she sees it:

> Christ as wisdom centers specifically on Christ hanging on the cross, a wisdom which undermines and turns on its head any wisdom based on power or prestige. Jesus, our wisdom, died on the cross, and the meaning of Sophia is transformed.[91]

Yet this reversal does not represent a kind of reverse rationalism by which we would somehow revel in incoherence and boast of contradiction. God's chosen actions may interrupt to overturn our sense of what is valuable and wise, but that is *God's* doing, so "none may boast in the presence of God" (1 Cor. 1:29). Alexandra Brown's close exegetical study of these opening chapters of 1 Corinthians marks the difference:

> Paul's Word is apocalyptic in part because it calls for an end to the world defined by the Corinthian categories of wisdom and power. . . . But the Word he offers can move his hearers into the transfigured wisdom and power of the cruciform existence only if it *both* creates cognitive dissonance (dislocation) *and* provides the positive impetus to *re*-locate in the new world it prescribes.[92]

Is not this reversal truly restoration? Human sin throws out of synch our knowing (so that we think too much, or too little, of ourselves with respective imbalance regarding the other). God's transforming revelation calls us as knowers back into the proper human place in the creation. There the other is given for us—given truly to be known as someone (something) that is truly other. Luther's description of a theologian of the cross surely rings with reversal, but that is so because this theologian, unlike the "theologian of glory," "calls the thing what it actually is."[93]

Consider, for example, experience. In both academy and market place the Western world has let David Hume define experience. Suppose we do say with Hume's Philo that "our ideas reach no farther than our experience."[94] If we then let Hume reduce our reliable experience to discrete sense perceptions, what then? If my knowing of an apple is a venturesome association of seeing something round and red, feeling something smooth, tasting something tart; what can we confidently say of knowing other persons, or God? Do we not seem reduced to regarding such knowing as unwarranted (and hence to minimizing its role in our lives) or to throwing aside all common sense experience of the world in an enthusiastic embracing of whatever fantasy claims us?[95] But what if it is true, using the language of this chapter's first section, that the other is given to us for our knowing as well?

Alfred North Whitehead well describes the difference in understanding experience:

> All modern philosophy hinges round the difficulty of describing the world in terms of subject and predicate, substance and quality, particular and universal. The result always does violence to that immediate experience which we express in our

actions, our hopes, our sympathies, our purposes, and which
we enjoy in spite of our lack of phrases for its verbal analysis.
We find ourselves in a buzzing world, amid a democracy of fellow creatures. . . .[96]

Whitehead's alternative to Hume carries a strong reference to time's
three tenses. It involves:

> a sense of emotional feeling, belonging to oneself in the past,
> passing into oneself in the present toward oneself in the future;
> a sense of influx of influence from other vaguer presences in the
> past.[97]

(1) What of the past? It is not dead, but living. To return to the
apple, consider this longish but eloquent testimony to memory by
James Ashbrook:

> It is the mind and senses together that ritually make the first
> bite into the first apple of the season real and ritual to me, so
> that the season, the taste, the recognition of change all cele-
> brate the occasion as ritual event calling on memory as it reaf-
> firms me living in this event of the apple season from the past,
> and moves me along in the reality of life in this new apple sea-
> son. Memory draws from my gut, from my physical senses,
> from my brain, from my knowledge of time's passage in the
> instance of the apple season, forming an experience of life that
> is my life, that bears my history. (I draw on memories of apples
> stored for winter in the straw above the horses' barn, the wind-
> fallen apples in the orchard; the memory of baking apples for
> supper the night I received news of my sister's death, so I don't
> bake apples anymore because of this memory. I remember
> going with my father with a wagon load of apples to the cider
> mill, sensing his excitement of this event, which now I call his
> richness in the world.) All of these are part of apple memory.[98]

We do remember now. The remembered past enters our present.

(2) What can we know in the present? We come to know what is
disclosed to us in our experience.[99] In this experienced world we
eschew Hume's clean distinction between fact and value, and ask
ourselves "instead why we do believe certain statements of fact."[100]
We are interested in "*How* one holds a truth, one's intention in
regard to truth, the use to which a truth is put" and like questions.[101] And, following Luther, in calling a thing what it actually is,
we will be moved to call evil evil and good good. In such moral judgments we are not far from the domain of faith. In that domain is a

living experience to be tapped for transforming knowledge. Why did Luther say that "experience alone makes the theologian"?

God's commitment to the creation is such that there is indeed a gift, the gift of relationship. Christian faith is about a relationship. In that relationship transforming knowledge is available. Consider, for example, the knowing that can be present in prayer. Ann Belford Ulanov writes well of this:

> In prayer, we re-collect ourselves and feel touched by what or who we know ourselves to be. We recover a sense of ourselves, now disidentified somewhat from the different roles we take on during each day. For finally in prayer, I am I, for better or for worse, before God, and not mother or teacher or wife or lover or some identity I share with my depressed or anxious or dulled feelings.[102]

(3) The knowing received through living experience is freedom's knowing, marked by what I have called the pulse of life toward the future. Humans are called to exercise their imagination to claim the true and the possible and the two need to be held together.[103] In the knowing of freedom there is gift for the creature, the gift of life. Life is newly given through the knowing that comes in relationship with the other, for this conversation does have, as Pannenberg puts it, "a life of its own."[104] This is not an easy gift for the knower, for in the knowing of freedom there is responsibility that may well provoke resistance, as Daniel Taylor realizes:

> Overcoming these resistances requires an unusual balance of self-confidence, humility, and integrity. It requires holding tightly to the value of the struggle, while holding loosely the conclusions we draw while in the midst. It calls for discerning between the opposition which must be overcome and that which calls us to a higher standard. . . . We should pursue God tenaciously; we should neither exaggerate our knowledge of His ways, which are not our ways, nor ignore the benefits of His grace which are offered us at every moment.[105]

There is a way between the ditches of naïve value-free realism and cynical relativism. To the former we suggest that human knowing is embodied in a particular time and place and as such is purposeful. Yet there is hope in this. To the latter, we say "in our knowing we may not have a ground, but we have a path."[106] Thus the grace we know is not simply "mazing," for we have a direction.[107]

This "in-between" posture of critical realism is a gift to us.[108] The
Christian can own up to ambiguity courageously, if not comfortably.
She can welcome change in principle, recognizing that fidelity to the
truths once delivered to the saints requires the flexibility of fresh formulation. Materially, the faith in the Creator that nourishes this
appreciation of temporality reaches out to welcome the world as
well. Explicit Christian faith is not a credential required for contributing to the conversation concerning what God is doing in the
world. That the centering Christian story of Jesus does not supplant
this welcome was made clear by Bonhoeffer:

> In Christ we are offered the possibility of partaking in the real-
> ity of God and in the reality of the world, but not in the one
> without the other. The reality of God discloses itself only by
> setting me entirely in the reality of the world, and when I
> encounter the reality of the world it is always already sus-
> tained, accepted and reconciled in the reality of God. This is
> the inner meaning of the revelation of God in the man Jesus
> Christ.[109]

This faith brought Bonhoeffer to his counsel for Christians in "a
world come of age":

> And we cannot be honest unless we recognize that we have to
> live in the world *etsi deus non daretur*. And this is just what we
> do recognize—before God! God himself compels us to recog-
> nize it. . . . The God who lets us live in the world without the
> working hypothesis of God is the God before whom we stand
> continually. Before God and with God we live without God.[110]

Bonhoeffer's succinct visionary counsel left itself vulnerable to the
wide range of interpretation that has followed. I hear in these words
not a ban on God talk but a recognition that such talk depends on
"the knowing of freedom." In the relationship "before" and "with"
God the Christian is given the freedom to a knowing together with
those others who live in this world. The remarkable level of activity
in the science and religion discussions, directed to trying to formulate an understanding of God's action in the world, is in principle a
fully fitting practice. We are empowered to resist the lesson William
Placher would draw from the history of theology:

> . . . theologians get in trouble when they think they can clearly
> and distinctly understand the language they use about God.[111]

Writing from prison in the middle of this century in the passage just
cited, Bonhoeffer went on to speak of how:

> God lets himself be pushed out of the world on to the cross. He
> is weak and powerless in the world, and that is precisely the
> way, the only way, in which he is with us and helps us. . . . only
> the suffering God can help.[112]

At the end of the century there are indications that theologians
have begun to fathom his point. Mainstream theologians deeply
rooted in the tradition write openly of the vulnerability of God in
Christ.[113] That christological insight drives the theologian toward a
reflective frontier in the doctrine of God. We can come to grasp the
context of the Patristic talk of impassibility:

> Impassibility then implies perfect moral freedom, and is a
> supernatural endowment belonging to God alone. . . . It is
> clear that impassibility means not that God is inactive or unin-
> terested, not that He surveys existence with Epicurean impas-
> sivity from the shelter of a metaphysical insulation, but that
> His will is determined from within instead of being swayed
> from without. It safeguards the truth that the impulse alike in
> providential order and in redemption and sanctification comes
> from the will of God.[114]

Even in the working of that will, human beings come to be
involved. With the parable of the importunate widow before the
unjust judge, Jesus admonished his disciples to pray and never lose
heart (Luke 18:1-8).[115] In any case, surely the suffering of God in
Christ is crucial for all God talk.[116] When seeking to indicate with
what humankind should occupy itself regarding the knowing of
God, Martin Luther turned to Jesus weeping over Jerusalem:

> It is God incarnate, moreover, who is speaking here: "I would .
> . . you would not"—God incarnate, I say, who has been sent
> into the world for the very purpose of willing, speaking, doing,
> suffering and offering to all men [sic!] everything necessary for
> salvation.[117]

If we would not learn of the truly suffering God from the biblical
theologian Luther, we could learn it from the biblical writings themselves, as Terence Fretheim reveals in his much cited work *The Suffering of God*. Pondering the relationship between the two
testaments, he writes of "a decisive continuity in the history of God":

> . . . For one who "experiences" the metaphors across the Testa-
> ments, the history of God is seen to be coherent, consistent,
> and marked by certain constants that are finally unsurpassably
> exemplified in the life and death of Jesus Christ. "He who has
> seen me has seen the Father" can, in at least one significant

sense, be turned around to say: "He who has seen the Father has seen the Christ."[118]

Or one could follow the lead of Whitehead, who as a philosopher could not neglect the fact that "Christ is nailed to the cross." Thus he found in the "Galilean origin of Christianity" a "suggestion" regarding God "which does not fit very well with any of the three main strands of thought . . . the ruling Caesar, or the ruthless moralist, or the unmoved mover."[119]

Well, from one source or another, perhaps contemporary theologians have learned this lesson, to affirm the reality of divine suffering.[120] Perhaps we are beginning to recognize this not as a discrete item for a catalogue of divergences but as a central focus shaping all God talk. William Placher sees the matter so:

> Christian talk about God ought to start with love, not power
> and introduce the language of power only in the context of love
> and only in a way that keeps challenging and subverting it by
> way of reminder of how easily it might be misunderstood.[121]

In exercising the gift of the calling to ongoing theological reflection we still have much more learning to do in this matter. We have not shown convincingly how, in Bonhoeffer's phrasing, a suffering God *does* help.[122] Douglas John Hall articulates the challenge:

> . . . There are situations where power is of no avail. . . . May we
> not also dare to say that, from the standpoint of a faith tradition which posits love, not power, as God's primary perfection,
> they are most of the situations in which God finds God's Self
> too?[123]

This honest question has surely been raised by writers who are not professional theologians. We closed this chapter's first section with psychologist Robert Kegan's reference to a God who does not control how we will turn out, who is fascinated with how we will live. So, too, poet Denise Levertov has written:

> . . . God then
> encompassing all things, is
> defenseless? Omnipotence
> has been tossed away, reduced
> to a wisp of damp wool?
>
> . . . is it implied that we
> must protect this perversely weak

animal, whose muzzle's nudgings
suppose there is milk to be found in us?
Must hold to our icy hearts
a shivering God?[124]

In this searching question thus voiced from well beyond seminary walls the contemporary theologian does not lack challenge. Perhaps it is difficult to see that challenge as the gift that it is. But gladly or grudgingly, one hopes for a creative constructive response. The conversation on the science and religion front is a start; such work offers the scope needed for faith's claims about God the creator.[125] That work may help the theologian realize that the "omnis" of classical theism need not stand or fall together. Worldly conversation may lead the Christian theologian to claim more freshly and intelligibly the omnipresence of God. The creator cannot be evicted from the universe; this the Christian knows in knowing the centering story of Jesus. In knowing this divine freedom binding itself to the creation, the Christian has cause to amplify the verb with which we began by speaking of empowerment. In God's unfailing presence there is power. If Cheryl Sanders is right that empowerment has to do with conveying the authority to act, in this relationship there *is* empowerment.[126]

So, having coming through the spiraling rhythm of interruption, calling, and relationship, we are moved to ask, "What, then, is now to be done?"

6. So, What Is Now to Be Done? (To Serve the Creator's Will)

He unrolled the scroll and found the place where it was written:
The Spirit of the Lord is upon me,
  because he has anointed me
  to bring good news to the poor.
He has sent me to proclaim release to the captives
  and recovery of sight
  to the blind,
  to let the oppressed go free,
  to proclaim the year of the Lord's favor. (Luke 4:17b-19)

So what? What is the upshot of this writing and reading of transformation? What follows from this description? What will follow it? Karl Marx did not doubt what was needed:

The philosophers have only *interpreted* the world in various ways; the point is to *change* it.[1]

Marx, master of modern suspicion, may lately have lost credibility, not to mention authority. But many postmodern voices still echo his emphasis in calling us to a solidarity in action without benefit of metaphysical comfort.[2] Are there not demands that clearly call out for decisive action? Christians do have a stubbornly persisting interest in interpretation, but are not without an interest in what follows the interpretive act. On the sixth Sunday after Easter, many Christians, together in worship, pray these words:

God, from whom all good things come: Lead us by the inspiration of your Spirit to *think those things that are right* and by your goodness *help us to do them. . . .*[3]

But may not description and interpretation somehow impede right action? Surely they may, in two ways: (1) The story of Christendom is filled with instances where the faith is understood in such a way that nothing transformative can be done now, at least by the worthless wretches human beings represent. Or in what may only appear to be an opposite dynamic, the believer acts, but with an absoluteness that puts him apart from or even against others.[4] (2) Between such apparent extremes back in the messy middle, Christians sometimes wonder, when can one reasonably declare the interpretive tasks completed and so present oneself as a candidate to act? May this be one way in which Yeats sadly is right that "the best lack all conviction, while the worst are full of passionate intensity"?[5]

How shall one respond to these challenges? To the first perhaps one can only continue to give voice to the corrective contained in Luke's words in which Jesus speaks of his mission as *present* liberation, and then add the biblical calling of believers into that mission. That is what I have tried to do in writing in these pages of the interruption and calling in relationship that the Christian experiences.

But what of the second challenge—that the Christian, poring over the wealth of revelation, never quite seems ready to act? One may note, in passing, that this is not a difficulty known only by Christians. Rather, Robert Coles in a letter to parents and teachers notes "the double irony of it all":

> The irony that the study of philosophy, say, even moral philosophy or moral reasoning, doesn't by any means necessarily prompt in either the teacher or the student a daily enacted goodness; and the further irony that a discussion of that very irony can prove equally sterile, in the sense that yet again one is being clever—with no apparent consequences, so far as one's everyday actions go.[6]

What can a book, what can words, do? Quite a little; it is not a small thing to change the heart.[7] But the proper aim of theology, like philosophy, includes moving the changed heart to action. Another doing must follow. It has in the lives of many, with surprising results. Henry David Thoreau, jailed upon his refusal to pay taxes to support public worship in Massachusetts, was asked by Emerson about why he had gone to prison. Thoreau's response: "Why did you not?"[8] Perhaps Thoreau's often cited counsel to "simplify, simplify" has a methodological meaning as well.[9] One prone to endless interpretation can be interrupted, called, and empowered in relationship, energized simply to act. Toward that second doing, in-deed, I offer three simplifying suggestions.

Locating Worlds—Where Are We? Finding a Place

> . . . The earth was a formless void and darkness covered the face of the deep, while a wind from God swept over the face of the waters. (Gen. 1:2)

> Then the channels of the sea were seen,
> and the foundations of the world were laid bare
> at your rebuke, O Lord,
> at the blast of the breath of your nostrils. (Ps. 18:15)

> What has come into being in him was life, and the life was the
> light of all people. The light shines in the darkness, and the
> darkness did not overcome it. (John 1:4)

Chapter 1 spoke of a groaning creation. Two chasms in the terrain of contemporary consciousness were laid bare. People experience disorientation when evicted from the modern "Cosmopolis," where self and world were neatly synchronized.[10] And Loren Mead and others sound the challenge to Christians to realize that we no longer live in "Christendom."[11] These assertions invite this interpretation, drawing on chapter three: we live in a condition of interruption, individually and collectively. Perhaps announcements of the end of modernity and of Christendom are too clean. Elements of each remain, and we cling to them, as to our memories. But we know something is broken, or at least approaching its end. Something has been lost, for good or ill. So what are Christians to do? Can our being thus interrupted be the beginning of a God-pleasing transformation? Shall we tremble . . . weep . . . laugh . . . repent . . . fall silent?[12] A good first step is to find out where we are. We must locate the worlds in which God may now be calling us to act.

To locate these worlds we must listen long and hard. Is such listening too quiescent a stance for a church with a gospel to proclaim? It may seem so, but in this confusing time we do well to heed Wittgenstein's remark that the winner of the race is the one who can run most slowly.[13] To listen first will serve us well, for the word does not mean something without a world. The word surely resists domestication in any given world, but it seeks to become flesh in concrete contexts. There is transformative power in the word to shape reality, to create new initiatives in any context. The charge against early Christians was that they were "turning the world upside down," for they were "acting contrary to the decrees of the emperor, saying 'there is another king named Jesus'" (Acts 17:6-7). But we cannot change what we do not locate. The speaker of the word is called to attend to whatever world is given. In such attending the listening Christian will not himself go unchanged. After all,

God is the creator who will not be simply absent from whatever world is there to be found. It should not shock us *that* God speaks to the church from well outside its apparent borders, though *what* we then hear may well constitute an interruption.

Words from worlds outside the church may bring up within it words from the church's formative story, the story of God's continuing work in the world. Attending to these words within the telling of that story may bring light to our task:

> . . . The earth was a formless void and darkness covered the face of the deep, while a wind from God swept over the face of the waters. (Gen. 1:2)

Feeling the losses involved in our condition of interruption, the Christian may seem to dwell in a dark and formless void. But the Christian also feels a breeze, or rather the Christian *believes* that the breath of the Spirit of God has not been stilled.

> Then the channels of the sea were seen,
> and the foundations of the world were laid bare
> at your rebuke, O Lord,
> at the blast of the breath of your nostrils. (Ps. 18:15)

The Christian may even see, beneath the rubble, the foundations of the Creator's making laid bare. Then she is in position to claim the gain in these losses.

> What has come into being in him was life, and the life was the light of all people. The light shines in the darkness, and the darkness did not overcome it. (John 1:4)

Contemporary people know not a little of death in the reality of interruption, the darkness of death and of sin. But all life is not ended. It is God who gives life and that life is "the light of all people." The light shines in the darkness, and the darkness does not overcome it.

Why, then, are we to listen in order to locate worlds? Faith in a still-creating God listens expectantly to locate the inarticulate groanings in need and quest that constitute a calling. This listening and locating will in fact not be quiescent. It will not be, because we will be listening to the other, to the others.[14] It is the coming into view, into earshot, of the other(s) that marks the passing of modernity and of Christendom. To listen to the other(s) is not a motionless stance, for—as Emmanuel Levinas has reminded us—we do not occupy the same site.[15] And they themselves surely dwell in no single world. It is worlds we must locate. This pluralism presses upon us with empirical force,[16] but faith in the God who creates in love for the other(s) should have made us ready for such a finding. That faith indicates the inadequacy of painting pluralism with a single evaluative brush, as Michael Welker notes:

> With a minimum of theological instinct, theologies and church leaders have, on the basis of a simplistic understanding of "unity" (e.g., monohierarchical unity), condemned pluralism as if it were a unitary phenomenon. In so doing they have demonstrated an absence of the power to distinguish between individually disintegrative pluralism and the life-enhancing, invigorating pluralism of the Spirit.[17]

This recognition of difference does not come easily to the modern spirit that lingers in us. Victor J. Seidler asks (and answers) the question of to what extent "a liberal moral culture, established in the image of the Enlightenment, makes us fearful of difference." Acceptance or assimilation into the dominant culture depends on the willingness of those who are different to disappear, to conceal the aspects of themselves that signal their differences and so threaten us.[18] But our resistance to difference is increasingly ineffectual. The willingness of African Americans, women, gays, and lesbians to remain either submerged or speechless is vanishing. In meeting the no longer invisible and silent other, something more than novelty is involved. We find that the conversation and the culture are changing, becoming more pluralistic as such diverse groups "insist on defining their own terms of acceptance and identity."[19] If we listen to the voices of people we have previously excluded, we will hear cries of pain that do not leave the moral standing of the dominant culture unquestioned.[20] We experience these eddies of anxiety within the broader turbulence generated by the awareness of human suffering our Enlightenment frameworks tended to deny.[21]

When we are interrupted by the other(s), we will not remain motionless. In our listening posture, we will move, or be moved. Perhaps our movement will approximate what Daniel Yankelovitch has called the "lurch and learn paradigm" for social change. He suggests that rather than moving forward in a smooth linear trend or swinging back and forth in place like a pendulum, social change occurs as we may move toward our opposites, then modify our movements in ways that may improve our aim or may be a momentary stagger in a backward direction. We lurch toward and away from, even against, the others, but they are harder and harder to simply ignore.[22]

Such singular, lurching responses do not serve our learning. To adore the other serves us no better than to abhor her. Similarly, Mark Kline Taylor has pointed out how unsatisfactory it is to disengage "admiration" and "liminality." In the absence of acknowledgment of the concrete differences we face in each other, the liminality of change becomes just one mode of living and thinking after another. Yet without the "sense of suspension, shock, and disorientation" that are marks of liminality, our admiration of difference would amount to a catalog of differences, of other worlds that make no direct impact on our lives.[23] In the movement of transformation, admiration and liminality, the delight and the risk in coming face to face with others, must be held together.

Our locating activity requires us to adopt what Robert Bellah has called a "radical middle" position, between an "inclusive" relativizing of all moral judgments and the turning of the wagon trains inward in an essentially defensive posture.[24] How do we do that? Faith finds itself drawn to make concrete distinctions and commitments in the light of the worldly realities actually encountered. For example, to take the category we have been stressing, the other, and a case in point, Native American people, such concrete locating will move beyond the reservation setting suffused with longing for the vanquished coherence of the tribal world. Faith faces the challenge of recognizing the urban Indian and coming to terms with the reality and meaning of life for such displaced persons in a world where cultural boundaries are shifting significantly.[25]

This locating will test our capacity to make distinctions in ways that cannot be limited to the task of empirical description. Consider the challenge presented by the contemporary mixture of modern and postmodern worlds. The Christian will welcome the waning of certain features of modernity such as the rigid separation of self and world supporting an over-reliance on technical fixes, and the tendency toward narrow disciplinary specialization in the academy. Such modern chopping up of life can be lost, happily. But surely Christians will not celebrate and support any erosion of such modern values as the freedom of the individual, scientific discovery, and democracy.

We will also need to make distinctions in locating what might be emerging as the postmodern. Certainly one can join with Ted Peters in finding hope in the cry this infant consciousness sounds:

> We moderns, say the postmodern critics, have separated human consciousness from the world of extended objects, separated value from truth. We have separated humans from nature, from God, and from one another; and should we finally detonate our nuclear weapons—weapons that represent the height of the modern achievements in technological thinking—then we may even separate ourselves from our own future. Our world continues to break into more and more pieces. Voices from many quarters can be heard crying out, "Enough of this! Let's put the world back together again!"[26]

That postmodern cry for connection is encouraging. We still need to heed the wise warning we have already heard against a possible postmodern "henophobia" (fear of the one) in which the celebration of difference could weaken attention to human integrity and justice.[27]

It is not easy to make the needed distinctions by which genuine difference and real connection can be held together. It will be with some fear and trembling that we set about the locating: making maps and making judgments. But we may be more hopeful than fearful in this time of transition. How so? The modern and the postmodern are currently often to be found dancing together. The choreography can be rather confusing as objections and enthusiasms, both new and old, keep company. Yet perhaps that very instability can create an opening for Christian dialogical witness. As we locate a world, we can "negotiate" with it.[28] A Christian who, in Kosuke Koyama's striking phrasing, worships a "spacious" God who "can speak all languages" can reach out to very different worlds. Koyama comments that the mind made spacious by such a God "listens, explores, accommodates, translates, and adjusts."[29] Moreover, if Christianity largely exists in a marginalized status in relation to such fragmentary worlds as struggle to be born and to survive, perhaps that is an apt place for a transformative faith to find itself. An alien can be restlessly at home in any world.[30] And we may be less tempted to negotiate from weakness just now, when one may no longer speak of or seek to identify with "the" world with its united front.

The calendar provides a case in point. As we approach the millennium, the idea of a dramatic denouement for history is embraced, ridiculed, and replicated in secular dress. What is sought but not found here may be a serious engagement with the very idea of decisive historical change in which the issues of good and evil are addressed. Christian faith drives the believer also to be interested in history and time. Things happen in time: Abraham left the Ur of Chaldee in time; Sarah laughed and had a son in time; Moses climbed a mountain and came down in time; a Jew named Jesus was born, was crucified, and was raised from the dead in time. In time a Martin Luther nailed some theses on a door in Wittenberg, and in time another man named Martin Luther marched on Washington. Christianity is a timeful religion: things do happen. To go to the base of the matter, God does happen. There are things in this time that feel qualitatively different. Consideration of that idea calls for serious assessment of what we humans are to make of time, in our thinking and acting.

What is clear is that it is not yet clear precisely *what* we should make of this time. Christians will not be without conversation partners in this effort. The challenge is to sort out and combine the contributions from such diverse participants as the Enlightenment's often scientistic emphasis on evolutionary progress, a feminist protest that "such physics is a bad model for physics,"[31] and a New Age focus on the near-death experience as illumining a consciousness that pervades the universe but does not cease at death.[32] In a time when the "end" of everything is being announced[33] but Bill Gates cheerfully points out *The Road Ahead*,[34] the Christian is summoned to calmer pondering. We speak a sobering word regarding such fundamental notions as the irreversibility of past, present, and future. But we also speak about the possibility of genuine change, of what can be thought and hoped regarding human becoming in such a universe. What human beings have made is only what humans have made; the Creator is working still.[35]

In locating a world the Christian now can "open the book" and "find the place." Actually, one has already found the place, the place where one is. In locating a world at least in the making the Christian is moved to the book. The book, the faith once delivered to (and lived by!) the saints (Jude 3; cf. 1 Cor. 15:3) has of course been in play in the locating. But with some measure of clarity about context in place, the Christian turns with explicit attentiveness to the text.

Word and world come together. The point is not to write the book, but to open it. But what we then find may surprise, even interrupt, us.[36]

What will be required and entailed is a focusing of faith.

Focusing Faith—Who Are We? Opening the Book

> I do not call you servants any longer, because the servant does not know what the master is doing; but I have called you friends, because I have made known to you everything that I have heard from my Father. (John 15:15)
>
> I am the vine, you are the branches. Those who abide in me and I in them bear much fruit, because apart from me you can do nothing. (John 15: 5)

Christians talk in two ways of focusing faith: (1) the faith that is believed (*fides quae creditur*), the confessions of faith, and (2) the faith by which we believe (*fides qua creditur),* the commitment and venture of faith. With regard to both the propositions and the passions of faith, focus is needed and can be secured.

Certainly Christianity carries a body of truth claims, a *fides quae.* Christians are a people "of the book," and in the way of their master they make it a practice to open the book and read. Jesus calls the disciples not servants but friends, because he has "made known to you everything that I have heard from my Father" (John 15:15). Christians claim to know something and are committed to carry that knowing forward in their lives. Thus there arises that vast body of "second order" tradition, in Ray Hart's startling phrase, theology's "linguistic debris."[37] Regarding these words of the tradition he observes that "the theologian has a penchant for keeping a supply of them in excess of demand."[38] But the theological tradition is not principally a pile of propositions sitting statically on some professor's dusty shelves. Once again, the Christian seeks to carry forward a certain knowing in living. Joseph Sittler said, "theology is something the church *does,* not only something it *has.*"[39] Sittler found Theodore Roethke's line fitting: "I learn by going where I have to go."[40] The doing of theology finds its dynamic focus as the Christian seeks to bring word and world together.

Where does this leave us? Does it leave us without a place to stand? Don't we have something to stand for? Very well, perhaps dogma is best understood as an eschatological goal.[41] But until the end the Christian seeks a timely focus, a way to concentrate on what is needed. Such a focus is not fashioned out of the air, for not everything that is blowing in the wind is the Spirit of God. We need the wisdom of the past for the tasks of the present. Christians share this insight with others engaged by the human prospect. Thus social scientist Michael Walzer points out that even in prophetic criticism, the prophet depends on what was previously given.[42] New shape for old wisdom has always been part of the work of God's people. Gerhard von Rad has written extensively of the living traditioning process for the people of Israel and finds the old and the new coming together in this way:

> In each specific case, Israel spoke in quite a different way about the "mighty acts" of her God. In so saying, we do not mean the truism that in the course of her history her faith itself underwent considerable changes. . . . No, Israel constantly fell back on the old traditions connected with the great saving appointments, and in each specific case she actualized them in a very arbitrary, and often novel, way. There are three entirely different conceptions of the "call of Abraham" set beside one another (Gen. 15:1-6, 7-17). The tradition of the covenant with David first appears in what is probably a very ancient text (2 Sam. 23); afterwards it makes its contribution to the Succession Document, thereafter it is taken up into the Deuteronomic history (in the concept of the "lamp of David"), and finally it is used by the Chronicler. It is therefore a case of the same appointments being actualized in a different way at different times and probably also at different places. Set in different perspectives, the appointments disclosed different contents and—what is equally important—they each opened up aspects of the future which were equally specific.[43]

In this focusing one both claims and tests the tradition.[44] One does test. One is seeking to focus, to "see clearly," the message that meets the actual needs at hand. Materials of two sorts fail the test. (A) There are materials that do not help one clearly to see, to hear, the good news of a gracious God. While the stringent economy of Jesus' charge to his disciples (Luke 10:7: "Carry no purse, no bag, no sandals. . . .") should not be applied too literally, a sense of priority will serve us well. We will ask, "Does the specific formulation under consideration enable one more clearly to see and hear the good news of God? If so, how?" Formulations that do not speak to the situation at hand need not be jettisoned; there may be a wisdom in keeping what we do not just now see the point of. But we may well de-emphasize such formulations. (B) There are materials that actually contradict that good news and that cannot responsibly be retained.[45] These formulations not only deflect the people of God from urgent business, they directly damage members of God's wide family of humankind. A church living under the banner of "always to be reformed" (*semper reformanda*) will claim the gift and task of self-criticism.[46]

So what is called for now, theologically? Where do we need to go for a focus in thought that will serve transformation? Testing and claiming move us to ask about how the *fides quae* understands God's Christ in relation to the Creator's project with humankind, and even all creation. We can briefly sketch these two points, indicating as well some promising partners for the conversation.

(1) To know Christ is, indeed, to know his benefits.[47] But if that is so, is there not something incongruous in the circumstance that the church seems much more definite about the *person* of Christ than about his *work?* If he was truly God and truly human, then we should find a way to speak of the power of his coming for God and for us. How is that done in forensic formulations that leave the work of Christ suspended in the air, halfway between the actual lives of either God or humankind? Earlier I have given some hints as to what a better approach might entail;[48] here I am simply pleading for the priority of such soteriological reflection. We need first to know that and how Christ saves and then to define who he is on that basis. With Schleiermacher we will say of the person of Christ what we need to say, given our experience of the saving work of Christ.[49]

Theological speech about Jesus has not only failed in the first way mentioned, by lacking connection with genuine human need and hope. We have spoken about Jesus and his "work" in ways that have brought actual harm to human beings. The questions put to various atonement theories, particularly by feminists, reveal that damage. If Christ is truly victor, does that suggest suffering is not really real? If Christ's work was one of satisfaction through the obedience that yields suffering and death, what model is there held up?[50] The questions are known to us, *in* us. The answers are not. But fragments of a formulation may be visible.

(1a) The way ahead will not take us through the denial of suffering. Dorothee Soelle begins her now classic text *Suffering* with a decisive critique of what she calls Christian masochism and sadism. But she does not call the reader to the suffering-free state of death. In the Christian "mystical way":

> . . . The soul is open to suffering, abandons itself to suffering, holds back nothing. It does not make itself small and untouchable, distant and insensitive; it is affected by suffering in the fullest possible way. The extreme and distorted form of this stance is masochism. Its distortion consists in anticipating the pleasure that deliverance affords; the way is mistaken for the goal. But a true acceptance of suffering is never a self-sufficiency which would be at peace and satisfied already now in the devil's inn.[51]

(1b) And what of the suffering work of Christ? Elizabeth Johnson acknowledges this reality can be misused, but she warns of "the pathological tendency in the present culture of First World countries to deny suffering and death in human experience." And so she argues:

> In this context speech about redemptive suffering and the power of the suffering God is genuinely countercultural, and of benefit to women who know in their own experience a full cup of anguish.[52]

A key here will be to knit God-talk and Jesus-talk firmly together, against persistent tendencies to say directly or suggest subtly that it was God who killed Jesus. When the stone the builders rejected becomes the cornerstone, *that* is the Lord's doing (Matt. 21: 33-44). The one who sent the son is the object, not the author, of the rejection of the son.[53]

(1c) It is possible, even necessary, to claim in and through the testing the reality of Christ's suffering. But it is not sufficient. If our test asks how our faith serves the life of the creation, we must attend to the question of how the living relates to that suffering. Joy Bussert makes that point pastorally:

> Although the cross as a symbol of comfort and hope does give significant meaning and dignity to the suffering, it is not enough. I find in working with battered women that all too often the direct application of this theological perspective to a woman's life experience actually serves to glorify suffering and reinforces her belief that it is "Christ-like" to remain in a violent

relationship. We need, instead, to begin articulating a faith that will provide women with resources for strength rather than resources for endurance.[54]

Thus to focus on the work of Christ will entail both naming the suffering of God *ex memoria passionis*[55] and a recognition that death could not hold the Nazarene. Something happened in the suffering of cross and resurrection that changed God. God has borne human flesh, suffered and died, and will not be the same ever after. Here the earlier mentioned references to Christ's actual efficacy (Schleiermacher's assumptive *"Urbild,"* Cobb's "field of force") cry out for further development.[56] The cross is dark enough, but Eberhard Jungel is right that the Christian does not find the encounter with an interrupting God to be simply deadly:

> This . . . is the Easter experience of a God who allowed the continuity of his own life to be interrupted through the death of Jesus Christ.[57]

(2) Thus we come to the second point: this Jesus is *God's* Christ. It is God, maker of heaven and earth, who comes in this one. We are brought to face the question, "Who is God?" or more precisely, "What do we mean by 'God'?" It is "for Jesus' sake" that we engage the God question, lest we offer the faint praise of claiming that God can be active only in this one or draw on the treasury of his human personality without sufficient metaphysical credit balance. Such diverse forms of "Jesusology" we mean to avoid by putting the God question. But what do we mean *by* God?

We have meant things that have not been helpful to human beings dealing with pain and struggling for life and growth. How helpful is it to learn that:

> The sorrow and pain that God experiences are wholly vicarious; they consist entirely in his imaginative response to the sin and suffering that afflict his creatures.[58]

We have said such things and still say them, harmfully. We have listed all the omnis for God endlessly, and seem to have forgotten Jesus weeping over Jerusalem: "How often would I have gathered you as a hen gathers her brood; I would, but you would not" (Luke 13:34b RSV). In writing of the Nazi holocaust Arthur Cohen is perhaps too optimistic:

> By the time of the *tremendum* of this century, the suppositions of classical theism had already passed through the testing fires

of radical criticism that left them depleted. Only by recourse to a precipitous rush to mystery could the assertion of an absolute and monarchic God, whose relations to creation were at best formal and external, be reconciled with the scriptural disclosure of a loving, merciful, and just God.[59]

People still rush to mystery and cling to the strange comfort to be had in trusting a God who rules absolutely over a world no better than this. One wonders too if church leaders have not succumbed to the temptation to model themselves in the image of such a God. Surely it is past time to get at the God question by asking what kind of being can hang on a cross. In fashioning our theological focus an ellipse forms with two foci: First, our God talk needs the direction given by the crucified Jesus. We need the figure of Jesus as the norm for our lists of divine attributes. Then our Jesus talk needs the support and stability provided by the universal scope of the Creator's work. Surely Christ's proper work is to bring life abundantly to wide worlds; whatever is true for God because of Jesus is true for the Creator in relation to all creatures.

In understanding that Creator's work, Christian theologians will have company. We will be stretched to participate in the "science and religion" discussion of divine action mentioned earlier.[60] But a still more challenging conversation may occur with the "proximate other," those non-Christians taking up the explicitly religious topic of the presence—or absence—of God. As word and world come together in conversation, what contribution could come from those who confess their faith very differently or offer no confession in God at all? What will one say of or to the Buddhist for whom the ultimate reality is Emptiness? What difference will it make to realize that in this reading the ground of our existence is nothingness, *Sunyata*? Could there be in this speaking some kind of witness to a God who creates out of nothing?[61] Perhaps in this strangely religious talk of nothingness we are not far from meeting forms of atheism that do not present a religious face. We have learned to value the critique of the atheist who shows us how specific forms of Christian formulation and practice have damaging effects. But may the atheist, in religious clothes or not, make a constructive contribution to our God conversation? Paul Ricoeur has suggested as much in pondering the significance of the awareness of the "nonethical":

> To think nonethically, we must start at a point where the
> autonomy of our will is rooted in a dependence and an obedi-
> ence which are not infected by accusation, prohibition, and
> condemnation. Listening is just such a pre-ethical situation. It
> is a mode of being which is not yet a mode of doing, and for
> this reason it escapes the alternatives of submission and
> revolt.[62]

Could Mark C. Taylor be right that "it is a certain negativity that
draws us together while holding us apart and holds us apart while
drawing us together"?[63] Could this be what Paul Tillich was getting
at in insisting that God does not "ex-ist," does not "stand out" as an
item in the world of things?[64] For that matter, could we come in this
conversation to realize that God is not a person in the way that we
are persons?

These questions are difficult. They are easier to ask than to
answer. But they are questions that must be engaged if Christians are
to open the book of their faith and find the place that speaks to folks
occupying worlds to be located here and now. It helps to know that
Christians need not expect to have the answers in place *before* the conversation. To be that amply equipped might be to miss the living
speaking of God. That was the wise counsel of the Division for Global Mission of the Evangelical Lutheran Church in America in making "Commitments for Mission in the 1990s":

> We are committed to inter-faith conversations and dialogue
> and through these encounters we will seek to understand per-
> sons of other faiths; we will listen to what God has to say to us
> through these conversations and through them we will witness
> to the crucified and risen Christ.[65]

What focus in faith, then, fits the shape of the needy and seeking
worlds in which we find ourselves located? I am suggesting that for
this focus we claim and test the Christian elliptical witness to God
the creator as that finds expression in the Christ who comes to bring
life abundantly. This focus fits, for it connects with the wide worlds
in their promise and their problems. The range is right, for where
there is life the Christian believes this God to be present. So orient-
ed, the Christian is ready and willing to have the dialogue begin.
Does Confucianism, for example, speak of transformation of selfhood
without belief in a God with a definite, historically particular will?[66]
The Christian will seek out that person to participate in conversation, to learn and to teach. In this there will be speaking of God.

The conversation will have constitutive theological status for the Christian. We find out what to say of God through listening and speaking together. It will not be possible for the theologian neatly to distinguish "apologetics" and "dogmatics." Do scientists, soft and hard, puzzle over the self, asking "Who are we?"[67] The Christian joins the puzzling with a theological focus that provides a framework for sorting out the human findings and failings. Do chemical dependency counselors, indeed do alcoholics, ask about a "higher power"? The Christian is ready to join with these other human beings to speak and yes, to learn of God, and of why other words or names for God may help. Are voices raised urging that the human prospect must at long last be engaged in the light of the universe's story?[68] The Christian recognizes that a theological agenda is thereby identified. The Christian comes to these conversations with a sense of definite direction, for she claims a Creator who wills relationship, genuine difference in true connection. Distinctions can be made; discernment is possible. Nor is such faith in the creator an opening move crafted for apologetic purposes but soon to be superseded by worthier themes of greater weight. At the end when the living creatures give glory and honor and thanks to the one who is seated on the throne, who lives forever and ever, this is what the elders sing:

> You are worthy, our Lord and God,
> to receive glory and honor and power,
> for you created all things,
> and by your will they existed and were created. (Rev. 4:11)

As the Christian comes upon others speaking of creation, he may think he hears a tone of desperation. If one is desperate, "without hope," perhaps one may be driven to make what one can out of what is simply given to us. Or more than one can. I think I hear more than urgency in Thomas Berry's claim that "From its beginning the universe is a psychic as well as a physical reality," particularly when he goes on to say this:

> The earth, within the solar system, is a self-emergent, self-propagating, self-nourishing, self-educating, self-governing, self-healing, self-fulfilling community.[69]

The Christian may wonder if universe and earth depend on nothing more. If one holds desperately to such a view of beginnings, one may be driven to see so strong a continuance that even evil finds its place in the "original blessing" as a way of "befriending darkness and letting go, letting be."[70] To be desperate in this way may not be a sin, but for the Christian it would be a mistake. The Christian turn to creation is really a deepening, a spiraling down to that which grounds and animates the distinctive Christian reading of things and at the same time links the Christian with all the others.

These last lines ring with confidence. We believe there is transformative power in a faith so focused. We could say with Bonhoeffer that "in the traditional words and acts we suspect that there may be something quite new and revolutionary, though we cannot as yet grasp or express it."[71] Moreover, we know that "the faith once delivered" was not sealed in a vault but given into human hands for use, for interpretation and application. Rosemary Radford Ruether speaks of this in pondering the fact that Christianity is a historical religion:

> It is a living community in history, which does not just have a past, but a present and a future. Like any living community, it has pasts that it remembers, that are foundational for its identity. But, just as a living person continually reevaluates and even revises what it remembers in response to new demands and new perceptions of meaning, so the church, as a historical community, continually reevaluates how it reads its past memories and even revises that which it remembers.[72]

In accepting the task of interpretation, the Christian accepts the gift of sustenance. He recognizes the challenge in the conversation(s), but he speaks and listens with confidence.

Or with arrogance. What of the dawning sense that our faithful propositions fail to fathom reality fully? What are we to do with the raw realization that God finally eludes all our formulations? Or even with the grudging recognition that we human beings tend to trap ourselves in a world of words, while life runs its own independent course? At such moments we still repair to focusing faith. But now I have in mind the *fides qua creditur*, the faith by which we believe. What are we to do after we have described the structure of transformation and located inhabited worlds? Well, yes, we are to think the faith in a focused way. But beyond and particularly beneath that, we are to live the faith. Faith gives focus to our living.

Of this faith, this way of being in the world, we will have less to *say*. In this faith we are not merely located, knowing where we are. We are rooted and know who we are. We are children of God. In this being there is a knowing, to be sure. I have uttered and written more than a few God sentences. But before and beyond our sentences is a relationship in which silence makes sense, early and late.[73] The gospel of John's organic metaphor of the vine and the branches illumines this relationship. Like the branch, the Christian has a living relationship with the source of new life. It should not surprise, then, that what flows in that relationship cannot be dammed up in some cognitive pool of propositions leaving the rest of the knower's life unchanged. The vine and branches metaphor comes from the same chapter of John's gospel in which Jesus speaks of his disciples not as servants, but as friends. Friends have a real relationship, a transforming one.[74] With friends there is life that flows from the one to the other freely.

And yet the two are not simply one. Friendship entails freedom and so responsibility. With responsibility comes risk. It is not merely theory that we can fail to live the life of faith. What stands out about *fides qua* is the frequent paucity of its presence in the lives of believers.[75] Take the example of what is surely a major resource for the life of faith: prayer. Arland J. Hultgren stresses that the Christian is sustained in prayer by the relationship with "the living God who wills the redemption of all that he has made and acts in history and at history's end to accomplish it."[76] But he has also noted those passages that link God's forgiving of us with our forgiving of others.[77] Dorothee Soelle has made the connection most directly and concretely. Who is the "other" to be found in the Our Father? Of course she knows of heaven, but she refuses to forget earth:

> Because we care about the brotherhood of all
>   not just of Christians or of some other group of all
> those too who will live after us
>   in our cities with our water
> those who bear our mark unto the third and fourth generation
> of all
>   the dead who lived before us and whose dreams we betrayed
> . . . because we care about our brothers and sisters
>   that's why we sometimes say OUR FATHER. . . .[78]

Similarly, the Christian is not Robinson Crusoe on a solo expedition to or even with God. The community is crucial as a gift sustaining the believer.[79] That the gift is given can be sensed, whether one models the church as institution or communion, as herald or as sacrament.[80] But with the gift comes a task. Larry Rasmussen can speak of the church as "haven or way station," but not without claiming categories like "pioneering creativity" and "moral critic."[81] That responsibility calls the believing community to turn outward and to look inward. Clark M. Williamson makes the first of these moves:

> The marks of the church, classical and reformed, must be reconceived that they might reflect the singular promise and command of the God of Israel made known to us in Christ Jesus and that they might lead the church to understand itself and to act as an agent of justice and liberation in the world. . . . At the heart of the Jesus movement and the theology of Paul was a denunciation of every effort to place limits and conditions on the gracious love of God. That God justifies the ungodly, that this is true for all "others" if it is true for Christians . . . this is at the heart of Christianity's apostolic witness.[82]

And Loren Mead has made the second in his recent call to the churches to "rebuild the wall" of identity and "restore the temple" in authentic worship.[83] In both looking in and looking out we focus on the *being*, not the doing, of the church. This call to responsibility is not a summons to the frantic activity of giving people all they want in the congregation's "program."[84] Instead, authentic worship strengthens the church and its members in a particular identity and presence in and for the sake of the world.

But to what task, then, does the gift of the *fides qua* call the Christian? What becoming serves the being of this life? We can identify the focus by recalling phrases known in Christian memory: welcome the stranger and love the enemy. Considerable attention has been given to the theme of Christian hospitality by writers such as Parker Palmer, Patrick Keifert, John Koenig, and Christine Pohl.[85] I will not try to summarize this generally accessible literature, but let Thomas Ogletree's comprehensive challenge stand:

> In its metaphorical usage, hospitality does not refer simply to literal instances of interactions with persons from societies and cultures other than our own. It suggests attention to "otherness" in its many expressions: wonder and awe in the presence of the holy, receptivity to unconscious impulses arising from our being as bodied selves, openness to the unfamiliar and unexpected in our most intimate relationships, regard for char-

acteristic differences in the experiences of males and females, recognition of the role social location plays in molding perceptions and value orientations, efforts to transcend barriers generated by racial oppression.[86]

Only that? What if the person at hand is not only different from us, but actually set against us as enemy? This, Walter Wink suggests, should be "the ultimate religious question today":

"How can we find God in our enemies?" What guilt was for Luther, the enemy has become for us: the goad that can drive us to God. . . . we can no more save ourselves from our enemies than we can save ourselves from sin, but God's amazing grace offers to save us from both.[87]

Wink goes on to show how the way to God is through the enemy, because in meeting the enemy we can come to face what (in them and in us) separates us from God and come to recognize the God who loves both us and our enemies. Noting Jesus' words (Matt. 5:44-45; cf. Luke 6:27, 35; Rom. 12:20), "Love your enemies . . . *that you may be children of your Father in heaven,"* Martin Luther King found this challenge: "We must love our enemies because only by loving them can we know God and experience the beauty of his holiness."[88] If we are called not merely to desist from violence but actively to "will the well being" of the enemy,[89] we will be driven back into meditation, prayer, and spiritual guidance to learn what we can about our enemies, ourselves—and, ultimately, God.

That will be quite enough with which to occupy ourselves. Such a direction reaches out with range sufficient to focus the whole Christian life of individuals and churches. But what if, in the meantime, the worlds in which we are located cry out, for believers who are so focused to work with others *now?* What if the Christian cannot first focus on full faith development and only later respond to the worldly cry? What might then need to be done?

Sharing and Shaping a Future—What Are We Up To?

Word and World

Thus says the Lord of hosts, the God of Israel, to all the exiles . . . Build houses and live in them; plant gardens and eat what they produce. Take wives and have sons and daughters. . . . But seek the welfare of the city where I have sent you into exile, and pray the Lord on its behalf, for in its welfare you will find your

> welfare. . . . For surely I know the plans I have for you, says the
> Lord, plans for your welfare and not for harm, to give you a
> future with hope. (Jer. 29:4-7, 11)
>
> See, now is the acceptable time; see, now is the day of salvation!
> . . . As servants of God we have commended ourselves in every
> way: . . . with the weapons of righteousness for the right hand
> and for the left. . . . Open wide your hearts also. (2 Cor. 6:2b,
> 4a, 7b, 13b)

Suppose Christians have some sense of who they are and where they
are. We ask a final time: so what? What follows? How are the word
(they open) and the world (they locate) to come together?[90] Jeremiah has a word for exiles that speaks to Christians who find themselves
interrupted: seek the welfare of the city, work for the health of the
planet. In this "meantime," this ambiguous middle time, this is
what calls the Christian and the Christian congregation. Paul's counsel to the Corinthians carries comparable challenge.He describes not
a tranquil existence but "afflictions, hardships, calamities, beatings,
imprisonments, riots, labors, sleepless nights, hunger" (2 Cor. 6:4-
5). But he believes that "now is the day of salvation" and, working
with God, he calls the Corinthians into active duty "with weapons of
righteousness for the right hand and for the left." Today that challenge will call for carrying the resources of the tradition out into the
public square.

As Christians enter that public square, what may they expect to
find? They will find it both empty and crowded. That it is empty is
the point of the adjective usually chosen to complete the reference:
naked public square. In this way Richard John Neuhaus vividly
described the doctrine and practice "that would exclude religion and
religiously grounded values from the conduct of public business."[91]
Neuhaus has followed up his protest with a persistent refusal to keep
quiet. Stubbornly, he stands in the city and speaks of *First Things*.[92]
Others have joined this chorus in lament, folks like Stephen Carter
and Robert Benne on the right and Cornel West and Jim Wallis on
the left.[93]

So is the square now crowded with religious appeals? It might
appear so, for do not our politicians end every speech with "God
bless America"? But Carter of Yale Law School warns against a hasty
conclusion:

>In truth, the seeming ubiquity of religious language in our
>public debates can itself be a form of trivialization—both
>because our politicians are expected to repeat largely meaning-
>less religious incantations and because of the modern tendency
>among committed advocates across the political spectrum to
>treat Holy Scripture like a dictionary of familiar quotations,
>combing through the pages to find the ammunition needed to
>win political arguments.[94]

This religious costuming, not to say posturing, keeps company with
a deep drive to regard the highly personal reality of religion as essentially private. Larry Rasmussen refers to our own experience in this
land:

>[Religion] . . . is sufficiently privatized that often we do not
>know the religious and moral convictions of the people we rub
>up against all the livelong day. They may dress like us, share
>our funny accent, and chuckle at the same ethnic jokes, but we
>will not know whether they are Catholic charismatic, soft New
>Age, Buddhist, utterly secular humanist, deep ecologist, or
>pious Lutheran. And we will not find out until there is some
>casual or intimate setting and conversation in which they
>choose to share what they normally do not.[95]

This public needs to be addressed, for the culture groans for transformation. Of course there are those who hear the groaning and
attempt to respond without an explicit appeal to religion. They
work hard at this, and do well. Yet perhaps they overextend themselves. Charles Taylor, tracing in over five hundred pages the "making of modern identity," concludes by wondering:

>. . . whether we are not living beyond our moral means in
>continuing allegiance to our standards of justice and benevo-
>lence. Do we have ways of seeing-good which are still credible
>to us, which are powerful enough to sustain these standards?
>. . . Is the naturalist seeing-good, which turns on the rejec-
>tion of the calumny of religion against nature, fundamentally
>parasitic?[96]

William Dean has a similar question. Noting the passing of the
American exceptionalist myth, he asks:

>Is the old optimism associated with the myth of exceptionalism
>to be replaced simply by a newly dominant pessimism . . . ?[97]

Dean links that pessimism with the radically pluralistic character of
our culture. The presence of plural voices is really beyond dispute.

Racial diversity is a striking illustration. Part of the pressure derives from immigration:

> During the 1980s, America's native-born population advanced by only about 4 percent, while the Asian population increased at twelve times that rate and the Hispanic population at five times.[98]

In California, by 2001 (projections indicate), "the Hispanic, Asian, and Afro-American population will swell to 17.1 million—nearly half of the state's population."[99]

The visible difference of skin color may fail to reveal the more subtle conflict of world views. The public square may well be described as empty, for no unifying moral vision drives decisions and empowers the people's participation. Yet in another sense, the public square is crowded with candidates for serious moral conversation informed by religious values. The debate about the role of religion in politics needs to continue.[100] The plurality of voices need not hinder but can enrich the conversation, and the Christian joins that conversation surely as one of the many, but as one with a distinctive gift to contribute. Alasdair MacIntyre, who cannot credibly be charged with ignoring plurality in tradition, virtue, and rationality, has shown how disputes can be rationally resolved.[101] What is "rational" in this process is *not* some neutral or even common standard, but the movement toward the other by respecting *their* formulation of what constitutes the problem in their tradition and what would remedy the situation.[102] This is asking a lot, even if one still speaks with one's own voice. Why and how would one attempt it?

Ronald F. Thiemann makes a particularly strong statement of the need and the possibility for diverse voices of faith to meet in conversation in the public square.[103] He notes that Protestant Christianity, while not legally established, has "enjoyed" a kind of cultural establishment yielding a "non-christological theism." That theism sustained civic virtue. But with the increase of genuine religious pluralism and secularism this American civil religion lost its ability to shape that virtue. Thiemann notes that James Madison argued for the free exercise of religion *theologically*. To be guided by one's conscience is to fulfill one's duty toward the Creator. Invigorated theological speech in the public square comes to create new possibilities for the ethics and activities of the civic body. Drawing on Thomas Nagel's "criteria of publicity," Thiemann specifies three "norms of plausibility" for use in evaluating argument in the public domain: (1) public accessibility (premises open to public scrutiny), (2) mutual respect (acknowledging the moral agency of those with whom one disagrees), and (3) moral integrity (principled consistency in speech and action). Believers and unbelievers alike can hold hope for this process, because the basic communal orienting convictions rooted in faith "do not differ in kind or in function from the fundamental commitments that orient the lives of nonreligious persons."[104] Thus he calls for people of diverse faiths and of no explicit faith to meet in the service of such fundamental American values as freedom, equality, and mutual respect.

The Christian theological perspective offered in these pages fits well with Thiemann's proposal. Faith in God the creator finds an expression in duty, in accordance with Madison's description. In this way, faith provides a basis for the hope that commitment to and capacity for such conversation will be present within and beneath our pluralistic situation. That hope applies to the individual, the congregation, and the denomination. Christians claim their own distinctive identity, and so will not be repelled by the sheer presence of pluralism. Christian faith brings one to the table, the square, with hopefulness that the conversation will be genuinely productive for the human prospect. At the same time, a Christian who joins in the confession of sins will know that the conversation requires discerning judgment.[105] It is crucial that mutual criticism find a place within that conversation.

The Christian joins the conversation as one of the many, careful to divest himself of any lingering privilege.[106] I did speak of a distinctive Christian gift for the conversation. William Dean has suggested that the contemporary sense of vacuity in our culture might be addressed by recognizing that we are a nation of immigrants.[107] Coming from somewhere else is the American condition. Some came earlier, perhaps crossing a now disappeared land bridge in the Bering Straits area to enter this hard land. Others have come much later, but to a land no easier as government policy and popular opinion pull back the welcome of a sustaining hand. We do not have a sense of established foundation, but so what? We do have a sense of possibility and movement. Christians are not without instruction when it comes to aliens; they are called to memories of Egypt (Exod. 22:21;

23:9). But, more than that, the Christian is in a position to recognize that "we are all immigrants." To be immigrants is the *human* condition. The Christian knows this, for *fides quae* and *fides qua* come together to push out the boundaries of life. Life at the boundary calls for that. John B. Cobb Jr. observes:

> If there be no standpoint more inclusive than those of human beings, these human standpoints will tend to be treated as final or absolute, justifying anthropocentrism, ethnocentrism, or even egocentrism. Or, this lack of an inclusive standpoint can so lead to the relativization of all truth and reality that every idea and action is considered equally good and equally bad with every other.[108]

Our fundamental citizenship, our ultimate loyalty, is not to be found with any human state. We come from God and we go to God.

On the way we settle a while. Christians may be tempted to claim this "better country" citizenship in such a way as to yield disengagement from social striving and acquiescence to the status quo. But why reduce all importance to the ultimate? Even as aliens we are called to seek the welfare of the city, "to plant gardens and eat what they produce." This immigrant status is the human condition, not the private property of Christians. Yet Christians know a marginal existence that encourages and can bring serious experimentation to the public square. Perhaps there is marginality acquired in this understanding, a marginality that according to Jung Young Lee does not seek to be the center:

> As the followers of Christ, we will always be marginal people. Liberation from the margin does not mean to be at the center that dominates the margin. Liberation means to transfer from one form of marginality to another form of marginality, that is to transfer from the marginality of human centrality to the new marginality of divine presence in the world.[109]

Freed from the burden of the center, the off-centered Christian can connect with those energies and entities that serve the Creator's will. And the Christian seeks such cohorts with hope, because her faith focuses in a Christ in whom all things hold together (Col. 1:17). This, verily, is the Creator's doing: all things were created "through him and for him" (Col. 1:16).

And what is the Christian, so positioned, to do? For a final time we turn to the reality of our creatureliness. In this creaturely condition we stand together and attend to four points.

(1) Our temporality: to be a creature is to be caught up in the movement from the past through the present into the future. The Christian claims this thrust of temporality with hopefulness, for she believes the Creator is at work in the coming of the new. Perhaps the Christian in hope may make common cause with something in the American spirit, the pioneer or pragmatic impulse. The pioneers had to face the challenge of truly new circumstances. They were on the move and they kept on moving.[110] They were "horizontal" people, poor candidates for confinement in a vertical space where hierarchical relations assume prominence.[111] Thus Sydney Mead wrote of the "lively experiment" of America in which settlers could:

> confront all traditional institutions with tolerance, with amusement, with anger, . . . with impatience, but never with submissiveness.[112]

More than that, such an American will confront institutions with hopefulness, looking to the future in evaluation:

> . . . An institution is to be judged by the amount and quality of the awareness of the tension between its ideal and its actuality that its members exhibit, and by the realism of the efforts they are making to reduce the gap.[113]

But let us sound a warning. There are two ditches alongside this road into the future. Certainly the person confessing faith in a continuing Creator will not cling to some past golden age.[114] To the contrary, he may plausibly get involved in rewriting the history standards for the schools. But it would be as much mistaken to align oneself with an Enlightenment belief in progress. If science and technology are typically designated as the engines of that progress, Mary Shelley's *Frankenstein* should help us recognize that human science is no sure savior. What is sure is that the future comes. We have no choice about that; it comes reliably or relentlessly. We do not create the future; at best, we shape it.

In the light of this fundamental temporality, we will often do well to seek not a position but an orientation. Thus Roger Fisher of the Harvard Negotiation Project and the Camp David Accords urges us to focus on "interests not positions."[115] That seems wise, but interests do carry content. We will be interested in children, for they are our future. We will evaluate policy decisions against this question: "How will this support or hinder children's chances for a full human life?" We will take an interest in those present realities in which the future is prefigured. We will be mindful that the growth and development of our children are shaped by their experiences in relationship to us and to their worlds. Our nurture of them will extend to our concern for the health of those worlds. So we will buy computers for our schools and homes, but we will ask how wisdom and not merely information can be supplied on *The Road Ahead.*[116] Wisdom will call us to listen to the children in our lives as well as exhorting them, knowing as we do that our listening creates the potential space for the growth in them of the spirit of "wisdom and understanding, counsel and might,"[117] the *logos* of the future. We will worry about the role of librarians and journalists who are called upon to be both gatekeepers of information and protectors of its free flow, and about the economic inequality of access to the information age.[118]

(2) Our finitude: to be a creature is to come up against limits, insistently and inescapably. In the 1990s we have celebrated the twenty-fifth anniversary of the "one small step" of the moon landing, and we have witnessed popular hysteria over the discovery of possible life on Mars. What shall we make of such scientific developments? It is tempting to revel in the achievement (if we can go to the moon, what can't we do?) and the prospect (life is not a "sport" in the universe, for a welcoming new environment awaits us). We must resist that temptation. The life on Mars is life that became extinct, and the young president who challenged us to the new frontier is dead by an assassin's bullet. Metaphysical and moral limits interrupt our celebrations.

Such limits should not surprise the Christian. A Christian reading of reality places this precious and precarious venture of creation within qualitative limits: it is God who is alpha and omega. But we become forgetful, perhaps willfully. In that instance perhaps the pessimism of the postmodern can be a useful teacher for us. Grand schemes of historical understanding and social organization are not so likely to tempt us these days. Perhaps we will be willing to join with others so taught in applying the "organic principle" that "in any sort of work there is a point past which more quantity necessarily implies less quality."[119] Perhaps Christians and others will be prepared to recognize limits to economic growth and to consider measurement indices that serve a commitment to sustainability.[120]

(3) Our responsibility: to be a creature is to be called to care for the creation. Thus Christians will support the empowerment and

accountability of individual citizens. While a federal campaign to recruit volunteers may invite skepticism, the essential appropriateness of such involvement should be recognized. Moreover, this emphasis on personal responsibility has implications beyond the individual. Initiative in matters political need not be limited to formally constituted entities. The influence of NGOs (non-governmental organizations) in world affairs is well demonstrated, as in the Oslo Initiatives contributing to Arab/Israeli accommodation.[121] Similarly one will resist self-justifying status for governmental units. One can formulate the logic of this resistance in the "principle of subsidiarity":

> Each higher society is *subsidiary*, that is, designed to be of help to the lesser societies beneath it. It is not the other way around: the *persons* who comprise the more fundamental societies are not means to serve the *societies*. Nor are the closely knit natural communities such as the municipality to be used as means by the larger but more remote organizations like the regional or provincial government (our "states") or the national state.[122]

That logic will lead one to favor at least relative economic independence for smaller organizational units.[123]

And yet, we all occupy one nation and dwell on one globe. The Christian can contribute to the strengthening of individual initiative and responsibility in that public square. That will not happen without turning away from powerful strains in traditional religion: that individual initiative represents prideful self-assertion, that efforts for social amelioration are pointless because nobody (but God?) can "fix it all."[124] But the prophet Micah (6:8) may yet teach us that "to do justice" may well be linked with "walking humbly with your God." And it is not only the Corinthians (1 Cor. 1:25) who might learn from Paul that power is not always what it seems to be, that "Lilliputian influence" can count incalculably for social transformation.[125] Taken together with Christian faith's affirmation of the temporal, one glimpses an emerging stress on spontaneity and creativity that leads Cornel West to speak of the "jazz freedom fighter."[126] But one does not strive alone.

(4) Our relatedness: to be a creature is to be face-to-face with the other(s). The individual exists always in relationship and so we will only shape the future as we share the present. It is after all the common good that we seek in the public square. But how are we to avoid the tyrannical imposition of a single vision on the less powerful in a

pluralistic population?[127] We will do so only as we realize that "the quest for a common good takes place within and not against the experience of plurality."[128] Or in Seyla Benhabib's three words: "Participation precedes universalizability."[129] Perhaps universalizability will still exceed our reach, but the call is to work together to build "trust," the social capital so desperately needed in this land.[130] Driven more by need than by optimism, one seeks to appeal to such "American" values as freedom, equality, and mutual respect to support a genuine public conversation.

Such a conversation will not be fruitful without the genuine participation of presently marginalized voices. At this point the Christian will be particularly engaged, because she knows how often God's blessing comes to and through the stranger (e.g., Deut. 14:28-29; 26:10-13; Luke 4:25-27; 14:16-24). The Christian will gladly join with others in "the third sector," knowing that "whoever is not against us is for us" (Mark 9:40). The joining will not evaporate in thin air but plod ahead on solid ground. In this journey the "other" will be not just agent, but end. *What* we work for will surely call for opposition to rising tides of ethnocentrism and heterosexism, open in hate crimes and cloaked in immigration policy. We cannot leave unaddressed the unresolved American racial paradox represented by a Thomas Jefferson who could write the celestial sentences of the Declaration of Independence, while owning more than a few slaves on the earth of Monticello. Earth is not only a metaphor. Seen in wider focus, the planet stands as a silent witness and mute neighbor to challenge the Christian conscience.[131]

The concreteness and inclusiveness of the cosmological reference may be the occasion for closing this statement. In a series of publications Paul Santmire has called Christians to recognize their ecological responsibility. The recognition is deeply rooted in their confession of faith in a Creator God. In a brief article in "The Common Good" issue of *dialog* Santmire stated the point with exemplary directness:

> The rationale for the incarnation is both the perfecting and the restoring of the creation, both carrying the whole creation forward to its eternally intended ultimate future and bringing the sinful, Death-wielding human creature back on board, as it were, as a soul mate in the covenantal history of God with all

things, as that history moves toward its divinely mandated, eternal future of consummated shalom. . . . And so, together with countless others, who take the name of Christ, I see that I am called to serve in my own human and natural milieu in exemplary fashion as a citizen of that future city of God that is set upon a hill, whose light cannot be hid.[132]

Such eloquence and so grand a sweep in vision may ring true, yet somehow appear too daunting to the Christian. There will perhaps be a temptation to settle back into the daily struggle of the local parish, to get on with the business of the neighborhood. That is a temptation *not* to be resisted. Hard work is needed to keep the doors open, to make the meetings work. The Christian may strain to see the whole picture, but the cosmos truly becomes concrete in specific transforming moments in the course of each day. It indeed seems a battle. That is not so new. I suspect that the church in Corinth was not an easy place to serve. Paul found it necessary to employ "the weapons of righteousness for the right hand and for the left." But in the struggle it helps to remember the Sabbath day, to observe the year of Jubilee, and to say with the apostle "now is the acceptable time; see, now is the day of salvation!" It is the Creator of heaven and earth who calls people into service in the church council and the city council. And it was not just doors that were to be open. Paul's word to the Corinthians was this: "Open wide your hearts!" Who can say what will happen for those who heed that call? For them the time ahead will be neither boring nor easy. Interrupted and called, held in relationship always, they have the gift and task of transformation.

 Notes

Preface

1. See his *Toward the Critique of Hegel's Philosophy of Law* and the eleventh of his *Theses on Feuerbach*. Both are available in *Writings of the Young Marx on Philosophy and Society*, ed. L. D. Easton and K. H. Guddat (Garden City, N.Y.: Doubleday Anchor, 1967), 249ff., 402.

2. See the sermon "Two Kinds of Righteousness" in *Martin Luther's Basic Theological Writings*, ed. T. F. Lull (Minneapolis: Fortress, 1989), 156–57.

3. I take the economical phrase "the Christian thing" from David H. Kelsey's *To Understand God Truly: What's Theological about a Theological School* (Louisville: Westminster/John Knox, 1992).

4. See *God—The Question and the Quest* (Philadelphia: Fortress, 1985) and *Faith and the Other* (Minneapolis: Fortress, 1993).

5. Alfred North Whitehead, *The Concept of Nature* (Cambridge: Cambridge University Press, 1920), 163.

6. Tyron L. Inbody, *The Transforming God: An Interpretation of Suffering and Evil* (Louisville: Westminster John Knox, 1997).

7. See, for example, ibid., 67, 148.

8. Ibid., 180.

9. *Whatever Happened to the Soul? Scientific and Theological Portraits of Human Nature*, ed. W. S. Brown, N. Murphy, and H. N. Maloney (Minneapolis: Fortress, 1998).

1. The Creation Groaning for Transformation

1. Dorothee Soelle writes wisely: "My task as a theologian encompasses three operations: to translate whatever can be translated into modern scientific language; to eliminate anything that contradicts a commitment to love; to name, and stupidly (*blöde*) to repeat, what I can neither translate nor put aside as superfluous. I'm using the word *blöde* ('stupidly') first in its older sense, namely 'feebly,' for our feeble eyes are not capable of seeing what we are speaking about. Then too, I'm using the word in its current sense, because the repetition of sentences we neither understand nor think through is a sign of stupidity." See her *Suffering*, trans. E. R. Kalin (Philadelphia: Fortress, 1975, 1981), 8. She has helped us to understand much about suffering and how to change what can be changed. I hope that I too can offer something by way of translation and understanding, but I agree that one should not dismiss that in the groaning which resists such efforts.

144

2. Cornel West, *Prophetic Fragments* (Grand Rapids: Eerdmans, 1988), 157.

3. Robert D. Kaplan, "The Coming Anarchy," *The Atlantic Monthly* (February 1994): 45.

4. On the second matter I am particularly grateful to staff at the Domestic Abuse Project in Minneapolis for making this point so emphatically. They use the notion of a "bell curve" of responsibility, such that at some point in the escalating curve of anger, choice was possible.

5. Kaplan, op. cit., 58.

6. John B. Cobb Jr. and Herman E. Daly, *For the Common Good: Redirecting the Economy toward Community, the Environment, and a Sustainable Future* (Boston: Beacon, 1989, 1994), 1. Citing various State of the World reports put out by the Worldwatch Institute, Daly and Cobb speak appropriately of "the wild facts" that "constitute an assault on unthinking economic dogma."

7. Paul R. Sponheim, *Faith and the Other: A Relational Theology* (Minneapolis: Fortress, 1993), v.

8. Charles Taylor, *Sources of the Self: The Making of Modern Identity* (Cambridge, Mass.: Harvard University Press, 1989), 42; cf. 40, 113.

9. Ibid., 33. See chapter 5 on the "Moral Topography" of the self.

10. Ibid., 106.

11. Ibid., 35.

12. Robert Bellah, et al., *Habits of the Heart: Individualism and Commitment in American Life* (Berkeley: University of California Press, 1985), 75–76. A decade later Robert Benne finds the description still fitting and comments on the implications: "At root this individualism posits an innocent and harmless self. The exertion of utilitarian interest or expressive need will not harm others by either intent or neglect. Indeed, the exertions and expressions of individual selves will lead to a miraculous harmony among self-interested and self-expressing parties. The liberation of the self means at the same time the liberation of others. So the illusion avers." Robert Benne, *The Paradoxical Vision: A Public Theology for the Twenty-First Century* (Minneapolis: Fortress, 1995), 20.

13. See particularly the second and sixth of the "Meditations on First Philosophy" in René Descartes, *The Philosophical Writings,* trans. J. Cottingham, R. Stoottff, and D. Murdoch, 2 vols. (Cambridge: Cambridge University Press, 1984).

14. Stephen Toulmin, *Cosmopolis: The Hidden Agenda of Modernity* (New York: Free Press, 1990), 108.

15. In *The Dilemma of Modernity: Philosophy, Culture, and Anti-Culture* (Albany: SUNY Press, 1988) 71–72, Lawrence Cahoone puts the point this way: "The gradual loss of the transcendental, the breakdown of the subjectivist-transcendental synthesis that had made subjectivism workable since

the seventeenth century, initiated a profound alteration of the subjectivist categories themselves. The subject and object categories were thereby freed to be universally and radically applied, unencumbered by God or reason or any other trans-subjective factor. . . . It becomes impossible to conceive of subjectivity and objectivity as being independent existences *and yet* as being interrelated, mutually involved" (emphasis his).

16. Judith V. Jordan, "Empathy and Self Boundaries," 67, in Judith V. Jordan et al., *Women's Growth in Connection: Writings from the Stone Center* (New York: Guilford, 1991), 67–80.

17. Jean Baker Miller, "The Development of Women's Sense of Self," 12, in Jordan, op. cit., 11–26.

18. John B. Cobb Jr. "Two Types of Postmodernism: Deconstruction and Process," *Theology Today* 47, no. 2 (July 1990): 151.

19. The legacy of Thomas Kuhn seems very much still with us. See his second edition of *The Structure of Scientific Revolutions* (Chicago: University of Chicago Press, 1970). A more flamboyant statement is Paul Feyerabend's *Against Method* (London: Humanities, 1975). See also Richard Rorty's very influential text *Philosophy and the Mirror of Nature* (Princeton: Princeton University Press, 1979). While Rorty would have us live without "metaphysical comfort," he is still quite prepared to make moral claims for solidarity. See his "Solidarity or Objectivity?" in *Post-Analytic Philosophy*, ed. J. Rajchmann and C. West (New York: Columbia University Press, 1985).

20. Jean Bethke Elshtain, *Augustine and the Limits of Politics* (Notre Dame, Ind.: Notre Dame University Press, 1995), 2.

21. On the notion of "trace" see Jacques Derrida, "How To Avoid Speaking Denials," *Languages of the Unsayable: The Play of Negativity in Literature and Literary Theory*, ed. S. Budick and W. Iser (New York: Columbia University Press, 1989), 3–70, and Mark C. Taylor, *Nots* (Chicago: University of Chicago Press, 1993). Catherine Keller is particularly helpful in her analysis of Derrida and Foucault in "'To Illuminate Your Trace': Self in Late Modern Feminist Theology," *Listening* 5, no. 3 (1990): 211–24.

22. See Brenda E. Brasher, "Thoughts on the State of the Cyborg: On Technological Socialization and Its Link to the Religious Function of Popular Culture," *Journal of the American Academy of Religion* 59, no. 4 (fall 1996): 809–30.

23. Robert D. Putnam, "Bowling Alone: America's Declining Social Capital," *Journal of Democracy* 6 (January 1995): 65–78.

24. Ibid., 70.

25. An anticipatory example is Jean Bethke Elshtain's *Democracy on Trial* (New York: Basic Books, 1994).

26. Nancy T. Ammerman, "Bowling Together: Congregations and the American Civic Order," Seventeenth Annual University Lecture in Reli-

gion at Arizona State University, Feb. 26, 1996. See also her *Congregation and Community,* forthcoming from Rutgers University Press. The Roper Center's journal, *The Public Perspective,* has argued from numerous polls that the evidence actually documents an increase in participation in communities. This seems a classic case of "dueling statistics."

27. Wuthnow has devoted considerable attention to the small group movement. See, for example, his *Sharing the Journey: Support Groups and America's New Quest for Community* (New York: Free Press, 1994), and a companion volume he edited, *"I Came Away Stronger": How Small Groups Are Shaping American Religion* (Grand Rapids: Eerdmans, 1994).

28. Robert Frost, "Fire and Ice," *The Poetry of Robert Frost,* ed. E. C. Lathem (New York: Holt, Rinehart, & Winston, 1979), 220.

29. See Christopher Lasch, *The Revolt of the Elites and the Betrayal of Democracy* (New York: Norton, 1995), and Elizabeth Kamarck Minnich, *Transforming Knowledge* (Philadelphia: Temple University Press, 1990), respectively.

30. Many find the growing dominance of the Walt Disney empire a striking example. Does *Pocahontas* turn the story of what happened to the Indians into a love story? See Judith Adams, *The American Amusement Park Industry: A History of Technology and Thrills* (New York: Twayne, 1991).

31. Wiesel's most influential work is perhaps *Night* (trans. S. Rodway [New York: Bantam, 1960, 1986]), his eyewitness account of the Holocaust, which was first published in Yiddish under the title, "And the World Has Remained Silent." The "popularity" of the United States Holocaust Memorial Museum in Washington, D.C., is important, but hard to assess. That such museums require evaluation is demonstrated by Oren Baruch Stier in "Virtual Memories: Mediating the Holocaust at the Simon Wiesenthal Center's *Beit Hashoah* Museum of Tolerance," *Journal of the American Academy of Religion* 64, no. 4 (winter 1996): 831–51. Stier notes the California museum's "technologically sophisticated, anti-artifactual, multimedia approach" and wonders about a process of "displacement": "The ground *has,* in fact, gone out from under us, and without any artifacts holding us down and helping to maintain a sense of history and coherence, . . . we travel weightless through the spectacle, unsure of what exactly has been represented or seen" (845; emphasis his).

32. The examples I have chosen are ones from my own territory, Minneapolis-St. Paul (respectively, The Citizens League, Minnesota Advocates for Human Rights, and the City, Inc.). But such examples are to be found throughout this nation. Consider the remarkably rapid growth of Habitat for Humanity. Or one thinks of growing ecological awareness, as symbolized by then-Senator Al Gore's book *Earth in the Balance* (Boston: Houghton Mifflin, 1992) and in the academy by less visible but significant

efforts to break out of captivity to the limits of scholarship rigidly divided by the disciplines.

33. For one example, see the report by Auke Tellegen and other members of the Twins Studies at the University of Minnesota in *Journal of Personality and Social Psychology* 54, no. 6 (1988): 1–39. See also David Lykken's report of a study of 1,500 pairs of twins, "Happiness Is a Stochastic Phenomenon," *Psychological Science* 7, no. 3 (May 1996): 186–89.

34. See Ted Peters, "Should We Patent God's Creation?", *dialog* 35, no. 2 (spring 1996): 117–32. Peters, a participant in the Human Genome Project, has written and lectured widely on this subject.

35. Such is the contention of Jon Katz in *Virtuous Reality* (New York: Random House, 1996).

36. Stephen D. O'Leary, "Cyberspace as Sacred Space: Communicating Religion on Computer Networks," 786, *Journal of the American Academy of Religion* 44, no. 4 (winter 1996): 781–808. I am aware that Bill Gates's recent book is titled *The Road Ahead* (New York: Viking Penguin, 1995).

37. I am borrowing from Milan Kundera. See his *The Unbearable Lightness of Being,* trans. M. H. Heim (New York: Harper, 1985).

38. Albert Borgmann marks the problem in writing of "the device Paradigm":

When liberation by disburdenment yields to disengagement, enrichment by way of diversion is overtaken by distraction, and conquest makes way first to domination and then to loneliness.

Borgmann, *Techonology and the Character of Contemporary Life* (Chicago: University of Chicago Press, 1984), 47, 76. I have been aided by Larry Rasmussen's discussion of Borgmann's work in *Moral Fragments and Moral Community: A Proposal for Church in Society* (Minneapolis: Fortress, 1993).

39. Bill Bradley's disillusionment with matters political parallels the more specifically technological deficiency. See his *Time Present, Time Past* (New York: Knopf, 1996). Class differences make the issue of campaign finance reform particularly pressing. Upon leaving President Clinton's cabinet after the November, 1996 elections, Labor Secretary Robert Reich delivered himself of a similar assessment of the gap between rich and poor, relating that to such specific matters as community funding for schools. One ponders the interrelatedness of the issues I have briefly identified, the relationship of greed and violence, the bottom-line market attitude and inequality of access to state-of-the-art information technology.

40. The two O. J. Simpson trials come to mind, as one wonders what differences technology made in the perception-and-reality mix. Or one thinks of the tendency toward more sexually explicit and violent material on television and the Internet.

41. Martin E. P. Seligman, *What You Can Change and What You Can't* (New York: Knopf, 1994).

42. The Harvard conference sponsored with the Mind/Body Medical Institute Care Group of Beth Israel Deaconess Medical Center took place March 15-17, 1997, in Los Angeles. The second conference mentioned focused on "Spirituality in the Work Place" and was held in May, 1996, also in California.

43. Vaclav Havel, *Foreign Affairs* (March–April 1994). See also his highly influential *Letters to Olga* (New York: Knopf, 1988).

44. David Whyte, *The Heart Aroused: Poetry and the Preservation of the Soul in Corporate America* (New York: Doubleday, 1994).

45. Martin E. Marty's four-volume series on Modern American Religion (of which three have been published as of this writing) will be the decisive work for the historical background for any such analysis. Marty is particularly helpful in his discussion of organized religion and religious traditions. There is as well the vast penumbral reality of popular religion. See Charles H. Lippy, *Modern American Popular Religion: A Critical Assessment and Annotated Bibliography* (Greenwood, 1996). Lippy lists and annotates more than 550 studies.

46. Harvey Cox, *Fire from Heaven: The Rise of Pentecostal Spirituality and the Reshaping of Religion in the Twenty-First Century* (Reading, Mass.: Addison-Wesley, 1995), xvi: "Before the academic forecasters could even begin to draw their pensions, a religious renaissance of sorts is under way all over the globe."

47. Harold Bloom, *The American Religion: The Emergence of the Post-Christian Nation* (New York: Simon and Schuster, 1992), 37.

48. Mary Farrell Bednarowski, *New Religions and the Theological Imagination in America* (Bloomington: Indiana University Press, 1989), 127–28.

49. Samuel S. Hill, "Born Again," D. G. Reid, et al., eds., *Dictionary of Christianity in America* (Downers Grove, Ill.: InterVarsity, 1990), 177.

50. Erling Jorstad, *Popular Religion in America: The Evangelical Voice* (Westport, Conn.: Greenwood, 1993), 7. Jorstad focuses on four "bodies of believers": evangelicals, fundamentalists, Pentecostalists, and charismatics. He does note some evidence for a "slowdown within evangelical popular religion." Martin E. Marty and R. Scott Appleby have provided us with the definitional study of fundamentalism in the five-volume Fundamentalism Project they edited. See particularly *Accounting for Fundamentalism: The Dynamic Character of Movements,* vol. 4 (Chicago: University of Chicago Press, 1994). In *The Glory and the Power: The Fundamentalist Challenge to the Modern World* (Boston: Beacon, 1992), a companion volume to the PBS television and National Public Radio series, Marty and Appleby speak of

fundamentalism as " a pattern of belief and behavior that has emerged in all the major world religions over the past twenty-five years and is gaining prominence and influence in the 1990s" (3). Their series is scrupulous in its attention to this global diversity. Other helpful studies of resurgent fundamentalism in American religious life are by Joel Carpenter and Nancy Ammerman.

51. Jorstad, op. cit., 13.

52. Marty and Appleby, *Accounting for Fundamentalism,* 56 (emphasis theirs).

53. Martin E. Marty, *The Irony of It All,* Modern American Religion, vol. 1 (Chicago: University of Chicago Press, 1986), 218. He notes how Billy Sunday "used the modern techniques of organizing and publicity while rejecting modernism of all hues" (215). As a summary, consider this: "Whenever religious conservatives, the countermoderns, reacted to modernity and its changes, their responses have turned out not to be merely conservative but innovatively reactive. They have been seen as inventors of new, particular, competitive 'old-time religions'" (319).

54. See Cox, op. cit., 303: "The great irony of Christian fundamentalism, for example, is that it shares the same disability that plagues and cripples the modern rational mind—literalism. In their frantic effort to oppose modernity, Christian fundamentalists have inadvertently embraced its fatal flaw."

55. A now classic case is what Robert Bellah et al. term "Sheilaism," the highly personal religion of a woman of that name. See *Habits of the Heart,* 221.

56. This is the title Martin E. Marty chooses for his study of modern American religion from 1919 to 1941.

57. See Robert N. Bellah and Frederick E. Greenspahn, eds., *Uncivil Religion: Interreligious Hostility in America* (New York: Crossroad, 1987).

58. For example, see "A Collection of Responses from ELCA Academicians and Synodical Bishops to *The Church and Human Sexuality: A Lutheran Perspective*" (Chicago: Division for Church and Society, ELCA, 1994). The strongest poison did not appear in this volume, but in (often anonymous) letters and telephone calls, where the language of war was readily employed.

59. Cf. Marty and Appleby, *Accounting for Fundamentalism:* "Indeed, with a few exceptions, fundamentalists have enjoyed the greater success in reclaiming the intimate zones of life in their own religious communities than in remaking the political or economic order according to the revealed norms of the traditional religion" (3).

60. Robert N. Bellah, "Conclusion: Competing Visions of the Role of Religion in American Society," *Uncivil Religion,* 219.

61. See Paul Tillich, *Systematic Theology,* 3 vols. (Chicago: University of Chicago Press, 1951–1963), vol. 1, 111–14.

62. Paul R. Sponheim, "'The Other Is Given': Religion, War and Peace," *Word and World* 15, no. 4 (fall 1995): 434 (emphasis in the original). The quotation is from Dag Hammarskjold, *Markings* (New York: Knopf, 1964), 154. Since completing this article I am grateful to Professor Christine Pohl of Asbury Theological Seminary, Lexington, Kentucky, for further analysis of the confusion involved. She makes the point that seeing ourselves as co-workers with God, the moral authority of the end "spills over into the process of getting there" so that we become uncritical of the means we use (personal communication).

63. Bloom, op. cit., 15.

64. Ibid. Thus literary critic Bloom observes that in the American religion there is no cross—or, if there is, it is the "emblem of the risen God, not of the crucified man" (264).

2. Creation Comprehending the Whole Work of God: A View from the Middle

1. H. H. Schmid, "Creation, Righteousness, and Salvation: 'Creation Theology' as the Broad Horizon of Biblical Theology," 115, *Creation in the Old Testament,* ed. B. W. Anderson (Philadelphia: Fortress, 1984), 102–17.

2. *Webster's Third New International Dictionary* (Springfield, Mass.: Merriam-Webster, 1986), 467.

3. Frank Kermode, *The Sense of an Ending: Studies in the Theory of Fiction* (Oxford: Oxford University Press, 1968).

4. See pages 16–17 in this volume.

5. I take this phrasing from the popular vocal group "Sweet Honey in the Rock." It first appeared in Kahlil Gibran's *The Prophet* (New York: Knopf, 1951). Gustaf Wingren, *Credo: The Christian View of Faith and Life,* trans. E. M. Carlson (Minneapolis: Augsburg, 1981), 20, makes a more expansive claim, writing of how secular people may still extend a measure of respect to those biological points (baptism, marriage, burial) which "correspond" to these qualitative elements. He adds: "Translated into biblical language this implies that the Creator gives, generates, awakens to life; and that he does this in opposition to that which damages, destroys, and distorts life."

6. To set that Christian speech in context, see Charles H. Long, *Alpha: The Myths of Creation* (New York: Braziller, 1963), especially chapter 4 on creation from nothing.

7. See Paul Tillich, *Systematic Theology,* 3 vols. (Chicago: University of Chicago Press, 1951–1963), vol. 1, 188. Cf. vol. 1, 253–54, and 2, 19–21.

8. See Jürgen Moltmann, *God in Creation: A New Theology of Creation and the Spirit of God,* trans. M. Kohl (Minneapolis: Fortress, 1993), 86–93.

9. The definitive twentieth-century work on creation is perhaps Langdon Gilkey's *Maker of Heaven and Earth* (Lanham, Md.: Doubleday, 1959, 1965). In his threefold summary of what *creatio ex nihilo* "is essentially 'about,'" we can see a commitment to speak to the middle (in the second and third points) and perhaps a challenge to that commitment (in the first): "These affirmations are: (1) That the world has come to be from the transcendent holiness and power of God, who because He is the ultimate origin is the ultimate ruler of all created things. (2) That because of God's creative and ruling power our finite life and the events in which we live have, despite their bewildering mystery and their frequently tragic character, a meaning, a purpose, and a destiny beyond any immediate and apparent futility; (3) That man's life, and therefore *my* life, is not my own to 'do with' merely as I please, but is claimed for—because it is upheld and guided by— a power and a will beyond my will" (25; emphasis his).

10. Pedro Trigo, *Creation and History*, trans. R. R. Barr (Maryknoll, N.Y.: Orbis, 1991), 24–25.

11. Dennis Olson, "God the Creator: Bible, Creation, Vocation," *dialog* 36, no. 3 (summer 1997): 172 (emphasis his). Cf. Schmid, op. cit.: "In the ancient Near East creation faith did not deal only, indeed not even primarily, with the origin of the world. Rather, it was concerned above all with the present world and the natural environment of humanity now" (102).

12. I take this phrasing from Robert John Russell's "Does Creation have a Beginning?", *dialog* 36, no. 3 (summer 1997): 187, where he is drawing upon the Hartle/Hawking model for quantum cosmology.

13. This is Russell's phrasing: "Because of his insistence on the distinction between a finite past and a beginning of time, Hawking has, in effect, helped us claim that the universe is indeed a creation of God even if it had no beginning" (ibid., 188). Cf. Hawking's much cited work, *A Brief History of Time* (New York: Bantam, 1988).

14. Langdon Gilkey, *Reaping the Whirlwind* (New York: Seabury, 1976), 247.

15. Philip Hefner, "The Creation," 312, *Christian Dogmatics,* 2 vols., ed. C. E. Braaten and R. W. Jenson (Philadelphia: Fortress, 1984), vol. 1, 265–358. I should note that Hefner immediately adds "we face here, in an inescapable manner, the limitations of human thought," and more helpfully goes on to develop the role of the human as "created co-creator."

16. The awkwardness is reduced if one does not argue that God foreknew that the "gift" of freedom would be misused. Still, in his *Historical and Critical Dictionary* (London: Harper, 1710) Pierre Bayle asks the classic question, how good is it to expose the creature to even the risk of such misuse? One avoids that question if one gives up the *ex nihilo*. See David Griffin, *God,*

Power, and Evil: A Process Theodicy (Phildaelphia: Westminster, 1976; Washington, D.C.: University Press of America, 1990) and *Evil Revisited: Responses and Reconsiderations* (Albany: SUNY Press, 1991). This is to move toward Paul Ricoeur's "theogonic" myth (Paul Ricoeur, *the Symbolism of Evil* (Boston: Beacon, 1967). Still the theodicy question returns, if one grants that God calls or lures toward greater freedom. Anna Case-Winters raises this question in *God's Power: Traditional Understandings and Contemporary Challenges* (Louisville: Westminster/John Knox, 1990), 156–61.

17. Cf. the discussion below ("The Creator Working Still" in Chapter 5) on whether God creates by will or desire.

18. Gustaf Wingren, *Creation and Law*, trans. R. Mackenzie (Philadelphia: Muhlenberg, 1961), 30.

19. J. Richard Middleton, "Is Creation Theology Inherently Conservative? A Dialogue with Walter Brueggemann," *Harvard Theological Review* 87, no. 3 (1994): 264–65.

20. See, for example, Daniel O'Connor and Francis Oakley, *Creation: The Impact of an Idea* (Cambridge: Cambridge University Press, 1964).

21. Hans-Jürgen Hermisson, "Observations on the Creation Theology in Wisdom," 119, *Creation in the Old Testament* (emphasis his).

22. Cf. Langdon Gilkey's warning in *Reaping the Whirlwind,* where he pleads that "dynamic vitality is fully as sacred as is form" (248–49). To separate God from creativity and flux is "to return to the Greek error of identifying the divine merely with order, Apollo, and to regard the Dionysian, the dynamic in our being, as nondivine."

23. Colin Gunton, "Atonement and the Project of Creation: An Interpretation of Colossians 1:15-23," *dialog* 35, no. 1 (winter 1996): 36 (emphasis his).

24. Ernst Bloch, *The Principle of Hope* (Boston: MIT Press, 1986). Thomas H. West has argued that Bloch's own work is impaled on a contradiction on the question of how we can look to the ultimate future with confidence. See his *Ultimate Hope without God: The Atheistic Eschatology of Ernst Bloch* (New York: Peter Lang, 1991), where he pits an "omega originism" in which the future remains open against an "alpha finalism" in which the aim is given from the beginning. In the next section I will argue for a delicate synthesis of two such strands in Christian thought.

25. Walter Brueggemann, *Israel's Praise: Doxology against Idolatry and Ideology* (Philadelphia: Fortress, 1988), 101.

26. See Terence E. Fretheim, *Exodus* (Louisville: John Knox, 1991) as well as his articles "The Plagues as Ecological Signs of Historical Disaster," *Journal of Biblical Literature* 110 (1991), and "The Reclamation of Creation: Redemption and Law in Exodus," *Interpretation* 45 (1991).

27. Middleton, "Is Creation Theology Inherently Conservative?", 277. Middleton emphasizes that he regards his critique as "a minor correction to a powerful and fresh biblical hermeneutic."

28. Walter Brueggemann, "Response to J. Richard Middleton," *Harvard Theological Review* 87, no. 3 (1994): 283. He notes the "plurivocity" (Ricoeur) of texts and cites Psalm 37 as material that can be read either as supporting the status quo or as "an act of radical hope by the disenfranchised."

29. Claus Westermann, *Creation,* trans. J. J. Scullion (Philadelphia: Fortress, 1974), 56.

30. See Lynn White's classic statement of this charge, "The Historical Roots of our Ecological Crisis," *Science* 155 (1967), 1203–7. Kathryn Tanner traces three strands associated with the creation doctrine (God rules and so do we, the great chain of being, stewardship), all of which can contribute to an anthropocentric focus. See her "Creation, the Environmental Crisis, and Ecological Justice" in R. Chopp and M. L. Taylor, eds., *Reconstructing Christian Theology* (Minneapolis: Fortress, 1994). A particularly well-balanced response to White's charge is Paul Santmire's *The Travail of Nature: The Ambiguous Ecological Promise of Christian Theology* (Philadelphia: Fortress, 1985).

31. Westermann, op. cit., 93; cf. 106.

32. Michael Welker, "What Is Creation? Rereading Genesis 1 and 2," *Theology Today* 48 (1991–92): 62. Welker notes that Genesis chapter one contains both a monistic or absolute conception expressed in the creation of light and darkness (1:3ff) and a pluralistic or relative conception in the notion of the alteration of day and night (1:14ff) (66). Cf., again, the juxtaposition of "heaven" and "the heavens."

33. Søren Kierkegaard, *Samlede Vaerker,* ed. A. B. Drachmann, J. L. Heiberg, and H. O. Lange; 15 vols. (Copenhagen: Guldendals, 1901–36), vol. 10, 132–33 (translation mine). Cf. *Christian Discourses*, trans. W. Lowrie (Oxford: Oxford University Press, 1939), 132–33, where Lowrie adds a note stressing that to exist "for" God is to "exist directly in the face of God."

34. *Søren Kierkegaard's Journals and Papers,* ed. H. V. and E. H. Hong, 6 vols. (Bloomington: Indiana University Press, 1970), vol. 2, #1251.

35. Ibid.

36. Elizabeth A. Johnson, *She Who Is: The Mystery of God in Feminist Theological Discourse* (New York: Crossroad, 1992), 228. Her fuller statement: "Insofar as each is directed toward the other with reciprocal interest and intimacy, the relation is mutual. Insofar as the world is dependent on God in a way that God is not on the world, the relation is not strictly symmetrical."

37. Søren Kierkegaard, *The Sickness unto Death*, trans. H. V. Hong and E. H. Hong (Princeton: Princeton University Press, 1980), 126.

38. Whitehead's fuller statement in *The Concept of Nature* (Cambridge: Cambridge University Press, 1920; Ann Arbor: University of Michigan Press, 1957), 163, is this: "The aim of science is to seek the simplest explanations of complex facts. We are apt to fall into the error of thinking that the facts are simple because simplicity is the goal of our quest. The guiding motto in the life of every natural philosopher should be, Seek simplicity and distrust it."

39. See *Teaching Christianity (De Doctrina Christiana)*, trans. E. Hill in *The Works of St. Augustine* (Brooklyn: New City, 1996), vol. 11, book 1, iii–iv, 107–8. One may appreciate this structure formally without endorsing the rather Platonic emphasis, evident in filling out the order of being, that locates what is to be enjoyed and what is to be used.

40. *The Formula of Concord*, "Epitome," Article I on original sin in *The Book of Concord*, ed. and trans. T. G. Tappert (Philadelphia: Fortress, 1959), 468.

41. See John Calvin, *Institutes of the Christian Religion*, 2 vols., trans. H. Beveridge (Grand Rapids: Eerdmans, 1964), vol. 2:3, 5.

42. Cf. William Placher, *A History of Christian Theology* (Philadelphia: Westminster, 1983), 51–52.

43. Jürgen Moltmann, *God in Creation*, 5. Thus Wingren, *Creation and Law*: ". . . The first Creation was Creation in Christ even before Christ's Gospel and the proclamation of the Gospel. . . ." (42).

44. Regin Prenter, *Creation and Redemption*, trans. T. I. Jensen (Philadelphia: Fortress, 1967), 404.

45. Herbert W. Richardson, *Toward an American Theology* (New York: Harper and Row, 1967), 130.

46. Ibid., 130–31.

47. Martin Luther, "The Small Catechism" in *The Book of Concord*, 352.

48. Westermann, *Blessing*, 83. Other passages he studies in this connection are (1) the "inheriting blessing" passages (1 Pet. 3:9; Heb. 12:17; 6:7-8, 12-14) and (2) Rom. 15:29, the "blessing of Christ" in the Christian community.

49. Søren Kierkegaard, *Philosophical Fragments or a Fragment of Philosophy*, trans. D. F. Swenson (Princeton: Princeton University Press, 1936), 44. See the helpful distinctions made by Frederick Dillistone, *The Christian Understanding of the Atonement* (Philadelphia: Westminster, 1968), 288–91, between Christ's work "for God" and "for us" (my paraphrase).

50. See Gustaf Wingren, *Man and the Incarnation* (Philadelphia: Muhlenberg, 1959), 80ff, drawing on Book 4 of Irenaeus' *Adversus Haereses*.

51. Wolfhart Pannenberg, *Anthropology in Theological Perspective*, trans. M. J. O'Connell (Philadelphia: Westminster, 1985), 525 (emphasis mine). This question of whether Pannenberg "turns the time line around" is discussed in the well-titled volume *Beginning with the End: God, Science and Wolfhart Pannenberg*, ed. C. R. Albright and J. Haugen (Chicago: Open Court, 1997). See particularly my chapter, 360–77, and Philip Clayton's, 378–95. Robert John Russell has referred to Pannenberg's "complex and unusual ontological reversal in which the future is given priority over the past as the determining reality" and remarked that this represents "the greatest challenge to dialogue with physicists." See his "Contingency in Physics and Cosmology: A Critique of the Theology of Wolfhart Pannenberg," 40, *Zygon* vol. 23, 23–43.

52. Pannenberg, op. cit., 20.

53. Ibid., 519. I think too of Pannenberg's locution for God, the "all-determining" reality. I continue to have these reservations, despite Pannenberg's insistence (in personal conversation) that I have misunderstood him.

54. Moltmann, *God in Creation*, 62.

55. Ibid., 63.

56. See note 24 above for Ernst Bloch's struggles at this point.

57. I take this list from Dennis Olson, op. cit., 173.

58. See David Little, "Calvin and the Prospects for a Christian Theory of Natural Law," *Norm and Context in Christian Ethics*, ed. G. H. Outka and P. Ramsey (New York: Scribner's, 1968), 175–98. Little draws effectively on the work of anthropologist Clyde Kluckhohn, as well as other field studies.

59. Douglas John Hall is a theologian who has not neglected this issue. His *Imaging God: Dominion as Stewardship* (Grand Rapids: Eerdmans, 1986) and *The Steward: A Biblical Symbol Come of Age* (Grand Rapids: Eerdmans, 1990) make a case for the concept of stewardship, though I wonder whether his emphasis on human life *with* (not *above* or *in*) nature does not lead us beyond the bounds of that concept.

60. Marjorie Suchocki's *In God's Presence: Theological Reflections on Prayer* (St. Louis: Chalice, 1996) is a very accessible treatment of this theme. See, notably, her discussion of intercessory prayer in which "we risk being used by God as answers to our own prayers" (50).

61. Michael Root, "Creation, Redemption, and the Limits of System," 24, *Creation and Method: Critical Essays on Christocentric Theology*, ed. H. Vander Goot (Washington, D.C.: University Press of America, 1981), 13–28. Root goes on to say: "The case may be that in fact human existence *is* only fulfilled in redemption, but that fact cannot be incorporated into a definition of human fulfillment without reading redemption into creation in an illegitimate way" (ibid., emphasis his).

62. Loren B. Mead, *Transforming Congregations for the Future* (Washington, D.C.: Alban Institute, 1994), 115.

63. *The Oxford Poets: Gerard Manley Hopkins*, ed. C. Phillips (Oxford: Oxford University Press, 1986), 128.

64. See Jaroslav Pelikan, *Jesus through the Centuries: His Place in the History of Culture* (New Haven: Yale University Press, 1985). Pelikan's summary judgment is this: "Despite the phenomenal successes of Christian missions during the nineteenth and twentieth centuries, it seems incontestable that the percentage of Christians in the total world population is continually declining and therefore it seems inconceivable that the Christian church and the Christian message will ever conquer the population of the world and replace the other religions of the human race. If Jesus is to be the Man Who Belongs to the World, it will have to be by some other way" (230).

65. Geiko Muller-Fahrenholz, *God's Spirit: Transforming a World in Crisis*, trans. J. Cumming (New York: Continuum, 1995), xii. He notes that Luke's genealogy traces Jesus back to Adam and adds: "This identity of creative and messianic power is fundamentally important," citing the Nicene Creed's insistence that Jesus is "God of God, Light of Light" (38). Cf. Robert Jenson's discussion of Cosmic Spirit, 165–78, in *Christian Dogmatics,* where emphasis is placed on "the freedom of history, the spontaneity of nature and the beauty of all things."

66. Wingren, *Creation and Law,* 43.

67. George A. Lindbeck, *The Nature of Doctrine: Religion and Theology in a Postliberal Age* (Philadelphia: Westminster, 1984), 94.

68. See Arland J. Hultgren, *Christ and His Benefits: Christology and Redemption in the New Testament* (Philadelphia: Fortress, 1987), ch. 10, for a specification and application of criteria for assessing the four types of redemptive Christology to be found in the New Testament. Cf. also Hultgren's later effort in *The Rise of Normative Christianity* (Minneapolis: Fortress, 1994).

69. Claus Westermann, *Blessing in the Bible and in the Life of the Church*, trans. K. Crim (Philadelphia: Fortress, 1978), 11–13.

70. Pedro Trigo, *Creation and History,* trans. R. R. Barr (Maryknoll, N.Y.: Orbis, 1991), 86. In a similar move Walter Wink, following Paul Ricoeur, distinguishes the biblical creation story from the Babylonian myth in which "creation is an act of violence," such that "killing is in our blood." See his *Engaging the Powers: Discernment and Resistance in a World of Domination* (Minneapolis: Fortress, 1992), 14–15.

71. Ibid.

72. I take this phrasing from another of these remarkable twentieth-century Swedish theologians, Gustaf Aulén, in *The Drama and the Symbols* (Philadelphia: Fortress, 1970), 76.

73. Lesslie Newbigin, *The Gospel in a Pluralist Society* (Grand Rapids: Eerdmans, 1989), 230.

74. This is the fourth commitment, as listed in Mark W. Thomsen, *The Word and the Way of the Cross: Christian Witness among Muslim and Buddhist People* (Chicago: Division for Global Mission, ELCA, 1993), 16 (emphasis mine).

75. Ibid., 17. The rest of this commitment (the sixth) reads: "we are committed to Jesus Christ in both word and deed. We will preach the gospel and in Jesus' name we will seek to alleviate suffering and empower the weak and advocate for righteousness, justice and peace."

76. I have addressed this matter in *Faith and the Other: A Relational Theology* (Minneapolis: Fortress, 1993).

77. Hannah Arendt, *The Human Condition* (Chicago: University of Chicago Press, 1958), 247. She completes the paragraph with these words: "It is this faith in and hope for the world that found perhaps its most glorious and most succinct expression in the few words with which the Gospels announced their 'glad tidings': 'A child has been born unto us.'"

78. Cf. Welker, "What Is Creation?": "The task of laying bare, criticizing, and revising our guiding abstractions seems to me . . . to be an interdisciplinary task. It is an interdisciplinary task because the abstractions with which we have to do are located and operate in several contexts, namely in texts, in dogmatics, in the communication of religious communities, in common sense's external perspective on religion, and so on."

79. Martha Nussbaum, *The Therapy of Desire: Theory and Practice in Hellenistic Ethics* (Princeton: Princeton University Press, 1994), 229.

80. See James Baldwin, *Another Country* (New York: Dell, 1962).

3. To Be Interrupted: This May Be the Beginning

1. Thus Jacques Derrida, commenting on Kierkegaard's *Fear and Trembling* (for whom the pseudonym is Johannes de Silentio) writes: "Once I speak I am never and no longer myself, alone and unique." And yet Derrida knows that Abraham does speak. See *The Gift of Death*, trans. D. Willis (Chicago: University of Chicago Press, 1995), 60.

2. Alfred North Whitehead, *Process and Reality: An Essay in Cosmology,* corrected ed. by D. R. Griffin and D. W. Sherburne (New York: Free Press, 1978), 23 (emphasis his). A more controversial development of this point is Whitehead's claim that "there is a becoming of continuity, but no continuity of becoming" (35).

3. For criticism of the stress on small variation and slow change, see Brian Leith, *The Descent of Darwin* London: Collins, 1982).

4. Ian Barbour, *Religion in an Age of Science* (San Francisco: HarperCollins, 1990), 158.

5. See, for example, the chapter "O Grave, Where Is Thy Sting?" in *Hen's Teeth and Horse's Toes* (New York: Norton, 1983), for comment on the fact that "extinctions of species are not spread evenly over time, but are concentrated in a few brief periods of markedly enhanced, often worldwide decimation" (345).

6. Stephen Toulmin, *The Return to Cosmology: Postmodern Science and the Theology of Nature* (University of California Press, 1982), 260.

7. I have developed this point in *Faith and the Other* (Minneapolis: Fortress, 1993), ch. 2.

8. Frank Kermode, *The Sense of an Ending* (Oxford: Oxford University Press, 1967). Kermode particularly stresses the pulse pushing toward completion in connection with narrative, but I believe this reveals a deeper ontological tension.

9. The classic text is *The Sickness unto Death*, ed. and trans. H. V. and E. H. Hong (Princeton: Princeton University Press, 1980).

10. Søren Kierkegaard, *The Concept of Anxiety*, ed. and trans. R. Thomte (Princeton: Princeton University Press, 1980), 61.

11. See the introduction of *The Concept of Anxiety*, and for a more extended treatment *The Concluding Unscientific Postscript to the Philosophical Fragments*.

12. Kierkegaard, *The Sickness unto Death*, 29. Thus one seems driven toward the kind of distinctions the *Postscript* makes between different kinds of knowing.

13. I am citing his "Consciousness for the First Century," a paper prepared for the meeting *Year 2000 and Beyond*, for the Evangelical Lutheran Church in America. See also his *Flow: The Psychology of Optimal Experience* (New York: Harper, 1990).

14. Michel Foucault, *The Uses of Pleasure*, trans. R. Hurley (New York: Pantheon, 1985), 8.

15. Paul Ricoeur, *Paul Ricoeur on Biblical Hermeneutics*, ed. J. D. Crossan (Semeia 4; Missoula, Mont.: Scholars, 1975), 77.

16. A still very useful study is Wayne C. Booth's *A Rhetoric of Irony* (Chicago: University of Chicago Press, 1974), where particular emphasis is placed on the way in which irony calls for decision, while metaphor may not—at least not dramatically. Gary Handwerk's *Irony and Ethics in Narrative* (New Haven: Yale University Press, 1985) offers a close study of how "the foundation of thought and society, and their continued creative and adaptive capacities, all depend upon the power of ironic incomprehensibility to unify humanity" (15). This becomes a community of query and doubt.

17. Alfred North Whitehead, *Adventures of Ideas* (New York: Free Press, 1967), 277.

18. William James, *Principles of Psychology* (New York: Dover, 1950). I have this reference from M. Jamie Ferreira in *Transforming Vision: Imagination and Will in Kierkegaardian Faith* (Oxford: Oxford University Press, 1991), 51, in which she seeks to read Kierkegaard himself as at times offering a view of "pathos-filled transitions" which are forms of "broadened will" without being self-conscious acts of "will-power" in the face of equally plausible alternatives. There is much of value in this line of development for the next chapter as we ponder the role of imagination in transformation. But it remains important to retain a distinction between will and reason, as Arnold Come clearly shows in *Kierkegaard as Humanist: Discovering My Self* (Montreal and Buffalo, N.Y.: McGill-Queen's University Press, 1995), 154.

19. John Dewey, *How We Think* (Boston: Heath, 1910), 72.

20. Ibid., 31 (emphasis his).

21. G. W. F. Hegel, *The Phenomenology of Mind*, trans. J. B. Baillie (London: Macmillan, 1931), 92–93.

22. Martha Nussbaum, *The Fragility of Goodness: Luck and Ethics in Greek Tragedy and Philosophy* (Cambridge: Cambridge University Press, 1986), 3.

23. Ibid., 5, quoting *The Republic* 612A.

24. Ibid., 20 (emphasis hers). It is particularly Aristotle to whom she looks.

25. Eberhard Jungel, "The Truth of Life: Observations on Truth as the Interruption of the Continuity of Life," 232–33, in *Creation, Christ, and Culture: Studies in Honor of T. F. Torrance*, ed. R. W. A. McKinney (Edinburgh: T. and T. Clark, 1976), 231–36 (emphasis his). My reading of Jungel has been informed by the unpublished doctoral dissertation of Jonathan P. Case, "Disputation and Interruption: Truth, Trinity and the Death of Christ in Pannenberg and Jungel," Luther Seminary, 1995. Case particularly contrasts Jungel's understanding with that of Aristotle, whose "idea of possibility is entirely secondary to and dependent on the actual" (100; citing *Aristotle's Metaphysics*, 1049b–1050b). He does not refer to Nussbaum's reading of Aristotle.

26. Ibid., 234. Cf. Patrick Sherry, *Spirit and Beauty: An Introduction to Theological Aesthetics* (Oxford: Clarendon, 1992), 49, on Baudelaire's theme, "the beautiful is always strange."

27. Edward Farley, *Good and Evil: Interpreting a Human Condition* (Minneapolis: Fortress, 1991), 45. Farley's examples seem to me to slip somewhat away from the sheer given of alterity. He mentions "the parent unable to simultaneously attend to the needs of all the children, the inability of an engaged couple to adjust their career plans to each other, and the impossibility of a firm to appoint all of its qualified people as its Chief Executive Officer" (ibid.).

28. Carol Gilligan, *In a Different Voice: Psychological Theory and Women's Development* (Cambridge: Harvard University Press, 1982), 108. She refers

to Piaget and Erikson respectively. She also cites Robert Coles's extensive studies of *Children of Crisis*: ". . . Crisis can lead to growth when it presents an opportunity to confront impediments to further development" (115).

29. I still find instructive William R. Rogers's "Order and Chaos in Psychopathology and Ontology: A Challenge to Traditional Correlations of Order to Mental Health and Ultimate Reality, and of Chaos to Mental Illness and Alienation" in P. Homans, ed., *The Dialogue between Theology and Psychology* (Chicago: University of Chicago Press, 1968), 249–62.

30. Robert Kegan, *The Evolving Self: Problem and Process in Human Development* (Cambridge: Harvard University Press, 1987), 105. Kegan's formulation is that "every balance's irritability is simultaneously testimony to its capacity to grow and its propensity to preserve itself."

31. I have this formulation from James Fowler's *Faithful Change: The Personal and Public Challenges of Modern Life* (Nashville: Abingdon, 1996), 9–10.

32. Hannah Arendt, *The Human Condition*, 178. See also George T. L. Land, *Grow or Die: The Unifying Principle of Transformation* (New York: Dell, 1973), on the relationship between entropy and syntropy.

33. Ian Barbour, "Creation and Cosmology," 131, in T. Peters, ed., *Cosmos as Creation: Theology and Science in Consonance* (Nashville: Abingdon, 1989), 115–51.

34. See Martha Ellen Stortz, "Beyond Justice: Friendship in the City," *Word and World* 14, no. 4 (fall 1994): 409–18.

35. Emmanuel Levinas, *Totality and Infinity: An Essay on Exteriority*, trans. A. Linguis (Pittsburgh: Duquesne University Press, 1969), 251 (emphasis his).

36. David Tracy, "The Hidden God: The Divine Other of Liberation," *Cross Currents* (spring 1996): 5.

37. See Anton T. Boisen, *Religion in Crisis and Custom: A Sociological and Psychological Study* (reprint; Westport, Conn.: Greenwood, 1973).

38. These are the three factors Keith Ward identifies as the sub-personal basis of creativity, rational purpose, and developing community. See his *Rational Theology and the Creativity of God* (New York: Pilgrim, 1982).

39. Ambiguity is indeed the epistemological correlate to the ontological reality of freedom.

40. Simone de Beauvoir, *The Ethics of Ambiguity*, trans. B. Frechtman (New York: Philosophical Library, 1948), 129.

41. For a basic statement of the distinctions between moral, metaphysical, and natural evil, see my "Sin and Evil" in Braaten and Jenson, eds., *Christian Dogmatics*, vol. 1, 359–464.

42. Paul Ricoeur, *The Symbolism of Evil*, trans. E. Buchanan (Boston: Beacon, 1967), 251 (emphasis his). The matter is not unproblematic. Ricoeur remarks:

"The myth puts in succession that which is contemporaneous and cannot not be contemporaneous." Yet he adds, "But that is how it attains its depth" (ibid.).

43. Susan Shapiro, "Hearing the Testimony of Radical Negation," *The Holocaust as Interruption*, ed. E. Schüssler Fiorenza and D. Tracy (Edinburgh: T. and T. Clark, 1984), 6. She notes (7) that Elie Wiesel has remarked, "Only one of my books, *Night*, deals directly with the Holocaust; all the others reveal why one cannot speak about it."

44. Kierkegaard, *The Sickness unto Death*, 92–93. Cf. 89, 95–96.

45. Ibid., 68.

46. See Reinhold Niebuhr, *The Nature and Destiny of Man*, 2 vols. (New York: Scribner's, 1941, 1964), esp. vol. 1, 186–207.

47. Ibid., 186. Niebuhr suggests that the sin of sensuality is in some way derived from pride.

48. Edward Farley, *Good and Evil: Interpreting a Human Condition* (Minneapolis: Fortress, 1991), 132–33.

49. See Justo L. Gonzalez, *Mañana: Christian Theology from a Hispanic Perspective* (Nashville: Abingdon, 1990), 52, on "the manner in which the dominant is confused with the universal." Elizabeth Kamarck Minnich makes the same point regarding how we know in *Transforming Knowledge* (Philadelphia: Temple University Press, 1990), targeting such matters as "faulty generalization," "circular reasoning," and "mystified concepts." Another major front has been in philosophy of science with Sandra Harding (e.g., *Whose Science, Whose Knowledge: Thinking from Women's Lives* [Ithaca: Cornell University Press, 1991]) leading the way, together with Susan Bordo, Evelyn Fox Keller, and Donna Haraway.

50. Robert C. Solomon, *Continental Philosophy since 1750: The Rise and Fall of the Self* (Oxford: Oxford University Press, 1988), 6.

51. The specific analyses are *Madness and Civilization: A History of Insanity in the Age of Reason*, trans. R. Howard (New York: Random House, 1965); *The Birth of the Clinic: An Archaeology of Medical Perception*, trans. A. M. Sheridan Smith (New York: Random House, 1975); *Discipline and Punish: The Birth of the Prison*, trans. A. Sheridan (New York: Random House, 1979) and *The History of Sexuality*, trans. R. Hurley (New York: Random House, 1978, 1985).

52. Very appropriately in Joseph Conrad's novel *Heart of Darkness* (New York: Penguin, 1902, 1989), what specifically is dark is not altogether clear. It is difficult to sort out the moral and epistemological dimensions, but it is obvious that Kurt sees something that calls forth the cry, "The horror! The horror!" (111).

53. Arthur Cohen, *The Tremendum: A Theological Interpretation of the Holocaust* (New York: Crossroad, 1981). Cohen is particularly addressing "the Jewish myths of indestructibility and the moral obligation of tenacity" (53).

54. Michael Lodahl, *Shekinah Spirit: Divine Presence in Jewish and Christian Religion* (Mahwah, N.J.: Paulist, 1992), 135–43. For example, on "realized" eschatology see Mary Knutsen, "The Holocaust in Theology and Philosophy: The Question of Truth," in Fiorenza and Tracy, *The Holocaust as Interruption,* 67–74.

55. Thomas Merton, "A Devout Meditation in Memory of Adolf Eichmann," *Raids on the Unspeakable* (New York: New Directions, 1966), 45–49 (emphasis his).

56. In such a way Kierkegaard speaks of the demonic as "inclosing reserve *(det Indeslsuttede)*" in *The Concept of Anxiety,* 123ff.

57. Kierkegaard, *The Sickness unto Death,* 49–66.

58. Catherine Keller, *From a Broken Web: Separation, Sexism, and the Self* (Boston: Beacon, 1986), 39. The pioneering essay at this point remains Valerie Saiving's "The Human Situation: A Feminine View" in *Womanspirit Rising: A Feminist Reader in Religion,* ed. C. Christ and J. Plaskow (San Francisco: Harper, 1979).

59. In "Dialogue with Maya Angelou," *Facing Evil: Light at the Core of Darkness,* ed. P. Woodruff and H. A. Wilmer (LaSalle, Ill.: Open Court, 1988), 37–45, Maya Angelou makes this point: "I think there is a kind of activity in the evil. There is an energy in the evil. I think we have to call upon the good. We do not have to call upon the evil" (38). In the same volume see Gregory Curtis' discussion of the "integrity" and "attractiveness" of evil (94–95).

60. Albert Camus, *The Plague* (New York: Modern Library, 1948), 240.

61. See *The Christian Century,* March 25, 1959.

62. Alexandr Solzhenitsyn, *A World Split Apart,* commencement address at Harvard University, June 8, 1978 (New York: Harper, 1978).

63. See Robert Jay Lifton, *Death in Life: Survivors of Hiroshima* (New York: Random House, 1967) and *The Nazi Doctors: Medical Killing and the Psychology of Genocide* (New York: Basic Books, 1986). On the widespread presence of such numbing in ordinary circumstances, see *The Life of the Self* (New York: Basic Books, 1983), and *The Broken Connection* (New York: Simon and Schuster, 1979). Geiko Muller-Fahrenholz discusses cynicism, fundamentalism, and violentism as three forms of such numbing in *God's Spirit: Transforming a World in Crisis,* trans. J. Cumming (New York: Continuum, 1995), ch. 10–12.

64. Hannah Arendt, *Eichmann in Jerusalem: A Report on the Banality of Evil* (rev. ed.; New York: Penguin, 1994). Tellingly, she cites Eichmann's clichéd remarks at his execution (252).

65. For example, Jacob Robinson, *And the Crooked Shall Be Made Straight: The Eichmann Trial, the Jewish Catastrophe, and Hannah Arendt's*

Narrative (New York: Macmillan, 1965), 59, argues strongly against Arendt's emphasis on Eichmann's self-deception and stupidity: "From the historical documents available to us, the real Eichmann emerges: a man of extraordinary driving power, master in the arts of cunning and deception, intelligent and competent in his field, single-minded in his mission to make Europe 'free of Jews.'"

66. Robert Solomon, *The Passions: The Myth and Nature of Human Emotion* (Notre Dame, Ind.: University of Notre Dame Press, 1983), 418. See the nuanced discussion in Mary Louise Bringle, *Despair: Sickness or Sin?* (Nashville: Abingdon, 1990).

67. William Styron, *Darkness Visible: A Memoir of Madness* (New York: Random House, 1990), 47.

68. I particularly appreciate Dorothee Soelle's strong warnings at this point. See *Suffering*, trans. E. R. Kalin (Philadelphia: Fortress, 1975), esp. ch. 1.

69. A well-known example is Joanne Carlson Brown and Carole R. Bohn, eds., *Christianity, Patriarchy, and Abuse: A Feminist Critique* (New York: Pilgrim, 1989). Thus in ending the first chapter (titled "For God So Loved the World?"), they write: "Christianity is an abusive theology that glorifies suffering. Is it any wonder that there is so much abuse in modern society when the predominant image or theology of the culture is of 'divine child abuse'—God the Father demanding and carrying out the suffering and death of his own son? If Christianity is to be liberating for the oppressed, it must itself be liberated from this theology" (26).

70. Sharon Welch, "Dismantling Racism: Strategies for Cultural, Political, and Spiritual Transformation," 241, in R. Williams, ed., *Theology and the Interhuman* (Valley Forge, Pa.: Trinity Press International, 1995), 228–43.

71. Franz Kafka quoted in Mara Donaldson, *Holy Places Are Dark Places: C. S. Lewis and Paul Ricoeur on Narrative Transformation* (Lanham, Md.: University Press of America, 1988), xiii.

72. My source is Methodist bishop Peter Storey, who chaired the selection committee for the commission.

73. Paul Tillich makes this point effectively in the famous sermon I have taken for this section's title. See the first sermon in the collection *The Shaking of the Foundations* (New York: Scribner's, 1948.) A fuller statement is available in Langdon Gilkey's discussion of "The Estrangement of History, Nemesis and Judgment," *Reaping the Whirlwind: A Christian Interpretation of History* (New York: Seabury, 1976), 253–65. On the one hand, Gilkey speaks of a tragic "sense of history in which fate seems continually to engulf freedom." On the other hand he points out "that what we find surrounding us in the social world and what appears within ourselves as the given from

our own past are themselves the result, in part but in important part, of human creativity." Thus he writes of the "historical irony of creativity followed by nemesis" (254–55, 261).

74. See, for example, Heinrich Schmid, *The Doctrinal Theology of the Evangelical Lutheran Church*, 2d English ed., trans. C. A. Hay and H. E. Jacobs (Philadelphia: Lutheran Publication Society, 1899), ch. 4.

75. Abraham Heschel, *The Prophets*, 2 vols. (New York: Harper, 1962), vol. 2, 62.

76. Ibid., 72.

77. Eberhard Jungel, *God as the Mystery of the World*, trans. D. L. Guder (Grand Rapids: Eerdmans, 1983), 314.

78. Ibid., 315. Jungel also writes that "we are to read the statement 'God is love' as an exposition of the self-identification of God with the crucified man Jesus" (326). This seems to me to point us strongly to the preaching and teaching ministry of the church. That is the concern of Steven D. Paulson in "The Wrath of God," *dialog* 33, no. 4 (fall 1994): 245–51. Paulson juxtaposes Jungel to Luther: "In his understandable desire to bind God's being to revelation christologically, Jungel uses a theological definition of God's essence that replaces the one means God desires to use for mercy, the church's office of proclamation" (250). I would hope that the reality of God's love, however known, could be held in a principled way without becoming an abstraction.

79. In *Faith and the Other*, 93–94, I have written of how God acts "first" and "last" with respect to every event.

80. For example, see Walter Brueggemann, *A Social Reading of the Old Testament: Prophetic Approaches to Israel's Communal Life* (Minneapolis: Fortress, 1994), 42.

81. James Nohrnberg, *Like unto Moses: The Constituting of an Interruption* (Bloomington: Indiana University Press, 1995), 346.

82. Could a Christian learn here from a nontheistic reading? See Ernst Bloch, *Atheism in Christianity*, trans. J. T. Swann (New York: Herder and Herder, 1972), 123–95.

83. See, respectively, Harriet Lerner, *The Dance of Anger: A Woman's Guide to Changing the Patterns of Intimate Relationships* (New York: Harper, 1985), and Michael Walzer, *Interpretation and Social Criticism* (Cambridge: Harvard University Press, 1987).

84. Martin Luther, "Theses for the Heidelberg Disputation," 53, *Martin Luther's Basic Theological Writings*, ed. T. F. Lull (Minneapolis: Fortress, 1989), 30–49 (emphasis mine).

85. See B. B. Gerrish, "To the Unknown God: Luther and Calvin on the Hiddenness of God," *The Journal of Religion* 53 (July 1973): 263–93, and David Tracy, "The Hidden God: The Divine Other of Liberation," *Cross*

Currents (spring 1996): 5–16. Tracy notes that "in extreme situations Hiddenness I itself becomes Hiddenness II" (12).

86. Gerrish, op. cit., 278–79.

87. J. B. Metz, *Faith in History and Society: Toward a Practical Fundamental Theology,* trans. D. Smith (New York: Seabury, 1980), 171.

88. See the very helpful distinctions developed by Robert Albers in *Shame: A Faith Perspective* (New York: Haworth, 1995).

89. Derrida, *The Gift of Death,* 54.

90. Ibid.

91. The notion of the "wholly other" seems too broad an instrument to use in trying to draw out this sense of the holy, given the dominant interpretation of Rudolf Otto's work. What Otto says (*The Idea of the Holy: An Inquiry into the Non-Rational Factor in the Idea of the Divine and its Relation to the Rational,* trans. J. W. Harvey [New York: Oxford University Press, 1958], 26) offers some promise in the emphasis on "that which is quite beyond the sphere of the usual, the intelligible, and the familiar, which therefore falls quite outside the limits of the 'canny' and is contrasted with it," though his influence seems to have lain in what he then adds in speaking of "filling the mind with *blank* wonder and astonishment" (emphasis mine). I find helpful Charles Hartshorne's notion of "categorical supremacy." See *Philosophers Speak of God,* ed. Hartshorne and Reese (Chicago: University of Chicago, 1953), 7:

> God is a name for the uniquely good, admirable, great, worship-eliciting being. Worship, moreover, is not just an unusually high degree of merit. There is a difference in kind. God is "Perfect," and between the perfect and anything as little imperfect as you please is no merely finite, but an infinite step. The superiority of the deity to all others cannot (in accordance with established word usage) be expressed by indefinite descriptions, such as "immensely good," "very powerful," or even "best" or "most powerful," but must be a superiority of principle, a definite conceptual divergence from every other being, actual or so much as possible.

Already in *The Divine Relativity* (New Haven: Yale University Press, 1948) Hartshorne made very clear that such a being is, like us, capable of development—indeed, in relation to us.

92. Kierkegaard, *The Sickness unto Death,* 85.

93. C. S. Lewis, *Till We Have Faces* (Grand Rapids: Eerdmans, 1956), 308 (emphasis his). See also Mara Donaldson's helpful interpretation in *Holy Places Are Dark Places* (Lanham, Md.: University Press of America, 1988).

94. Ann and Barry Ulanov, *Primary Speech: A Psychology of Prayer* (Louisville: Westminster/John Knox, 1992), 145–55.

95. Gerard Manley Hopkins, *The Oxford Poets: Gerard Manley Hopkins* (New York: Oxford University Press, 1967), 71, 75.

96. Elizabeth A. Johnson drives this point home as well as anyone. Thus in *She Who Is: The Mystery of God in Feminist Theological Discourse* (New York: Crossroad, 1992), 131, she will speak of God as spirit, not forgetting that God is "more unlike than like anything we know in the world as spirit." She uses the same construction in speaking of the analogy of maleness (163) and that of mother (178). She has prepared for such emphasis by drawing together a catalog of testimony to the mystery of God, citing Augustine, Anselm, Hildegaard, Aquinas, Luther, Simone Weil, and Sallie MacFague (7).

97. William Styron, *Darkness Visible*, 64–66 (emphasis his).

98. Ibid., 81, 66. Styron then offers what I can only call a stunning testimony to the goodness of creation: "in a flood of swift recollection I thought of all the joys the house had known: the children who had rushed through its rooms, the festivals, the love and work, the honestly earned slumber, the voices and the nimble commotion, the perennial tribe of cats and dogs and birds, 'laughter and ability and Sighing,/And Frocks and Curls' [quoting Emily Dickinson]" (66–67).

99. Derrida, op. cit., 15.

100. Kierkegaard, *Christian Discourses,* 336 (emphasis his).

101. Johnson, *She Who Is,* 205.

102. Lewis, op. cit., 306.

103. This is the title of his story of "the shape of my early life": *Surprised by Joy* (New York: Harcourt, Brace, 1955), where he writes of the experience of joy as "a pointer to something other and outer," noting that "When we are lost in the woods the sight of a signpost is a great matter" (238).

104. Mark C. Taylor provides in *Nots* a striking collection of such testimonies—in architecture (e.g., David Liebeskind), in music (Arnold Schonberg), and in the recognition of the insidious character of silent disease.

105. Peter Berger, *A Rumor of Angels: Modern Society and the Rediscovery of the Supernatural* (Garden City, N.Y.: Doubleday, 1969), 86. Kierkegaard is particularly illuminating in characterizing humor as "the last terminus a quo in connection with the problem of determining the Christian." See *Concluding Unscientific Postscript,* 243.

106. One thinks of the frequent testimony to the healing power of laughter. One of the better known is Norman Cousins's *Anatomy of an Illness as Perceived by the Patient* (New York: Norton, 1979), ch. 1, where Cousins mentions marked differences in his blood's sedimentation readings before and after laughing episodes prodded by "Candid Camera" and Marx Brothers films.

107. Despite—or rather, because of—the poetic power of John Donne, I find very dangerous the lack of specificity in a passage like this:
Batter my heart, three-person'd God; for you
As yet but knock, breathe, shine, and seek to mend;

> That I may rise, and stand, o'er throw me and bend
> Your force to break, blow, burn and make me new. . . .
> Take me to you, imprison me, for I
> Except you enthrall me, never shall be free,
> Nor ever chaste, except you ravish me.

See *John Donne: The Complete English Poems* (New York: Knopf, 1991), 443.

108. I have discussed this in "On Being and Becoming before God: A Response to Daphne Hampson," *Word and World* 15, no. 3 (summer 1995): 332–41.

109. Anselm, *Proslogion, a Scholastic Miscellany,* ed. E. R. Fairweather (Philadelphia: Westminster, 1966), 70.

4. To Be Called: This May Be the Coming

1. Recall the summary of David Tracy of how "the real face of our period . . . is the face of the other": "Every form serves as an interruption of the rule of the same." See his "The Hidden God: The Divine Other of Liberation," *Cross Currents* (spring 1996): 5–6.

2. Mark C. Taylor, *Erring: A Postmodern A/Theology* (Chicago: University of Chicago Press, 1984).

3. Mark C. Taylor, "Denegating God," *Critical Inquiry* (summer 1994): 592.

4. Ibid.

5. This is a particularly Lutheran way of stating the matter. See, for example, Marc Kolden, *Called by the Gospel* (Minneapolis: Augsburg, 1983), 58–59.

6. John B. Cobb Jr. and Charles Birch, *The Liberation of Life: From the Cell to the Community* (Cambridge: Cambridge University Press, 1981), 185.

7. See pages 26–29 in this volume.

8. Robert Kegan, *The Evolving Self: Problem and Process in Human Development* (Cambridge: Harvard University Press, 1982), 7–8.

9. Richard Rorty, "The Priority of Democracy to Philosophy," 269, *The Virginia Statute for Religious Freedom*, ed. M. D. Peterson and R. C. Vaughan (New York: Cambridge University Press, 1988), 257–82.

10. Edith Wyschogrod, *Saints and Postmodernism: Revisioning Moral Philosophy* (Chicago: University of Chicago Press, 1990), 234.

11. Catherine Keller, "'To Illuminate Your Trace': Self in Late Modern Feminist Theology," *Listening* 5, no. 3 (1990): 218.

12. Ibid., 221. A fuller statement is available in her *From a Broken Web: Separation, Sexism, and Self* (Boston: Beacon, 1986).

13. This anthropological point is grounded cosmologically in Whitehead's thought. Thus in *Process and Reality* (New York: Free Press, 1978), we are told: "The primordial appetitions which jointly constitute God's pur-

pose are seeking intensity, and not preservation. . . . Thus God's purpose in the creative advance is the evocation of intensities. The evocation of societies [where human identity is located] is purely subsidiary to this absolute end" (105).

14. Søren Kierkegaard, *Concluding Unscientific Postscript to the Philosophical Fragments,* trans. D. F. Swenson and W. Lowrie (Princeton: Princeton University Press, 1944), 311. See also George Connell's *To Be One Thing: Personal Unity in Kierkegaard's Thought* (Macon, Ga.: Mercer University Press, 1985).

15. In *The Sickness unto Death* Kierkegaard's advice is that in despair "the word is: Get possibility, get possibility, possibility is the only salvation" (38–39).

16. James Loder, *The Transforming Moment: Understanding Convictional Experiences* (San Francisco: Harper, 1981), 32. Loder's overall term for this process is "interlude for scanning," and he notes that it entails "indwelling the conflicted situation with empathy for the problem and its parts."

17. Vincent M. Colapietro, "The Integral Self: Systematic Illusion or Inescapable Task?", *Listening* 5, no. 3 (1990): 197 (emphasis his). Cf. Hannah Arendt, *The Human Condition* (Chicago: University of Chicago Press, 1958, 1969), 237: "Without being bound to the fulfillment of promises, we would never be able to keep our identities; we would be condemned to wander helplessly and without direction in the darkness of each man's lonely heart, caught in its contradictions and equivocalities—a darkness which only the light shed over the public realm through the presence of others, who confirm the identity between the one who promises and the one who fulfills, can dispel."

18. Donald W. Winnicott, *The Maturational Processes and the Facilitating Environment* (New York: International Universities Press, 1965), 54 (emphasis his).

19. Donald W. Winnicott, *Playing and Reality* (New York: Basic Books, 1971), stresses how the mother in "mirroring" the infant begins with a very full identification with the infant.

20. Carol Gilligan, *In a Different Voice: Psychological Theory and Women's Development* (Cambridge: Harvard University Press, 1982), 173.

21. See Judith V. Jordan, Janet L. Surrey, and Alexandra G. Kaplan, "Women and Empathy: Implications for Psychological Development and Psychotherapy," 50, in Judith V. Jordan et al., *Women's Growth in Connection* (New York: Guilford, 1991), 27–50.

22. Judith V. Jordan, "Empathy and Self Boundaries," 79, in ibid., 67–80.

23. Robert Kegan, op. cit., 106. See also Kegan's *In over Our Heads: The Mental Demands of Modern Life* (Cambridge: Harvard University Press, 1994).

24. Some theologians would decline to speak of God's address to the becoming self apart from faith as calling. Thus in his classic study *Luther on Vocation*, trans. C. C. Rasmussen (Philadelphia: Muhlenberg, 1957), Gustaf Wingren writes "As far as we can determine Luther does not use *Beruf* or *vocatio* in reference to the work of a nonChristian. All have station (*Stand*) and office; but *Beruf* is the Christian's earthly or spiritual work" (2; cf. 91). I have chosen to use the word Calling in a more comprehensive way to include God's claim on every human creature. Wingren finds that claim strongly present in Luther under other terminology, as when he writes: "It is not only God's demand that presents itself ceaselessly in new form, but also his gifts. The goodness of God comes to us, among other ways, through other people, who are 'God's masks' whether or not they have faith" (144).

25. See Michael Walzer, *Thick and Thin: Moral Argument at Home and Abroad* (Notre Dame, Ind.: Notre Dame University Press, 1994). A helpful older discussion is David Little's "Calvin and the Prospects for a Christian Theory of Natural Law," *Norm and Context in Christian Ethics,* ed. G. Outka and P. Ramsey (New York: Scribner's, 1968), 175–98, where the cross-cultural anthropological work of Clyde Kluckhohn is brought to view.

26. Martin Luther, "Two Kinds of Righteousness" (1519), 156–57, *Martin Luther's Basic Theological Writings*, ed. T. F. Lull (Minneapolis: Fortress, 1989), 155–64.

27. Dietrich Bonhoeffer, *The Cost of Discipleship*, trans. R. H. Fuller (New York: Macmillan, 1959), 73.

28. All of these quotations are from the remarkable prayer with which Kierkegaard begins and ends *Purity of Heart*. See *Upbuilding Discourses in Various Spirits: Kierkegaard's Writings,* vol. XV, ed. and trans. H. V. Hong and E. H. Hong (Princeton: Princeton University Press, 1993), 7–8, 154.

29. Daphne Hampson, *Theology and Feminism* (Oxford and Cambridge, Mass.: Basil Blackwell, 1990), 127. See also her article "Luther on the Self: A Feminist Critique," *Word and World* 8, no. 4 (fall 1988): 334–42.

30. Lois Malcolm, "The Gospel and Feminism: A Proposal for Lutheran Dogmatics," *Word and World* 15, no. 3 (summer 1995): 295.

31. Kierkegaard uses the metaphor of love to speak of this. In the passion of erotic love "self-love has foundered. . . . But it can come to life again. . . . So also with the paradox's relation to the understanding. . . ." See *Philosophical Fragments,* ed. and trans. H. V. Hong and E. H. Hong (Princeton: Princeton University Press, 1985), 48.

32. Hampson, "Luther on the Self: A Feminist Critique," 339–40.

33. On 2 Cor. 3:18 ("We are being transformed. . . .") *Luther's Works*, vol. 14, ed. J. Pelikan (St. Louis: Concordia, 1958), 285–86.

34. Commenting on Zech. 3:8-9 in *Luther's Works*, vol. 20, 217.

35. William Henry Lazareth and Peri Rasolondraibe, *Lutheran Identity and Mission: Evangelical and Evangelistic?* (Minneapolis: Fortress, 1994), 126. In *Embodying Forgiveness: A Theological Analysis* (Grand Rapids: Eerdmans, 1995), 137ff., L. Gregory Jones helpfully points out the mistake involved in arguing that repentance must be prior to forgiveness.

36. I have this formulation from an unpublished (to my knowledge) paper by Vitor Westhelle, "Luther and Liberation: or, Doing Theology from the Left (Hand of God)."

37. Paul Ramsey, *Basic Christian Ethics* (Chicago: University of Chicago Press, 1950), 187. In an unpublished (to my knowledge) paper, "'Worthily of the Gospel of Christ (Phil. 1:27)': The Ecclesiastical Significance of Christ's Political Agency," my colleague David Fredrickson goes so far as to say: "Christ's obedience, even to the point of death and crucifixion, is given to humans, not God. Similarly, his voluntary slavery is directed to humanity" (8).

38. See Gene Outka's *Agape: An Ethical Analysis* (New Haven: Yale University Press, 1972), 276–78, for an analysis of how self-sacrifice as a focus leads to self-contradictory circumstances, if everyone were so to act.

39. Other passages offer diverse but supporting nuances. Cf. Terence Fretheim's comment (*Exodus* [Louisville: John Knox, 1991], 52) on the call of Moses (Exod. 3:1-7:7): "The recognition of holiness (3:6) does not lead to passivity in the presence of God. Disagreement, argument, and even challenge play an important role. The divine holiness is of such a character that it invites rather than repels human response, inviting Moses into genuine conversation. God does not demand a self-effacing Moses but draws him out and works with him, 'warts and all.' The oft-noted speech disability of Moses adds an ironic twist to this point. It is not only a human being who challenges God; an inarticulate one does so, and holds his own!" Or see Gustavo Guttiérez, *On Job*, trans. M. J. O'Connell (Maryknoll, N.Y.: Orbis, 1987), 86–87, for the observation that (even) Job does not withdraw his claim of innocence.

40. Michael Welker, *God the Spirit*, trans. J. F. Hoffmeyer (Minneapolis: Fortress, 1994), 249. Cf. Eberhard Jungel.

41. Jason Mahn has pointed out to me that the classical model of Alcoholics Anonymous involves such vertical images as "hitting bottom" and "a higher power." But what if the problem is horizontal in the sense that shame guards the boundaries of the self against the invasion by others? I am indebted to Mahn's paper "To Dance with Nonbeing: A Study in Alcoholism, Shame, and the Self," prepared for an elective seminar on Transformation. He draws significantly on Donald Capps, *The Depleted Self: Sin in a Narcissistic Age* (Minneapolis: Fortress, 1993).

42. Gustaf Wingren, *Creation and Law*, trans. R. Mackenzie (Philadelphia: Muhlenberg, 1961), 42–43.

43. Wingren, *Luther on Vocation*, 143.

44. Ted Peters, "Wholeness in Salvation and Healing," *Lutheran Quarterly* 5 (1991): 312. Peters is concerned that we attend to such matters as the global economy, alternative medical models, and the interdependence of the wholeness of the individual with that of the cosmos. Cf. also Terence Fretheim, "Salvation in the Bible vs. Salvation in the Church," *Word and World* 13, no. 4 (fall 1993): 363–72.

45. Walter Wink, *Engaging the Powers: Discernment and Resistance in a World of Domination* (Minneapolis: Fortress, 1992), 275.

46. Jones, *Embodying Forgiveness*, 262. Jones goes on to make the point that Christians are often guilty of denying or repressing these negative judgments: "Hence, through a curious irony, which Nietzsche was quick to note, too many Christians (and others) have linked together a repressed hatred and an ideology of forgiveness."

47. This is Marjorie Hewitt Suchocki's formulation in *The Fall to Violence: Original Sin in Relational Theology* (New York: Continuum, 1994), especially chapter 9, "Forgiveness and Transformation."

48. See Nahum M. Sarna, *JPS Commentary: Genesis* (Phildelphia: Jewish Publication Society, 1989), 19, for the helpful suggestion that this "geographical" feature is an "abrupt interruption," a "pause [that] functions as a tension-building device." There will be life outside Eden, and with that life comes risk. But not everything is at risk, as Terence Fretheim notes in *Genesis*, 351, in *The New Interpreter's Bible* (Nashville: Abingdon, 1994), 319-674: "The two humans will not move from a world of blessing to one devoid of blessing."

49. C. S. Lewis, *An Experiment in Criticism* (Cambridge: Cambridge University Press, 1961), 140–41.

50. In a Kierkegaardian way such twentieth-century figures as Levinas, Derrida, and Mark C. Taylor see that such true otherness is lost in an Hegelian scheme. Thus Taylor writes in *Tears* (Albany, N.Y.: SUNY Press, 1990), 93: "The Hegelian Idea that grounds all reality is a structural totality in which everything becomes *itself* in and through *its own* other. Because otherness and difference are essential components of self-identity . . . , relationship to otherness and difference is, in the final analysis, *self*-relationship. . . . Inasmuch as identity always owns otherness, difference is inevitably repressed" (emphasis his).

51. Kierkegaard makes this point repeatedly, notably by contrasting "recollection" and "repetition." See, for example, *The Concept of Anxiety*, 19–21. A helpful secondary discussion is available in Connell's *To Be One Thing*, 114–16.

52. Alice Walker, "Only Justice Can Stop a Curse," 341–42, *In Search of Our Mothers' Gardens* (San Diego: Harcourt Brace, 1983), 338–42. She adds "and because it has fresh peaches in it," and then, "In any case, Earth is my home."

53. Alfred North Whitehead, *Process and Reality*, 259. Of course, he adds: "The importance of truth is, that it adds to interest." Cf. Charles Saunders Peirce's "interest" in the "abductive." For example in *The Collected Papers of Charles Saunders Peirce*, ed. C. Hartshorne and P. Weiss (Cambridge: Harvard University Press, 1934), 5:172 ("Pragmatism and Pragmaticism"): "Deduction proves that something *must* be; Induction shows that something *actually is*; Abduction merely suggests that something *may be*" (emphasis his).

54. Simone Weil, *On Science, Necessity, and the Love of God*, trans. and ed. R. Rees (New York: Oxford University Press, 1968), 160.

55. Kierkegaard, *Concluding Unscientific Postscript*, 314. Another category one could employ here is "desire," as Margaret Farley does in *Personal Commitments: Beginning, Keeping, Changing* (San Francisco: Harper, 1986), 27, in speaking of choice as "my *ratification* of one desire (rather than its alternative), my allowing *this* desire (rather than its opposing alternatives) to issue in action."

56. Thus Gustaf Wingren, *Creation and Law*, 30; *Creation and the Gospel*, 28.

57. Gustaf Wingren, *Luther on Vocation*, 36–37.

58. Clark H. Pinnock, "God's Sovereignty in Today's World," *Theology Today* 53, no. 1 (April 1996): 21.

59. Gregory Baum, "The Holocaust and Political Theology," 37, in *The Holocaust as Interruption*, ed. E. Schüssler Fiorenza and D. Tracy (Stichting Concilium and Edinburgh: T. and T. Clark, 1984), 34–42.

60. Walter Brueggemann, *A Social Reading of the Old Testament: Prophetic Approaches to Israel's Communal Life*, ed. P. D. Miller (Minneapolis: Fortress, 1994). I trust it is clear that, unlike Brueggemann (41), I want to locate process thought in this trajectory rather than in the "royal" one.

61. Paul Ricoeur, *Time and Narrative*, 3 vols., trans. K. McLaughlin and D. Pellauer (Chicago: University of Chicago Press, 1984–1988), vol. 1, 3.

62. Leslie Marmon Silko, *Ceremony* (New York: Viking, 1977), 2. See also the reference to South Africa's "Truth and Reconciliation Commission" in note 72 of chapter 3. It seems clear that the stories told by victims and perpetrators have in their truth the power not only to interrupt but also to call to reconciliation.

63. I think of Thomas Berry and Brian Swimme's *The Universe Story* (San Francisco: HarperSanFrancisco, 1992). For the use of the category in therapy, see Patricia O'Hanlon Hudson and William Hudson O'Hanlon, *Rewrit-*

ing Love Stories: Brief Marital Therapy (New York: Norton, 1991). Michael Walzer writes of the power of story-telling for social criticism in *Interpretation and Social Criticism* (Cambridge: Harvard University Press, 1987), 65.

64. Ricoeur, op. cit.

65. I am taking issue with the theme of one of the most singable themes of "Joseph and the Amazing Technicolor Dreamcoat," the popular contemporary American musical by Andrew Lloyd Webber and Tim Rice.

66. Ricoeur, op. cit., 79.

67. Frank Kermode, *The Sense of an Ending* (Oxford: Oxford University Press, 1967).

68. Cf. Ricoeur, op. cit., 87, on "thinking about eternity and death at the same time."

69. See pages 28–33 in this volume.

70. See, for example, the research by Elizabeth Loftus of the University of Washington concerning "imagination inflation."

71. This is the phrasing borrowed from Ernest Becker and employed by Van A. Harvey in *Feuerbach and the Interpretation of Religion* (Cambridge: Cambridge University Press, 1995), 303 (emphasis his). Harvey does note that for Feuerbach nature is not Becker's nightmare on a planet soaked in blood, but "can be seen as eternal, infinite, omnipresent, wise, just, even good" (308).

72. Nietzsche, for example, attacks Christianity for teaching believers "to place themselves through piety in an illusory higher order of things and thus to maintain their contentment with the real order, in which their life is hard enough." See *Beyond Good and Evil: Prelude to a Philosophy of the Future,* trans. W. Kaufmann (New York: Random House, 1966), #61. Is this what it means to set one's mind "on the things that are above"? I have considered this familiar charge in *God: The Question and the Quest*, ch. 4.

73. Cf. Kenneth Burke's *A Rhetoric of Motives* (Berkeley: University of California Press, 1969) for a discussion of how the use of language involves both an "identification *of*" and an identification *with.*"

74. Ann Ulanov and Barry Ulanov, *The Healing Imagination: The Meeting of Psyche and Soul* (Mawah, N.J.: Paulist, 1991), 26.

75. The classic text is *Metaphors We Live By* (Chicago: University of Chicago Press, 1980). See also Mark Johnson's *The Body in the Mind: The Bodily Basis of Meaning, Imagination, and Reason* (Chicago: University of Chicago Press, 1987) and his *Moral Imagination: The Implications of Cognitive Science for Ethics* (Chicago: University of Chicago Press, 1993).

76. Robert Frost, *Robert Frost on Writing* (New Brunswick, N.J.: Rutgers University Press, 1973), 127. Cf.: "The artist must value himself as he snatches a thing from some previous order in time and space into a new

order with not so much as a ligature clinging to it of the old place where it was organic" (ibid.).

77. William Stafford, "Bi-Focal," as quoted in Donald Capps, *The Poet's Gift: Toward the Renewal of Pastoral Care* (Louisville: Westminster/John Knox, 1993), 152. That the poet has not only a gift but a task is made clear by the gifted poet Denise Levertov in *The Poet in the World*, 107–13: "When words penetrate deep into us they change the chemistry of the soul, of the imagination. We have no right to do that to people if we don't share the consequences" (114).

78. Garrett Green, *Imagining God: Theology and the Religious Imagination* (San Francisco: Harper, 1989) is critical of Sallie McFague for assuming a "prelinguistic religious experience" (129), but he is also concerned to reject the view "that choices among language games are arbitrary" (141). I find John Cobb's formulation helpful: "In short, language does create our worlds. But it does so by highlighting features of a common world that, in its totality, is so rich and complex that no language will ever encompass it all. Different languages highlight different features. Communities order themselves to the features highlighted in their language, neglecting others. But the neglected features are still there, and they still function even when they are not thematized. When communities that have developed quite differently interact, each may learn about features of its own experience that it has neglected and thus expand its own grasp of reality" (12, "Experience and Language," an unpublished paper available from the Center for Process Studies, Claremont, California). See also Hilary Putnam, *The Many Faces of Realism* (LaSalle, Ill.: Open Court, 1987) and Donald Davidson, *Inquiries into Truth and Interpretation* (New York: Oxford University Press, 1984).

79. Thomas Kuhn, *The Structure of Scientific Revolutions*, 2nd enl. ed. (Chicago: University of Chicago Press, 1970).

80. This is a point made by the Ulanovs in *The Healing Imagination*, 113f.

81. Craig R. Dykstra, *Vision and Character: A Christian Educator's Alternative to Kohlberg* (Mahwah, N.J.: Paulist, 1981), 83. See also Richard L. Eslinger, *Narrative Imagination: Preaching the Worlds That Shape Us* (Minneapolis: Fortress, 1995).

82. Ekkehard Muhlenberg, "*Synergia* and Justification by Faith," 34, in *Discord, Dialogue, and Concord: Studies in the Lutheran Reformation's Formula of Concord*, ed. L. W. Spitz and W. Lohff (Philadelphia: Fortress, 1977), 15–37 (emphasis mine).

83. Martin Luther, "Theses for the Heidelberg Disputation," 30–49, *Martin Luther's Basic Theological Writings*, ed. T. F. Lull (Minneapolis: Fortress, 1989), 44. See Green, *Imagining God*, on "The Hermeneutics of the Cross," 146–48. Alexandra Brown, *The Cross and Human Transformation*

(Minneapolis: Fortress, 1995) is a helpful exegetical study of this matter in 1 Corinthians.

84. Sullivan's address was delivered November 23, 1996, in New Orleans. See Lawrence Sullivan, "Coming to Our Senses: Religious Studies in the Academy," *Journal of the American Academy of Religion* 66, no. 1 (spring 1998): 1–12.

85. This is M. Jamie Ferreira's formulation in *Transforming Vision: Imagination and Will in Kierkegaardian Faith* (Oxford: Clarendon; New York: Oxford University Press, 1991), 111. Ferreira's work is a noteworthy argument against a narrowly voluntarist reading of Søren Kierkegaard. She does grant (pp. 48, 67, 117, 125) that we can use our will to stifle or cultivate the new seeing.

86. I have the phrase "lively possibility" from Marjorie Suchocki (in personal conversation). I think of Whitehead's distinction between "real" and "pure" potentiality in *Process and Reality*, 65–66.

87. I have these categories from Ferreira, op. cit.

88. *The Healing Imagination*, 130.

89. Walter Wink, *Engaging the Powers: Discernment and Resistance in a World of Domination* (Minneapolis: Fortress, 1992), 293.

90. Walter Brueggemann, *A Social Reading of the Old Testament*, 224. In *Hopeful Imagination: Prophetic Voices in Exile* (Philadelphia: Fortress, 1986), 18–20, Brueggemann applies this understanding, materially, to the very notion of "call," arguing from Jeremiah against the view "that one can live 'an uncalled life.'" Barry Kanpol makes an effective application of this point in "Critical Pedagogy and Liberation Theology: Borders for a Transformative Agenda," *Educational Theory* 46, no. 1 (winter 1996): 105–17, writing of "questioning the knowledge, skills, values, and attitudes (the cultural capital) set up by the dominant culture of which the school is a part" (111).

91. On these two ditches, see the Ulanovs, *The Healing Imagination*, 43–48. Eslinger, *Narrative and Imagination*, 91f, makes the point about memory well.

5. To Be Related: This Is the Empowering

1. I have used this phrasing in *Faith and the Other* (Minneapolis: Fortress, 1993), chapter 3.

2. See pages 48–49 in this volume.

3. See pages 70–71 in this volume.

4. Jonathan Strandjord uses Levinas and Whitehead to show both sides of the coin. He notes that Whitehead "fears in thought an impoverishing and progress-stalling Balkanization by the Many," while Levinas "warns against the inhumanity of any Empire of the One." See his unpublished

doctoral dissertation at Vanderbilt University (1996), "The Politics and Ethics of Beauty: A Theological Reconsideration of Conscience with the Aid of Whitehead and Levinas," 203.

5. See the first volume of Barbour's Gifford Lectures, *Religion in an Age of Science* (New York: Harper, 1990), 105–6.

6. Ibid., 104.

7. Ibid.

8. Jeffrey S. Wicken, "Theology and Science in the Evolving Cosmos: A Need for Dialogue," *Zygon* 23, no. 1 (March 1988): 52 (emphasis his). He adds: "Nucleic acids and proteins, for example, are relationally constituted by their functional roles in organisms, and their behaviors are constituted by those wholes. At a higher level of the organic hierarchy, the identities of organisms are relationally constituted by their ecosystemic roles." See also Jeffrey S. Wicken, *Evolution, Thermodynamics, and Information: Extending the Darwinian Program* (New York: Oxford University Press, 1987).

9. Alfred North Whitehead, *Process and Reality: An Essay in Cosmology*, corrected ed. by D. R. Griffin and D. W. Sherburne (New York: Free Press, 1978), 21.

10. As, for example, Wolfhart Pannenberg does in his *Systematic Theology*, 3 vols., trans. G. Bromiley (Grand Rapids: Eerdmans, 1991–1997), vol. 1, 84–101. See also "Cosmology," *dialog* 30, no. 4 (autumn 1991).

11. Gustaf Wingren, *Creation and Law*, trans. R. Mackenzie (Philadelphia: Muhlenberg, 1961), 101–2.

12. Whitehead, op. cit., 105.

13. See the studies by Tellegen and Lykken cited in note 33 in chapter 1 above.

14. See page 70 in this volume. In addition to the sources cited there, see the tellingly titled *Home Is Where We Start From* (New York: Norton, 1988).

15. Jean Baker Miller, "The Development of Women's Sense of Self," 13–14, in Judith V. Jordan et al., *Women's Growth in Connection* (New York: Guilford, 1991), 11–26, citing particularly the work of Daniel Stern. See page 70ff in this volume.

16. Jean-Michel Oughourlian, *The Puppet of Desire: The Psychology of Hysteria, Possession, and Hypnosis*, trans. E. Webb (Palo Alto: Stanford University Press, 1991), 11–12 (emphasis his).

17. René Girard, *Deceit, Desire, and the Novel: Self and Other in Literary Structure*, trans. Y. Freccero (Baltimore: Johns Hopkins University Press, 1965, 1976).

18. See Andrew N. Meltzoff, "Infant Imitation and Memory: Nine-Month-Olds in Immediate and Deferred Tests," *Child Development* 59: 217–25; "Imitation of Televised Models by Infants," *Child Development* 59:

1221–29; and "Infant Imitation after a 1 Week Delay," *Developmental Psychology* 24: 470–76. See also Mabel Rice and Linda Woodsmall, "Lessons from Television: Children's Word Learning When Viewing," *Child Development* 59: 420–29, where it is reported that children learned new words more easily when they saw them being used by others on television.

19. See the study by Sharon and Laurent Parks with Cheryl and James Keen, *Common Fire: Lives of Commitment in a Complex World* (Boston: Beacon, 1996).

20. This is the formulation Robert Kegan attributes to the "fifth consciousness" in *In over Our Heads: The Mental Demands of Modern Life* (Cambridge: Harvard University Press, 1994), 313. In *The Evolving Self: Problem and Process in Human Development* (Cambridge: Harvard University Press, 1987), 226, Kegan speaks of the "inter-individual" stage as involving "interdependent self-definition."

21. To speak so would be to select the "traducianist" interpretation of human birth and becoming, as distinguished from a "creationist" one. The question at issue is whether the human soul is created immediately by God or by parents. For a traditional statement of traducianism see Heinrich Schmid, *The Doctrinal Theology of the Evangelical Lutheran Church*, 2d English ed., trans. C. A. Hay and H. E. Jacobs (Minneapolis: Augsburg, 1899), 166, 248. A creationist statement is found in G. C. Berkouwer, *Man: The Image of God*, trans. D. W. Jellema (Grand Rapids: Eerdmans, 1962), 279–309.

22. Michael Eigen, "Winnicott's Area of Freedom: The Uncompromisable," 80, *Liminality and Transitional Phenomena,* ed. N. Schwartz-Salant and M. Stein (Wilmette, Ill.: Chiron, 1991), 67–88.

23. This is the phrasing used by N. Porteus, "Man, Nature of, in the OT" in *The Interpreter's Dictionary of the Bible* (Nashville: Abingdon, 1962), 3:243.

24. Donald W. Winnicott, *The Maturational Processes and the Facilitating Environment* (New York: International Universities Press, 1965), 54. Winnicott has made clear (43) that "the term 'holding' is used here to denote not only the actual physical holding of the infant, but also the total environmental provision prior to the concept of *living with*" (emphasis his).

25. Alfred North Whitehead, *Modes of Thought* (New York: Free Press, 1938, 1966), 114.

26. Poet Mary Oliver proposes a corrective strategy:

I don't want you just to sit down at the table.
I don't want you just to eat, and be content.
I want you to walk out into the fields
where the water is shining, and the rice has risen.
I want you to stand there, far from the white tablecloth.
I want you to fill your hands with the mud, like a blessing.

See *New and Selected Poems* (Boston: Beacon, 1992), 38.

27. See pages 7–8, 15–16 in this volume. A particularly striking testimony is Robert Wuthnow, ed., *"I Come Away Stronger": How Small Groups Are Shaping American Religion* (Grand Rapids: Eerdmans, 1994).

28. Larry Rasmussen, *Moral Fragments and Moral Community* (Minneapolis: Fortress, 1993), 59.

29. Kyle A. Pasewark, *A Theology of Power* (Minneapolis: Fortress, 1993), 336. On no proof being possible, see 333–35.

30. Edward Farley, *Good and Evil: Interpreting a Human Condition* (Minneapolis: Fortress, 1991).

31. Ibid., 37–40.

32. Ibid., 105. Farley notes these are not two passions, but one—"a passion for human face-to-face reciprocity and intimacy."

33. Ibid., 144 (emphasis his). A similar unifying depth is found in René Girard's notion of "metaphysical desire," the desire to be Another: "There is only one metaphysical desire but the particular desires which instantiate this primordial desire are of infinite variety" (op. cit., 83).

34. Farley, loc. cit.

35. Harold Ditmanson, *Grace in Experience and Theology* (Minneapolis: Augsburg, 1977), 110 (emphasis his).

36. Thomas C. Oden, *The Structure of Awareness* (Nashville: Abingdon, 1969), 81 (emphasis his). Carol Ochs, *Song of the Self: Biblical Spirituality and Human Holiness* (Valley Forge, Pa.: Trinity Press International, 1994), 22–28, ponders how sound, unlike sight, enters us to heal.

37. Michael Sandel, *Liberalism and the Limits of Justice* (Cambridge: Cambridge University Press, 1982), 172–73. For a thorough statement of the importance of community in economic thinking, see John B. Cobb Jr. and Herman Daly, *For the Common Good : Redirecting the Economy toward the Community, the Environment, and a Sustainable Future* (Boston: Beacon, 1989, 1994).

38. Farley, op. cit., 118 (emphasis his).

39. See Donald Capps, *The Depleted Self* (Minneapolis: Fortress, 1993), 79-80.

40. See Catherine Keller, *From a Broken Web: Separation, Sexism and the Self* (Boston: Beacon, 1986), ch. 3, for the setting of these categories from Heinz Kohut's "self psychology" in a more relational matrix. Robert H. Albers voices a similar question about the human potential movement in *Shame: A Faith Perspective* (New York: Haworth, 1995), 92–93, while moving toward more explicitly theological resources.

41. I am referring to the ethical discourse of *Either/Or*, 2 vols., ed. and trans. H. V. and E. H. Hong (Princeton: Princeton University Press, 1987), vol. 2, 177: ". . . the heavens seem to open, and the I chooses itself or, more

correctly, receives itself." For a reading of Søren Kierkegaard guided by this distinction see Edward Mooney, *Selves in Discord and Resolve* (New York: Routledge, 1996).

42. Kegan, *In Over Our Heads*, 355.

43. William Henry Lazareth and Peri Rasolondraibe, *Lutheran Identity and Mission: Evangelical and Evangelistic?* (Minneapolis: Fortress, 1994), 111.

44. Michael Walzer, *Exodus and Revolution* (New York: Basic Books, 1985), 12. Walzer notes that our word *revolution* is derived from this notion of eternal recurrence. His project is to connect revolution rather with Exodus, which "breaks in the most decisive way with this kind of cosmological story-telling" (13). Cf. Mircea Eliade's classic studies of that form of religion where in myth and ritual one abolishes time to return to that sacred age when God laid the foundations of the earth. See, for example, Mircea Eliade, *Patterns in Comparative Religion,* trans. R. Sheed (New York: Sheed and Ward, 1958).

45. Rasolondraibe, op. cit., 110–11 (emphasis his).

46. See pages 27–28 in this volume.

47. Robert Jenson, "The Triune God," 168, *Christian Dogmatics*, ed. C. E. Braaten and R. W. Jenson, 2 vols. (Philadelphia: Fortress, 1984), vol. 1, 79–196. Cf. 156 on "God's utter freedom."

48. Karl Barth, *Church Dogmatics*, trans. and ed. G. W. Bromiley and T. F. Torrance (Edinburgh: T. and T. Clark, 1936–1977), vol. 2:1, 272.

49. Ibid., 280.

50. Paul S. Fiddes, *The Creative Suffering of God* (Oxford: Clarendon, 1988), 71. Fiddes offers an extended discussion of creation by the will (Barth, Keith Ward) or desire (Nicholas Berdyaev) of God.

51. Ibid., 75.

52. Catherine Mowry LaCugna, *God for Us: The Trinity and Christian Life* (San Francisco: Harper, 1991), 355 (emphasis hers). Cf. 373, note 67: "Even if God's goodness is necessarily self-diffusive, the diffusion of God's goodness in the creaturely realm must be rooted in freedom, not necessity."

53. Stephen H. Webb, *The Gifting God: A Trinitarian Ethics of Excess* (New York: Oxford University Press, 1996), 9.

54. Eberhard Jungel, *God as the Mystery of the World*, trans. D. L. Guder (Grand Rapids: Eerdmans, 1983), 384 (emphasis his).

55. Jürgen Moltmann, *God in Creation*, trans. M. Kohl (Minneapolis: Fortress, 1993), 241.

56. Terence E. Fretheim, *Exodus* (Louisville: John Knox, 1991), 305 (emphasis his). My colleague has referred me to supporting readings by Freedman and Driver. Thus David Noel Freedman, "The Name of the God of Moses," *Journal of Biblical Literature* 79 (1960): "This is an *idem per idem* construction, precisely parallel to Exodus 3:14 ['I am who I am']. . . . The

stress in this passage is upon the verbal action: showing grace and mercy. There appears to be no suggestion of willfulness or arbitrary free choice in the Hebrew. . . ." (154). To quote Driver once more (S. R. Driver, *The Book of Exodus* [Cambridge University Press, 1911], 363): 'All that is said here is that God is gracious to those to whom he is gracious. . . . The second 'will' in each sentence is a simple future: it must not be emphasized as though it meant 'wish to' [Hence, in effect.] I am the gracious one, I am the compassionate one."

57. Jungel, op. cit., 328.

58. Moshe Halevi Spero, *Religious Objects as Psychological Structures: A Critical Integration of Object Relations Theory, Psychotherapy, and Judaism* (Chicago: University of Chicago Press, 1992), 194 (emphasis his). Spero is filling in clues from the early Freud's "succinct speculation."

59. Sammeli Juntunen of the University of Helsinki has effectively demonstrated the scope of this continuing creation motif in the thought of Martin Luther. See "Luther and Metaphysics: What Is the Structure of Being According to Luther?" in *Union with Christ: The New Finnish Interpretation of Luther,* ed. Braaten and Jenson (Grand Rapids: Eerdmans, 1998): "Luther's notion of being is clearly connected with this Ockhamistic *creatio continua.* According to him creation has not occurred only once. God always creates all things. . . . Important to notice here is, that Luther (in quite an other way than the ockhamist tradition to whom the reality of grace is always something accidental in the human substance) extends the scope of the *creatio continua* into the *esse gratiae.* . . . The *esse gratiae* of a person, like the *esse naturae,* is a continuous reception of the gifts of God. . . ." (139–40).

60. Lutherans are particularly keen to recognize some distinction here. Cf. the Formula of Concord's concern to distinguish different meanings of "Gospel" in *The Book of Concord,* trans. and ed. T. G. Tappert (Philadelphia: Fortress, 1959), 478:5.5–6. The warning against "confusion" is sounded precisely lest we "darken the merit of Christ and rob disturbed consciences of the comfort which they would otherwise have in the holy Gospel. . . ." (558:5.1). For comment on this confusion in "so much unevangelical ideology in influential ecumenical approaches to mission and evangelism today," see William Lazareth, *Lutheran Identity and Mission* (Minneapolis: Fortress, 1994), 39–41.

61. Still on Lutheran ground, Rasolondraibe thinks so. In *Lutheran Identity and Mission,* 101: "There may be a danger of triumphalism in a Christian integrist approach to social-political life. A Lutheran laissez-faire social ethic, however, is even more dangerous."

62. See pages 32–33 and page 155, note 49, in this volume.

63. In *God: The Question and the Quest* (Philadelphia: Fortress, 1985), chapter 7, I have written of this transformation as the advance to an "actual absolute."

64. In *Christ and His Benefits: Christology and Redemption in the New Testament* (Philadelphia: Fortress, 1987), Arland J. Hultgren borrows for his title from Philip Melanchton's *Loci Communes* of 1521. I find particularly helpful Hultgren's discussion of the "theopractic" and "Christopractic" dimensions of New Testament thought regarding the agent active in redemption. John 14 seems to place the distinction in perspective when Jesus reminds us that "I am in the Father and the Father is in me."

65. *The Book of Concord*, 432. Cf. Luther on how it is an erring use of the power of the keys if one "cannot say that I know for certain that I have loosed you before God, whether you believe it or not"("The Keys," *Luther's Works*, trans. E. Beyer and C. Bergendoff, vol. 40, 367).

66. Søren Kierkegaard, *The Sickness unto Death*, ed. H. V. Hong (Princeton: Princeton University Press), 121.

67. Søren Kierkegaard, *Philosophical Fragments*, ed. H. V. Hong (Princeton: Princeton University Press), 36.

68. Simo Peura, "Christ as Favor and Gift (*donum*): The Challenge of Luther's Understanding of Justification," in *Union with Christ*, ed. Braaten and Jenson, 44. Cf. pages 72–73 in this volume, on the "two kinds of righteousness." This theme is pervasively present in Luther's exegetical writings. For example, on John 3:4 (*Luther's Works*, vol. 22, 286): "And if you remain constant in this faith, then the Holy Spirit is there to baptize you, to strengthen and increase your faith and to implant a new understanding in your heart. He also awakens in you holy and new thoughts and impulses, so that you begin to love God, refrain from all ungodly conduct, gladly do God's will, love your neighbor, and shun anger, hatred, and envy." This theme of the actual transformation of the believer by the indwelling Christ need not be linked with the telos of theosis, though that connection seems to have been important for these Finnish Luther scholars in their conversation with Eastern Orthodox theologians.

69. Friedrich Schleiermacher, *The Christian Faith*, English trans. of 2d German ed. Ed. H. R. Mackintosh and J. S. Stewart (Edinburgh: T. and T. Clark, 1928), 435.

70. Ibid., 438.

71. Søren Kierkegaard, *Practice in Christianity*, ed. and trans. H. V. and E. H. Hong (Princeton: Princeton University Press, 1991), 238–39 (emphasis his).

72. John B. Cobb Jr., *Christ in a Pluralistic Age* (Philadelphia: Westminster, 1975), 117. He cites specifically the work of Walter Grundmann on the Pauline "in Christ." See Walter Grundmann, "The Christ Statements of the New Testament" in G. Kittel, ed., *Theological Dictionary of the New Testament*, trans. G. W. Bromiley (Grand Rapids: Eerdmans, 1964–1976), vol. 9.

73. Michael Welker, *God the Spirit,* trans. J. F. Hoffmeyer (Minneapolis: Fortress, 1994).

74. Ibid., 228.

75. Ibid., 242–43.

76. Ibid., 240. Welker offers the comparison of "a system differentiated into subsystems, a structure composed of structures or—more graphically— a complexly structured network whose component parts themselves form nets." Welker is very clear that "love defines not only person-to-person relations, but also relations of sociality and of community" (ibid., 250).

77. Ibid., 228.

78. Ibid., 323.

79. See, for example, Wolfhart Pannenberg, *Systematic Theology*, vol. 2, 83, where Pannenberg offers this formal description of the relationship between the disciplines: "We also see that the reality is the same because the theological (as distinct from the scientific) development of the concept is in a position to find a place in its reflection for the different form of description in physics, for which there can be empirical demonstration, and in this way to confirm the coherence of its own statements about the real-ity of the world." And again: "Theology has to have its own material reasons for applying a basic scientific concept like field theory to its own philosophical rather than scientific presentation. Only then is it justified in developing such concepts in a way appropriate to its own themes and independently of scientific usage." Welker's work provides those material reasons in convincing fashion. Pannenberg's theological employment has the Holy Spirit not "as the field but as a unique manifestation (singularity) of the field of the divine essentiality."

80. Thus John Polkinghorne, well published physicist-theologian, in a public lecture at Luther Seminary, St. Paul, Minnesota, on April 21, 1997, expressed puzzlement over Pannenberg's recruitment of this "essentially mechanical" notion of field of force.

81. A very different effort devoted to this purpose is Cheryl J. Sanders, *Empowerment Ethics for a Liberated People* (Minneapolis: Fortress, 1995), where seven approaches are identified: testimony, protest, uplift, cooperation, achievement, remoralization and ministry. But one could say that these represent the human outworking of the empowering relationship.

82. Robert John Russell, "Does the 'God Who Acts' Really Act? New Approaches to Divine Action in Light of Science," *Theology Today* 54, no. 1 (April 1997): 64–65. In this issue see also Owen C. Thomas' summary article "Chaos, Complexity, and God: A Review Essay" (66–76) for comment on the 400 page *Chaos and Complexity: Scientific Perspectives on Divine Action*, ed. R. J. Russell, N. Murphy, and A. R. Peacocke (Berkeley: Vatican

Observatory, 1995). Russell's opening chapter is a particularly helpful analytical summary of current approaches to divine action.

83. Welker, op. cit. , 228, 323.

84. Alfred North Whitehead's apt title, *Adventures of Ideas* (New York: Macmillan, 1933), comes to mind. Michael Walzer traces a series of adventures of one such idea, "Exodus," in *Exodus and Revolution*, 149: "This is a central theme in Western thought, always present though elaborated in many different ways. We still believe, or many of us do, what the Exodus first taught, or what it has commonly been taken to teach, about the meaning and possibility of politics and about its proper form: first, that wherever you live, it is probably Egypt; second, that there is a better place, a world more attractive, a promised land; and third, that 'the way to the land is through the wilderness.' There is no way to get from here to there except by joining together and marching."

85. Paul Ricoeur, *History and Truth* (Chicago: Northwestern University Press, 1965), 5. Here is Ricoeur's fuller statement of this point with regard to the Christian message: "The word is my kingdom and I am not ashamed of it. . . . As a university professor, I believe in the efficacy of instructive speech; in teaching the history of philosophy, I believe in the enlightening power, even for a system of politics, of speaking devoted to elaborating our philosophical memory."

86. Søren Kierkegaard, *On Authority and Revelation: The Book on Adler*, trans. Walter Lowrie (Princeton: Princeton University Press, 1955), 168.

87. See also Romans 11:33-36, where the evocation of the unsearchability of the Lord's judgments is linked with the Isaiah text but followed by a comprehensive witness to the Creator: "For from him and through him and to him are all things. To him be glory forever. Amen."

88. Michael Welker, *God the Spirit*, 230–31; cf. 268.

89. "The face of the self, the face of the other, and the face of Christ are all present in this verse. There are three distinct faces, and yet through the subtle mediation of the mirror they become one face and thus share the same emotion and character. . . . The person [in Greco-Roman society] progressing in virtue was to hold up and look at a worthy person from the past as if looking in a mirror; the image seen was simultaneously the goal to be striven toward and the face of the one looking. . . . The connection between gazing into a mirror and transformation into the mirror's image is particularly helpful for Paul's attempt to show how the Spirit's work in the church is the creation of identity with Christ and simultaneously with one another." From David Fredrickson's article, "Christ's Many Friends: The Presence of Jesus in 2 Corinthians 1-7," *Word and World Supplement Series* 3 (1997): 170.

90. "Opinion" (but also "expectation") is more firmly in place in classical Greek. See Henry George Liddell and Robert Scott, *A Greek-English Lexicon* (Oxford: Clarendon, 1843, 1983), 444. For New Testament usage, see Johannes P. Louw and Eugene A. Nida, *A Greek-English Lexicon of the New Testament Based on Semantic Domains,* 2 vols. (New York: United Bible Societies, 1988), I, 33/357 for "praise" and 33.468 for "promise." I am indebted to my colleague, James Boyce, for conversation concerning these associations.

91. Diane Jacobson, "Strengths and Weaknesses of Wisdom/Sophia Talk," 122, in *A Reforming Church: Gift and Task,* ed. C. P. Lutz (Minneapolis: Kirk House, 1995), 107–25.

92. Alexandra R. Brown, *The Cross and Human Transformation: Paul's Apocalyptic Word in 1 Corinthians* (Minneapolis: Fortress, 1995), 163 (emphasis hers).

93. Martin Luther, "Theses for the Heidelberg Disputation," 44, *Martin Luther's Basic Theological Writings,* ed. T. F. Lull (Minneapolis: Fortress, 1989), 30–49.

94. David Hume, *Dialogues Concerning Natural Religion,* ed. H. D. Aiken (New York: Hafner, 1948, 1974), 16.

95. Hume's ethical appeal to "sentiment," as distinguished from reason, seems difficult to assess at this point. See David Hume, *Inquiry Concerning the Principles of Morals* (Chicago: Open Court, 1953).

96. Whitehead, *Process and Reality,* 49–50. I am following Whitehead's invitation to recognize the "causal" knowing involved in "causal efficacy," from which Hume's misleadingly clear and distinct impressions are derived.

97. Ibid., 178.

98. James B. Ashbrook, *Minding the Soul: Pastoral Counseling as Remembering* (Minneapolis: Fortress, 1996), 170.

99. Here process thought and phenomenology make some common cause. For the latter see *The Phenomenology of the Truth Proper to Religion,* ed. D. Guerriere (Albany: SUNY Press, 1990).

100. Michael Polanyi, *Personal Knowledge: Towards a Post-Critical Philosophy* (Chicago: University of Chicago Press, 1958), 256.

101. Daniel Taylor, *The Myth of Certainty: The Reflective Christian and the Risk of Commitment* (Waco, Tex.: Jarrell Word, 1986), 129 (emphasis his).

102. Ann Belford Ulanov, "What Do We Think People Are Doing When They Pray?", *Anglican Theological Review* 60 (1978): 388. In this purgation we do "die to the world," Ulanov says, but "then something unexpected happens. All those objects, which are somehow lost to us, renounced as clearly 'not God,' though earlier hailed as 'truly God,' return to us in a new way. It is a way that makes space for an 'us' that can only be described as 'given' rather than as 'derived' or 'developed.' . . . Dead to the world, we

discover the living world returned to us. . . ." (392). Or, as I would say, the other is given.

103. See pages 83–87 in this volume.

104. Wolfhart Pannenberg, *Anthropology in Theological Perspective*, trans. M. J. O'Connell (Philadelphia: Westminster, 1985), 372.

105. Taylor, op. cit., 150.

106. I have come to this formulation in reading colleague James Burtness' discussion of Dietrich Bonhoeffer's emphasis on time, not space. See his "As Though God Were Not Given: Barth, Bonhoeffer, and the *Finitum Capax Infiniti,*" *dialog* 19 (1980): 249–55.

107. I am thinking of the much cited 1984 work of Mark C. Taylor, *Erring: A Postmodern A/Theology* (Chicago: University of Chicago Press), where with history ended (chapter 3), we are offered "mazing grace." I have indicated in chapter 4 (page 66, in this volume) that ten years later he hears a call, apparently giving some sense of direction.

108. See Jung Young Lee, *Marginality: The Key to Multicultural Theology* (Minneapolis: Fortress, 1995), ch. 2, for a discussion of the "in-between" and the "in-both," as such an epistemological understanding represents.

109. Dietrich Bonhoeffer, *Ethics*, ed. E. Bethge, trans. N. H. Smith (New York: Macmillan, 1955, 1965), 195.

110. Bonhoeffer, *Letters and Papers from Prison,* ed. E. Bethge (New York: Macmillan, 1953), 188.

111. William C. Placher, *The Domestication of Transcendence: How Modern Thinking about God Went Wrong* (Louisville: Westminster/John Knox, 1996), 181. Placher himself seems to me to be guilty of writing very clearly about God. I applaud his concern to avoid formulations that make "faith in God's sovereignty and grace the *enemy of human freedom*" or the "*enemy of transformative justice*" (182, emphasis his), but believe his call to heed revelation makes a full claim on the cognitive powers given humankind.

112. Bonhoeffer, loc. cit.

113. Thus Carl E. Braaten, *Christian Dogmatics,* vol. 1, 533, or William Placher himself in *Narratives of a Vulnerable God: Christ, Theology, and Scripture* (Louisville: Westminster/John Knox, 1994), 10: " Suppose God, more than anything else, freely loves, and in that love is willing to be vulnerable and to risk suffering."

114. G. L. Prestige, *God in Patristic Thought* (London: SPCK, 1964), 7. Jürgen Moltmann's *The Crucified God* (New York: Harper, 1974) perhaps did as much as any publication to awaken Western theology to this theme. See 229–30, on God's suffering as fullness, not deficiency. Earlier, Kazoh Kitamori's *Theology of the Pain of God* (Richmond, Va.: John Knox, 1965) is a challenging Japanese statement.

115. See Dorothee Soelle's description of the resistance of twentieth-century Christians to recognize God's suffering and our own involvement with it in *Suffering*, trans. E. R. Kalin (Philadelphia: Fortress, 1975), chapter 1.

116. Carl E. Braaten, *Christian Dogmatics*, vol. 1, 532, makes a helpful distinction at this point: "Even on orthodox grounds it does not make sense to divorce the suffering of Christ from the Father. Christ suffered in his person, and this person (*hypostasis*) is God the Son, of one being (*homoousios*) with the Father. If God was in Christ, then suffering became a part of the experience of God. . . . The distinction between the Father and the Son can be maintained without denying the Father a share in the incarnate fate of his Son Jesus Christ."

117. Martin Luther, "The Bondage of the Will," *Luther's Works*, vol. 33 (Philadelphia: Fortress, 1972), 145–46.

118. Terence E. Fretheim, *The Suffering of God: An Old Testament Perspective* (Philadelphia: Fortress, 1984), 5.

119. Whitehead, *Process and Reality*, 338, 343. The fuller statement in the earlier passage is "Philosophy may not neglect the multifariousness of the world—the fairies dance, and Christ is nailed to the cross."

120. But not without some dissent. For example, see Richard Creel, *Divine Impassibility* (Cambridge and New York: Cambridge University Press, 1986) and Ronald Goetz, "The Suffering God: The Rise of a New Orthodoxy," *The Christian Century* (April 16, 1986): 385–89.

121. Placher, op. cit., 17.

122. Or in Paul Fiddes' phrasing (note 50, page 180 in this volume) how *The . . . Suffering of God is Creative.*

123. Douglas John Hall, *God and Human Suffering: An Exercise in the Theology of the Cross* (Minneapolis: Augsburg, 1986), 99.

124. Denise Levertov, "Agnus Dei," from "Mass for the Day of St. Thomas Didymus," *Candles in Babylon* (New York: New Directions, 1982), 114.

125. In the *Chaos and Complexity* volume mentioned (note 84 above) see particularly Nancey Murphy's article "Divine Action in the Natural Order: Buridan's Ass and Schrodinger's Cat," 325–58.

126. Sanders, op. cit., 4. Thus Levertov, op. cit., 115, answers her own question about the human role:

So be it.

Come, rag of pungent

quiverings,

dim star.

Let's try

if something human still

can shield you,

spark
of remote light.

6. So, What Is Now to Be Done? (To Serve the Creator's Will)

1. Karl Marx, "Theses on Feuerbach," from the Notebooks of 1844–1855, *Writings of the Young Marx on Philosophy and Society*, ed. and trans. L. D. Easton and K. H. Guddat (Garden City, N.Y.: Doubleday Anchor, 1967), 402 (emphasis his).

2. Richard Rorty, for example, in "The Priority of Democracy to Philosophy," *The Virginia Statute for Religious Freedom*, ed. M. D. Peterson and R. C. Vaughan (Cambridge and New York: Cambridge University Press, 1988), 257–82: "The Kantian identification with a central transcultural and ahistorical self is thus replaced by a quasi-Hegelian identification with our own community, thought of as a historical product. For pragmatist social theory, the question of whether justifiability to the community with which we identify entails truth is simply irrelevant" (259).

3. *Lutheran Book of Worship* (Minneapolis: Augsburg, 1978), 22 (emphasis mine).

4. Rorty, op. cit., 273, raises a Deweyan objection: "For it is hard to be both enchanted with one version of the world and tolerant of all the others." Cf. note 19, page 146 in this volume.

5. William Butler Yeats, "The Second Coming," 185, *The Collected Poems of W. B. Yeats* (New York: Macmillan, 1956), 184–85.

6. Robert Coles, *The Moral Intelligence of Children* (New York: Random House, 1997), 182.

7. The phrase is Ricoeur's. See page 184, note 85 in this volume.

8. Cited in Richard Lebeaux, *Thoreau's Seasons* (Amherst: University of Massachusetts Press, 1984), 79. Lebeaux grants that the story is "perhaps apocryphal," but he can quote Thoreau's "Civil Disobedience": "Under a government which imprisons any unjustly, the true place for a just man is also a prison."

9. Henry David Thoreau, "Walden," *Henry David Thoreau* (New York: Library of America, 1985), vol. 2, 395.

10. See pages 4–7 in this volume.

11. Loren Mead, *The Once and Future Church* (Washington, D.C.: Alban Institute, 1991), especially chs. 2 and 3.

12. See pages 60–65 in this volume.

13. Ludwig Wittgenstein, *Culture and Value*, ed. G. H. von Wright, trans. P. Winch (Chicago: University of Chicago Press, 1980), 34c.

14. See pages 56–57 in this volume.

15. See pages 48–49 in this volume.

16. Denise Levertov locates the point in seeing "the world of the white herons," for there she learned:

> that it was not a fragile, only, other world,
> there were, there are . . . a host,
> each unique. Yet each having
> the grace of recapitulating
> a single radiance, multiform.
> She knows, further:
> . . . that the vision
> was given me: to know and share
> but knows as well that:
> its clarity dwindles in our confusion. . . .

See the poem "Many Mansions" in *Candles of Babylon* (New York: New Directions, 1982), 116, where the last words are "the amulet of mercy."

17. Michael Welker, *God the Spirit*, trans. J. F. Hoffmeyer (Minneapolis: Fortress, 1994), 27.

18. Victor J. Seidler, *The Moral Limits of Modernity: Love, Inequality, and Oppression* (New York: St. Martin's, 1991), 181–82. See also Walter Lowe's *Theology and Difference* (Bloomington, Ind.: Indiana University Press, 1993), significantly subtitled "The Wound of Reason."

19. Ibid., 182.

20. Cf. Gustaf Wingren, *Creation and Gospel* (New York: Edward Mellen, 1979), 121, where "the cry from the South" is understood as "God's dunning letters."

21. Seidler, op. cit., ix, notes the difficulty either Kantian or utilitarian moral theory has had in coming to terms with "the moral realities that we face after Auschwitz and Hiroshima" and comments that it has taken "over forty years in the wilderness to discern that our inherited Enlightenment frameworks might themselves be part of the problem."

22. Daniel Yankelovich, "Trends in American Cultural Values," *Criterion* 35, no. 3 (autumn 1996): 2–9.

23. Mark Kline Taylor, *Remembering Esperanza: A Cultural-Political Theology for North American Praxis* (Maryknoll, N.Y.: Orbis, 1990), 200.

24. Robert N. Bellah, "Competing Visions of the Role of Religion in American Society," 230, *Uncivil Religion*, ed. R. N. Bellah and F. E. Greenspahn (New York: Crossroad, 1987), 219–32.

25. Thus one might contrast such Indian authors as N. Scott Momaday, Leslie Marmon Silko, and Louise Erdrich with the newer voices of such writers as Greg Sarris (*Grand Avenue*) and Sherman Alexie (*Indian Killer*).

26. Ted Peters, *God—The World's Future: Systematic Theology for a Postmodern Era* (Minneapolis: Fortress, 1992), 14–15.

27. See page 68 for Edith Wyschogrod's analysis in *Saints and Postmodernism,* or page 66 on how *Erring* Mark C. Taylor seems now to hear a call.

28. This is the term Yankelovitch uses (op. cit.), pleading that we do so from strength rather than weakness.

29. Kosuke Koyama, "How Many Languages Does God Speak?", *Cross Currents* (summer 1996): 170, 172.

30. Charles E. Winquist makes this point, more broadly, about theology by employing Victor Turner's notion of the "liminal": "Theological thinking is relevant because it is other than ordinary discourse and because it is a discourse that can transgressively display the otherness of its semantic achievement. It is needed by its three publics as a form of public liminality, as a public critique, and as a display of alternative possibilities. . . . The danger is that what is liminal becomes stabilized and what is marginal becomes central. Theology needs to stay on the margins to be itself." See "Theology, Deconstruction, and Ritual Process," *Zygon* 18, no. 3 (September 1983): 307–8.

31. At the 1989 Nobel Conference at Gustavus Adolphus College, Sandra Harding gave her paper this provocative title. See also the collection *Sex and Scientific Inquiry,* ed. S. Harding and J. O'Barr (Chicago: University of Chicago Press, 1987). For an expression of this more inclusive approach in a very different discipline see Janet D. Spector's *What This Awl Means: Feminist Archeology at a Wahpeton Dakota Village* (St. Paul: Minnesota Historical Society, 1993).

32. See Mary Farrell Bednarowski's analysis in *New Religions and the Theological Imagination in America,* (Bloomington: Indiana University Press, 1989), ch. 4, "The Dead Learn Forever."

33. See, for example, Bill McKibben's *The End of Nature* (New York: Random House, 1989), Francis Fukuyama's *The End of History and the Last Man* (New York: Free Press, 1992), David Lindley's *The End of Physics* (New York: Basic Books, 1994), John Horgan's *The End of Science* (Abrams, 1996), and Paul Ormerod's *The Death of Economics* (New York: St. Martin's, 1995). "Sovereignty," "isms," "Japan incorporated," "laissez-faire," "affluence," "equality," "racism," "education," "work," "bureaucracy"—one must say the list seems nearly endless.

34. Bill Gates, *The Road Ahead* (New York: Viking Penguin, 1995).

35. See *Physics and the Ultimate Significance of Time,* ed. D. R. Griffin (Albany: SUNY Press, 1986) for such a pondering. The subtitle, "Bohm, Prigogine and Process Philosophy," suggests the key sources employed.

36. For a succinct and striking expression of this theme see Patrick Henry's "On Teaching Christianity: How to Make the Familiar Surprising," *Bulletin of the Council on the Study of Religion* 16, no. 1 (February 1985): 1–3.

37 Ray L. Hart, *Unfinished Man and the Imagination* (New York: Herder and Herder, 1968), 28.

38. Ibid.

39. Joseph Sittler, *Gravity and Grace* (Minneapolis: Augsburg, 1986), 11 (emphasis his).

40. Ibid., 27, quoting Roethke, "The Waking."

41. Cf. Karl Barth, who can hardly be charged with minimizing the *fides quae*, in *Church Dogmatics*, vol. 1, part 1, *The Doctrine of the Word of God*, trans. G. T. Thomson, ed. G. W. Bromiley and T. F. Torrance (Edinburgh: T. and T. Clark, 1936), 284–330.

42. Michael Walzer, *Interpretation and Social Criticism* (Cambridge: Harvard University Press, 1987), 71.

43. Gerhard von Rad, *Old Testament Theology*, 2 vols. (New York: Harper, 1965), vol. 2, 413 (emphasis mine).

44. I have written of this in "To Claim and to Test: Doing Theology in This Time and Place," *A Reforming Church: Gift and Task*, ed. C. P. Lutz (Minneapolis: Kirk House, 1995), 74–92.

45. Several authors make clear that this principle of criticism cannot be silenced within the covers of the Bible. Elisabeth Schüssler Fiorenza's *In Memory of Her* (New York: Crossroad, 1986) was a rather early but already very powerful statement. For a current call to self-criticism in reading the Bible, see Terence E. Fretheim and Karlfried Froehlich, *The Bible as Word of God in a Postmodern Age* (Minneapolis: Fortress, 1998).

46. See Martin Heinecken's series "Criticism in the Church" in *Certus Sermo*, an independent monthly review of the Northwest Washington Synod of the Evangelical Lutheran Church in America, ed. R. F. Marshall, J. R. Nelson, and R. G. Baker, no. 47–49 (March–May, 1994). The editors, taking their title from Luther's reference to the truth as a "sure word" (*Luther's Works* 29, 32, 33, 35), publish their often pointedly critical review "to stimulate a vigorous conversation in our parishes . . . [and] to nurture a deliberate and detailed vantage from the Bible and the Lutheran Confessions." But they state clearly that "the opinions expressed herein are solely those of the editors."

47. See pages 100–101 in this volume.

48. See pages 101–2 in this volume.

49. Friedrich Schleiermacher, *The Christian Faith*, Eng. trans. of 2d German ed. Ed. H. R. Mackintosh and J. S. Stewart (Edinburgh: T. and T. Clark, 1928), 389–90.

50. The sharp edge of these questions is particularly clear in Joanne Carlson Brown and Rebecca Parker, "For God So Loved the World," *Christianity, Patriarchy, and Abuse: A Feminist Critique,* ed. J. C. Brown and C. Bohn (New York: Pilgrim, 1989), 1–29. See also Daphne Hampson, *Theology and Feminism*

(Oxford and Cambridge, Mass.: Blackwell, 1990) for critique of the kenosis notion and the suggestion that [even] emphasis on Jesus as our mother devalues our natural mothers. It is not only explicitly feminist authors who voice such questions. See Douglas John Hall, *God and Human Suffering* (Minneapolis: Augsburg, 1986), 100ff., for comparable criticism focusing on the notion of power implied in traditional atonement theories.

51. Dorothee Soelle, *Suffering*, trans. E. R. Kalin (Philadelphia: Fortress, 1975), 101–2.

52. Elizabeth A. Johnson, *She Who Is: The Mystery of God in Feminist Theological Discourse* (New York: Crossroad, 1992), 254. Cf. Alexandra R. Brown, *The Cross and Human Transformation: Paul's Apocalyptic Word in 1 Corinthians* (Minneapolis: Fortress, 1995), 164, on the cross as an *empowering*, not a *dis*-empowering symbol: "What the cross reveals is Christ's own struggle for us against systemic sin and thereby God's loving will to stand with the suffering world against the 'rulers of this age' (1 Cor. 2:8)" (emphasis hers).

53. In his best selling book *The Will of God* (Nashville: Abingdon, 1944, 1972), 12, Leslie Weatherhead makes the point plain: "Was it God's intention from the beginning that Jesus should go to the Cross? . . . No. . . . He came with the *intention* that men [*sic!*] should follow him, not kill him" (emphasis his).

54. Joy Bussert, *Battered Women* (Lutheran Church in America Division for Mission, 1986), 65.

55. This is Johannes Metz' proposal for an "anti-history" in *Faith in History and Society* (New York: Seabury, 1980), 111.

56. See pages 102–3 in this volume. For the distinction between the exemplary ("*vorbildliche*") and *Urbildlichkeit* (with its "productivity"), see Schleiermacher, op. cit., 378–79.

57. Eberhard Jungel, "The Truth of Life: Observations on Truth as the Interruption of the Continuity of Life," 236, in *Creation, Christ, and Culture: Studies in Honour of T. F. Torrance*, ed. R. W. A. McKinney (Edinburgh: T. and T. Clark, 1976), 231–36.

58. H. P. Owen, *Concepts of Deity* (New York: Herder and Herder, 1971), 24. Owen continues: "Therefore, any suffering that God endures through his love for his creatures is immediately transfigured by the joy that is necessarily his within his uncreated Godhead" (ibid.).

59. Arthur Cohen, *The Tremendum: A Theological Interpretation of the Holocaust* (New York: Crossroad, 1981), 83.

60. See page 104 in this volume.

61. Masao Abe, noted Buddhist scholar, warns of making this move in any facile way: "This *Sunyata* is deep enough to encompass even God, the 'object' of mystical union as well as the object of faith. For *Sunyata* is not the

nothingness from which God created everything, but the nothingness from which God himself emerged." See "God, Emptiness, and the True Self," *The Eastern Buddhist*, new series 2, no. 2 (1969): 28.

62. Paul Ricoeur and Alasdair MacIntyre, *The Religious Significance of Atheism* (New York: Columbia University Press, 1969), 71.

63. Mark C. Taylor, *Nots* (Chicago: University of Chicago Press, 1993), 30. The scale seems right, for Taylor has "discovered that the problem of the not extends beyond the realm of thought and invades all domains of experience" (2).

64. See Paul Tillich, *Systematic Theology* (Chicago: University of Chicago Press, 1951), vol. 1, 205: "The ground of being cannot be found within the totality of beings, nor can the ground of essence and existence participate in the tensions and disruptions characteristic of the transition from essence to existence. . . . God does not exist. He is being-itself beyond essence and existence."

65. "Commitments for Mission in the 1990s," Division for Global Mission, Evangelical Lutheran Church in America, Commitment 4, in the preface of Mark W. Thomsen, *The Word and the Way of the Cross: Christian Witness Among Muslim and Buddhist People* (Chicago: Division for Global Mission, Evangelical Lutheran Church in America, 1993). Thomsen served as Executive Director of the division, and in a similar capacity in one of the predecessor churches.

66. See Tu Wei-Ming, *Confucian Thought: Selfhood as Creative Transformation* (Albany: SUNY Press, 1985).

67. See Natalie Angier, "Evolutionary Necessity or Glorious Accident? Biologists Ponder the Self," *The New York Times* (April 22, 1997): B9–10.

68. See Brian Swimme and Thomas Berry, *The Universe Story: From the Primordial Flaring Forth to the Ecozoic Era; A Celebration of the Unfolding of the Cosmos* (San Francisco: Harper, 1992). A less dramatic casting of the point is Mihalyi Csikszentmihalyi's "Consciousness for the Twenty-first Century," *Zygon* 26, no. 1 (March 1991) 7–25: ". . . A new spirituality will move the fulcrum of its worldview from the human being to the network of beings, to the process of evolution itself. Rather than soloist, humankind becomes a part of the choir. . . ."

69. These statements are drawn from the third and the seventh of Berry's "Twelve Principles for understanding the universe and the role of the human in the universe process." See Anne Lonergan and Caroline Richards, eds., *Thomas Berry and the New Cosmology* (Mystic, Conn.: Twenty-third Publications, 1987), 107–8.

70. This is Matthew Fox's formulation in *Original Blessing: A Primer in Creation Spirituality* (Santa Fe: Bear and Co., 1983), 23. I emphatically wish to join Fox in an emphasis on creation. But I believe the new creation (a

category he affirms, indeed, as the *Via Transformativa*) is the more remarkable, given the genuine interruption human evil represents.

71. Dietrich Bonhoeffer, *Letters and Papers from Prison,* ed. E. Bethge (New York: Macmillan, 1953, 1967), 161.

72. Rosemary Radford Ruether, "Is Feminism the End of Christianity? A Critique of Daphne Hampson's *Theology and Feminism,*" *Scottish Journal of Theology* 43, no. 3: 396.

73. See pages 62–64 in this volume on the response of silence and Elizabeth Johnson's knowing reference to the mystery of God.

74. For a substantial development of this theme see L. Gregory Jones, *Embodying Forgiveness* (Grand Rapids: Eerdmans, 1995), where the emphasis is clear at the outset: ". . . Those who genuinely seek to embody Christian forgiveness will find that it involves profoundly disorienting yet life-giving transformations of their life, their world, and their capacity for truthful communion" (xiii).

75. A notable study revealing such disappointing results is Search Institute's "Effective Christian Education: A National Study of Protestant Congregations," headed by Peter L. Benson, 1987–1990.

76. Arland J. Hultgren, "Expectations of Prayer in the New Testament," 27, *A Primer on Prayer,* ed. P. R. Sponheim (Philadelphia: Fortress, 1988), 23–35.

77. Ibid., 32–33.

78. Dorothee Soelle, "Answer to Our Leftist Friends Who Ask Us Why We Pray" in *Revolutionary Patience,* trans. R. and R. Kimber (Maryknoll, N.Y.: Orbis, 1977), 24. She continues in this vein throughout the prayer, concluding with this: "because we need faith for the kingdom we are and we build and encouragement for our work so that we don't plan in vain, that's why we sometimes say FOR THINE IS THE KINGDOM AND THE POWER AND THE GLORY and count on the fact that god is FOREVER for us."

79. Robert Wuthnow has developed this theme, empirically, in a number of recent studies. See particularly the case studies in *"I Come Away Stronger": How Small Groups Are Shaping American Religion* (Grand Rapids: Eerdmans, 1994).

80. These are four of the five models listed by Avery Dulles in his classic study, *Models of the Church* (Garden City, N.Y.: Doubleday, 1974). I am stressing that a church modeling itself after any of these four must be able to recognize the challenge in the model Dulles lists as fifth, the church as servant. For this model Dulles (93–96) draws on Teilhard de Chardin ("the main focal point of the energies of love in the world"), Dietrich Bonhoeffer ("The Church is the Church only when it exists for others. . . . The Church

must share in the secular problems of ordinary human life, not dominating, but helping and serving"), and Harvey Cox ("The church's task in the secular city is to be the diakonos of the city, the servant who bends himself to struggle for its wholeness and health").

81. Larry Rasmussen, *Moral Fragments and Moral Community*, (Minneapolis: Fortress, 1993), ch. 8, "A People of the Way."

82. Clark M. Williamson, *A Guest in the House of Israel* (Louisville: Westminster/John Knox, 1993), 260, 265.

83. Loren Mead, *Transforming Congregations for the Future* (Washington, D.C.: Alban Institute, 1994), 116–17. See also his very specific description of "ten features characteristic of a good congregation," 48–52.

84. For a vigorous statement of this warning see William L. Dols Jr., "The Church as Crucible for Transformation," *Jung's Challenge to Contemporary Religion*, ed. M. Stein and R. L. Moore (Wilmette, Ill.: Chiron, 1987), 127–45. Dols speaks of being starting to take precedence over doing with the result that in such a parish "the back of the service leaflet is blank because the former manic activities in the parish have ceased" (141).

85. Parker Palmer, *The Company of Strangers* (New York: Crossroad, 1985) and *Going Public*, (Washington, D.C.: Alban Institute, 1980); Patrick Keifert, *Welcoming the Stranger: A Public Theology of Worship and Evangelism* (Minneapolis: Fortress, 1991); John Koenig, *New Testament Hospitality: Partnership with Strangers as Promise and Mission* (Philadelphia: Fortress, 1985); Christine Pohl, "Welcoming Strangers: A Social Ethical Study of Hospitality in Selected Expressions of the Christian tradition," unpublished Ph.D. dissertation, Emory University, 1993, and her forthcoming publication on this topic.

86. Thomas Ogletree, *Hospitality to the Stranger* (Philadelphia: Fortress, 1985), 3. See also my book, *Faith and the Other* (Minneapolis: Fortress, 1993).

87. Walter Wink, *Engaging the Powers: Discernment and Resistance in a World of Domination* (Minneapolis: Fortress, 1992), 263.

88. Martin Luther King Jr., *Strength to Love* (Philadelphia: Fortress, 1963), 53 (emphasis his).

89. See pages 77–78 in this volume, and the call sounded by Marjorie Suchocki and L. Gregory Jones.

90. A comparable positioning is available in a remarkable collection of essays, *The Church between Gospel and Culture: The Emerging Mission in North America,* ed. G. R. Hunsberger and C. Van Gelder (Grand Rapids: Eerdmans, 1996), where the fuller phrases are "assessing our culture," "discerning the gospel," and "defining the church." I believe the authors gathered in this volume would regard my "locating" of worlds as rather too optimistic.

91. Richard John Neuhaus, *The Naked Public Square: Religion and Democracy in America* (Grand Rapids: Eerdmans, 1984), vii.

92. This is the title of the journal published at the Institute on Religion and Public Life in New York and edited by Richard John Neuhaus, who provides a regular column, "Public Square: A Continuing Survey of Religion and Public Life."

93. See Stephen Carter, *The Culture of Disbelief: How American Law and Politics Trivialize Religious Devotion* (New York: Basic Books, 1993); Robert Benne, *The Paradoxical Vision: A Public Theology for the Twenty-first Century* (Minneapolis: Fortress, 1995); Cornel West, *Race Matters* (Boston: Beacon, 1993); and Jim Wallis, *The Soul of Politics* (New York: New Press, 1994). Wallis was a leader in organizing the "Cry for Renewal" conference in Washington, D.C., in May, 1995.

94. Stephen Carter, op. cit., 44–45.

95. Larry Rasmussen, *Moral Fragments and Moral Community: A Proposal for Church in Society* (Minneapolis: Fortress, 1993), 104.

96. Charles Taylor, *Sources of the Self: The Making of the Modern Identity* (Cambridge: Harvard University Press, 1989), 503.

97. William Dean, *The Religious Critic in American Culture* (Albany: SUNY Press, 1994), 13.

98. Russell Chandler, *Racing Toward 2001: The Forces Shaping America's Religious Future* (Grand Rapids: Zondervan; San Francisco: HarperSanFrancisco, 1992), 28. Chandler has been a religion specialist with the *Los Angeles Times* for more than 18 years. He also knows of another pluralism, and writes of "The Changing Shapes of Churches and Religion" under the apt title "Clashing Cosmologies: Battle for the Worldview."

99. Ibid.

100. See, for example, Robert Audi and Nicholas Wolterstorff, *Religion in the Public Square: The Place of Religious Convictions in Political Debate* (Lanham, Md.: Rowan and Littlefield, 1997), in the "Point/Counterpoint" series.

101. See Alasdair MacIntyre, *Three Rival Versions of Moral Enquiry* (Notre Dame, Ind.: Notre Dame University Press, 1990), 181ff.

102. MacIntyre specifies two conditions needed in order for adherents of a particular tradition to see that an alternative tradition is superior. (1) The tradition should lead to irremediable failure in the light of its own standards in the face of some set of problems that its own goals require it to solve. (2) The alternative tradition must be able to provide the resources to explain why the first tradition failed by its own standard of achievement, and the resources for such explanation must not be available within the first tradition.

103. Ronald F. Thiemann, *Religion in Public Life: A Dilemma for Democracy* (Washington, D.C.: Georgetown University Press, 1996).

104. Ibid., 155.

105. Thus Langdon Gilkey has written clearly of the emergence of a "rough parity" among plural revelations in our land, but speaks even more emphatically of the need to resist forms of religion that are "intolerable because they are demonic." See "Plurality and Its Theological Implications," *The Myth of Christian Uniqueness: Toward a Pluralistic Theology of Religions*, ed. J. Hick and P. F. Knitter (Maryknoll, N.Y.: Orbis, 1987), 37–50.

106. See William Placher's plea to Christians to "keep rejecting the advantages that Christianity's residual cultural status could provide" in *Narratives of a Vulnerable God: Christ, Theology, and Scripture* (Louisville: Westminster/John Knox, 1994), 178.

107. William Dean, *The Religious Critic in American Culture* (Albany: SUNY Press, 1994), 177–80.

108. John B. Cobb Jr. "From Individualism to Persons in Community: A Postmodern Economic Theory," 141, *Sacred Interconnections: Postmodern Spirituality, Political Economy, and Art*, ed. D. R. Griffin (Albany: SUNY Press, 1990), 123–42.

109. Jung Young Lee, *Marginality: The Key to Multicultural Theology* (Minneapolis: Fortress, 1995), 101–2. While Lee stresses the specific Asian-American context, he here recognizes a fundamental Christian marginality, and roots that in a doctrine of creation: "Clearly, Christ is imprinted upon all creation. . . . Christ is the creative core of marginality, the point where creativity and marginality join" (103).

110. Cf. Oscar Handlin, *The Uprooted*, 2d enl. ed. (Boston: Little, Brown, 1951, 1973), 3, on the scope of this movement: "Once I thought to write a history of the immigrants in America. Then I discovered that the immigrants *were* American history" (emphasis his). This horizontal "feel" is also carried in the title of Perry Miller's *Errand into the Wilderness*, where the locale is admittedly something more somber than a garden.

111. Sydney Mead's formulation stresses non-confinement with regard to space, but includes temporal discontinuity as well. See *The Lively Experiment* (New York: Harper, 1963), 5–6: "Gone was the traditional sense of confinement in space, for space relative to people that mattered was practically unlimited. Thus the first immigrants experienced a new birth of freedom—the possibility of unconfined movement in space—while concurrently the time ties were tattered or broken by the breaking of the continuity of the regular passing of one generation after another in one place." J. Ronald Engel finds Mead stressing time as "life itself," but argues that Mead needed to look further at the American experience of space. See "The Theology of the Republic" in *The Lively Experiment Continued*, ed. J. C. Brauer (Macon, Ga.: Mercer University Press, 1987). I am grateful to colleague Todd Nichol for conversation around this theme.

112. Mead, *The Lively Experiment,* 7.

113. Sydney E. Mead, "Reinterpretation in American Church History," 229–30, *The Lively Experiment Continued.*

114. The temptation thus to locate governing values in some past period is certainly available in the American experience. Art critic Robert Hughes points to such obsessive nostalgia as over against an American belief in progress. He cites the neoclassical architecture of the new republic's civic buildings (e.g., Thomas Jefferson's Rotunda at the University of Virginia) and the pattern of millionaire plunderers of European antiquities. See *American Visions: The Epic History of Art in America* (New York: Knopf, 1997).

115. Roger Fisher and William Ury, *Getting to Yes: Negotiating Agreement without Giving In* (Boston: Houghton Mifflin, 1981), ch. 3. See page 79 and note 53, page 173 in this volume, for Whitehead's emphasis on the "interesting proposition." William Dean, op. cit., 178, finds reason for optimism in American history: "Americans seem to have specialized in improvisation, and this is manifest in their theater, their jazz, their basketball. America has never embraced the divine right of national leaders, a natural law, a controlled economy, or a hereditary class system—although it has established a monied elite. Longer than any other nation, it has embraced open forms in government, law, economics, and religion." But his optimism is qualified: "America's blessing is unencumbered revisability; its curse is unrelenting revisability" (179).

116. Gates, *The Road Ahead.*

117. These words are taken from the prayer for the Holy Spirit in the Baptismal rite and Affirmation of Baptism service in the *Lutheran Book of Worship* (Minneapolis: Augsburg, 1978).

118. See Langdon Winner, *The Whale and the Reactor* (Chicago: University of Chicago Press, 1986) on the need for a philosophy of technology. Winner asks (26) whether "scientific knowledge, technological invention, and corporate profit reinforce each other in deeply entrenched patterns, patterns that bear the unmistakable of political and economic power."

119. This formulation is Wendell Berry's in *The Gift of a Good Land* (San Francisco: North Point, 1981), 142. A striking critique of American insatiability is offered by Alan Durning in *How Much Is Enough? The Consumer Society and the Future of the Earth* (New York: Norton, 1992) and *This Place on Earth: Home and the Practice of Permanence* (Seattle: Sasquatch, 1996).

120. A notable example is The Index of Sustainable Economic Welfare as presented by John B. Cobb Jr. and Herman E. Daly in *For the Common Good: Redirecting the Economy toward Community, the Environment, and a Sustainable Future* (Boston: Beacon, 1989, 1994). The index includes such fac-

tors as "natural resource depletion," "environmental damage," "value of leisure," and the "value of unpaid household labor."

121. I refer to the efforts of the husband-and-wife team of Terje Rod Larsen and Mona Juul and of three other Norwegians. One negotiator said of his opposite: "This guy is my enemy but I trust him." One account is by Wilmar Thorkelson in *The Lutheran* (April 1994): 40.

122. Bernard W. Dempsey, *The Functional Economy* (Paramus, N.J.: Prentice Hall, 1958), 281 (emphasis his). Cf. Cobb and Daly, op. cit., 174ff.

123. Cobb and Daly make this point strongly. Similarly, in "America's Search for a New Public Philosophy," *The Atlantic Monthly* (March 1996): 57–74, Michael J. Sandel recommends "diffusing sovereignty" as over against the "modern" emphasis on the nation state: "Only a politics that disperses sovereignty both upward and downward can combine the power required to rival global market forces with the differentiation required of a public life that hopes to inspire the allegiance of its citizens" (74).

124. On the second point see particularly Sharon Welch, *A Feminist Ethic of Risk* (Minneapolis: Fortress, 1990).

125. In *Cosmopolis: The Hidden Agenda of Modernity* (New York: Free Press, 1990), 197–98, Stephen Toulmin develops this image in relation to such organizations as Amnesty International.

126. Cornel West, *Race Matters* (Boston: Beacon, 1993), 101.

127. This question is raised pointedly by liberals such as John Rawls or Ronald Dworkin. For a summary statement see John A. Coleman, "A Common Good Primer," *dialog* 34, no. 4 (fall 1995): 249–54.

128. This formulation is Philip Selznick's in *The Moral Commonwealth* (Berkeley: University of California Press, 1992), 526.

129. Seyla Benhabib, *Critique, Norm and Utopia: A Study of the Foundations of Critical Theory* (New York: Columbia University Press, 1986), 315. I am grateful to my colleague, Gary Simpson, for this reference.

130. Francis Fukuyama, *Trust: The Social Virtues and the Creation of Prosperity* (New York: Free Press, 1995).

131. Jürgen Moltmann voices this challenge forcefully in *God in Creation: A New Theology of Creation and the Spirit of God,* trans. M. Kohl (San Francisco: Harper and Row, 1985). Consider simply two sentences: "Nature must no longer be viewed as 'unclaimed property.' . . . The body must no longer be seen as something which we 'possess'" (3).

132. H. Paul Santmire, "Toward a Christology of Nature," *dialog* 34, no. 4 (fall 1995): 278–79.

Bibliography

Abe, Masao, "God, Emptiness, and the True Self," *The Eastern Buddhist* new series 2, no. 2 (1969).

Adams, Judith. *The American Amusement Park Industry: A History of Technology and Thrills.* New York: Twayne, 1991.

Albers, Robert. *Shame: A Faith Perspective.* New York: Haworth, 1995.

Albright, Carol Rausch and Haugen, Joel, eds. *Beginning with the End: God, Science and Wolfhart Pannenberg.* Chicago: Open Court, 1997.

Altmann, Walter. *Luther and Liberation.* M. Solberg, trans. Minneapolis: Fortress, 1992.

Ammerman, Nancy T. "Bowling Together: Congregations and the American Civic Order," Seventeenth Annual University Lecture in Religion at Arizona State University, Feb. 26, 1996.

Anderson, Bernhard W., ed. *Creation in the Old Testament.* Philadelphia: Fortress, 1984.

Angelou, Maya. "Dialogue with Maya Angelou" in *Facing Evil: Light at the Core of Darkness.* P. Woodruff and H. A. Wilner, eds. LaSalle, Ill.: Open Court, 1988.

Angier, Natalie. "Evolutionary Necessity or Glorious Accident? Biologists Ponder the Self," *The New York Times* (April 22, 1997): B9–10.

Anselm. *Proslogion, a Scholastic Miscellany.* E. R. Fairweather, ed. Philadelphia: Westminster, 1966.

Arendt, Hannah. *The Human Condition.* Revised edition. New York: Penguin, 1994.

———. *Eichmann in Jerusalem: A Report on the Banality of Evil.* New York: Viking, 1964.

Ashbrook, James B. *Minding the Soul: Pastoral Counseling as Remembering.* Minneapolis: Fortress, 1996.

Audi, Robert and Wolterstorff, Nicholas. *Religion in the Public Square: The Place of Religious Convictions in Political Debate.* Point/Counterpoint series. Lanham, Md.: Rowan and Littlefield, 1997.

Augsburger, David W. *Pastoral Counseling across Cultures.* Philadelphia: Westminster, 1986.

Augustine. *Teaching Christianity (De Doctrina Christiana).* E. Hill, trans. *The Works of St. Augustine.* Brooklyn: New City Press, 1996.

Aulén, Gustav. *The Drama and the Symbols: A Book on Images of God and the Problems They Raise.* S. Linton, trans. Philadelphia: Fortress, 1970.

Baldwin, James. *Another Country*. New York: Dell, 1962.

Barbour, Ian. "Creation and Cosmology," *Cosmos as Creation: Theology and Science in Consonance*, 115–51. T. Peters, ed. Nashville: Abingdon, 1989.

———. *Religion in an Age of Science*. San Francisco: HarperCollins, 1990.

Barth, Karl. *Church Dogmatics*. Ed. G. W. Bromiley and T. F. Torrance. Edinburgh: T. and T. Clark, 1963–1977.

———. "Letter to East German Pastor," *The Christian Century* (March 25, 1959).

Baum, Gergory. "The Holocaust and Political Theology," in *The Holocaust as Interruption*, 34–42. D. Tracy and E. Schüssler Fiorenza, eds. Stichting Concilium and Edinburgh: T. and T. Clark, 1984.

Bayle, Pierre. *Historical and Critical Dictionary*. London: Harper, 1710.

Bednarowski, Mary Farrell. *New Religions and the Theological Imagination in America*. Bloomington: Indiana University Press, 1989.

Bellah, Robert et al. *Habits of the Heart*. Berkeley: University of California Press, 1985.

Bellah, Robert and Greenspahn, F., eds. *Uncivil Religion: Interreligious Hostility in America*. New York: Crossroad, 1987.

Bell-Fialkoff, Andrew. *Ethnic Cleansing*. New York: St. Martin's, 1996.

Benne, Robert. *The Paradoxical Vision: A Public Theology for the Twenty-first Century*. Minneapolis: Fortress, 1995.

Benson, Peter. *Effective Christian Education: A National Study of Protestant Congregations*. Minneapolis: Search Institute, 1987–1990.

Berger, Peter. *A Rumor of Angels: Modern Society and the Rediscovery of the Supernatural*. Garden City, N.Y.: Doubleday, 1969.

Bernstein, Richard. *Beyond Objectivism and Relativism*. Philadelphia: University of Pennsylvania Press, 1983.

Berry, Thomas and Swimme, Brian. *The Universe Story: From the Primordial Flaring Forth to the Ecozoic Era; A Celebration of the Unfolding of the Cosmos*. San Francisco: HarperSanFrancisco, 1992.

Berry, Wendell. *The Gift of a Good Land*. San Francisco: North Point, 1981.

Bloch, Ernst. *The Principle of Hope*. Cambridge: MIT Press, 1986.

———.*Atheism in Christianity*. J. T. Swann, trans. New York: Herder and Herder, 1972.

Bloom, Harold. *The American Religion: The Emergence of the Post-Christian Nation*. New York: Simon and Schuster, 1992.

Boesak, Allan. *Farewell to Innocence*. Maryknoll, N.Y.: Orbis, 1976.

Boisen, Anton T. *Religion in Crisis and Custom*. Reprint. Westport, Conn.: Greenwood, 1973.

Bonhoeffer, Dietrich. *The Cost of Discipleship*. R. H. Fuller, trans. New York: Macmillan, 1959.

————. *Ethics.* E. Bethge, ed. N. H. Smith, trans. New York: Macmillan, 1955, 1965.

————. *Letters and Papers from Prison.* E. Bethge, ed. New York: Macmillan, 1953, 1967.

Book of Concord. T. G. Tappert, trans. and ed. Philadelphia: Fortress, 1959.

Booth, Wayne C. *A Rhetoric of Irony.* Chicago: University of Chicago Press, 1974.

Borgmann, Albert. *Technology and the Character of Contemporary Life.* Chicago: University of Chicago Press, 1989.

Braaten, Carl E. "The Person of Jesus Christ," *Christian Dogmatics,* vol. 1, 465–569. C. E. Braaten and R. W. Jenson, eds. 2 vols. Philadelphia: Fortress, 1984.

Braaten, Carl E. and Jenson, Robert W., eds. *Union with Christ: The New Finnish Interpretation of Luther.* Grand Rapids: Eerdmans, 1998.

Bradley, Bill. *Time Present, Time Past.* New York: Knopf, 1996.

Brasher, Brenda. "Thoughts on the State of the Cyborg: On Technological Socialization and Its Link to the Religious Function of Popular Culture," *Journal of the American Academy of Religion* 59, no. 4 (fall 1996): 809–30.

Brauer, J. C., ed. *The Lively Experiment Continued.* Macon, Ga.: Mercer University Press, 1987.

Bosch, David J. *Transforming Mission: Paradigm Shifts in Theology of Mission.* Maryknoll, N.Y.: Orbis, 1991.

Bringle, Mary Louise. *Despair: Sickness or Sin? Hopelessness and Healing in Christian Life.* Nashville: Abingdon, 1990.

Brown, Alexandra R. *The Cross and Human Transformation: Paul's Apocalyptic Word in 1 Corinthians.* Minneapolis: Fortress, 1995.

Brown, Joanne Carlson and Bohn, Carole, eds. *Christianity, Patriarchy, and Abuse: A Feminist Critique.* New York: Pilgrim, 1989.

Browning, Don. *A Fundamental Practical Theology.* Minneapolis: Fortress, 1991.

Brueggemann, Walter. *Hopeful Imagination: Prophetic Voices in Exile.* Philadelphia: Fortress, 1986.

————. *Israel's Praise: Doxology against Idolatry and Ideology.* Philadelphia: Fortress, 1988.

————. "Response to J. Richard Middleton," *Harvard Theological Review* 87, no. 3 (1994): 278–89.

————. *A Social Reading of the Old Testament: Prophetic Approaches to Israel's Communal Life.* P. D. Miller, ed. Minneapolis: Fortress, 1994.

Bryant, David. *Faith and the Play of the Imagination.* Macon, Ga.: Mercer University Press, 1989.

Budick, S. and Iser, W. eds. *Languages of the Unsayable: The Play of Negativity in Literature and Literary Theory.* New York: Columbia University Press, 1989.

Burke, Kenneth. *A Rhetoric of Motives.* Berkeley: University of California Press, 1969.

Burtness, James. "As Though God Were Not Given: Barth, Bonhoeffer, and the *Finitum Capax Infiniti,*" *dialog* 19 (1980): 249–55.

Bussert, Joy. *Battered Women.* New York: Lutheran Church in America Division for Mission, 1986.

Cahoone, Lawrence. *The Dilemma of Modernity.* Albany: SUNY Press, 1988.

Calvin, John. *Institutes of the Christian Religion.* 2 vols. H. Beveridge, trans. Grand Rapids: Eerdmans, 1964.

Camus, Albert. *The Plague.* New York: Modern Library, 1948.

Capps, Donald. *The Depleted Self: Sin in a Narcissistic Age.* Minneapolis: Fortress, 1993.

———. *The Poet's Gift: Toward the Renewal of Pastoral Care.* Louisville: Westminster/John Knox Press, 1993.

Carter, Stephen. *The Culture of Disbelief: How American Law and Politics Trivialize Religious Devotion.* New York: Basic Books, 1993.

Case, Jonathan P. "Disputation and Interruption: Truth, Trinity and the Death of Christ in Pannenberg and Juengel." Unpuplished Th.D. dissertation at Luther Seminary, St. Paul, Minnesota, 1995.

Case-Winters, Anna. *God's Power: Traditional Understandings and Contemporary Challenges.* Louisville: Westminster/John Knox, 1990.

Chandler, Russell. *Racing toward 2001: The Forces Shaping America's Religious Future.* Grand Rapids: Zondervan; San Francisco: HarperSanFrancisco, 1992.

Chopp, Rebecca. "Feminism's Theological Pragmatics: A Social Naturalism of Women's Experience," *The Journal of Religion* 67, no. 2 (April 1987).

———. *The Power To Speak.* New York: Crossroad, 1989.

Clebsch, William. *American Religious Thought.* Chicago: University of Chicago Press, 1973.

Cobb, John B., Jr. *Christ in a Pluralistic Age.* Philadelphia: Westminster, 1975.

———. "Experience and Language." Unpublished paper available from the Center for Process Studies, Claremont, California.

———. "From Individualism to Persons in Community: A Postmodern Economic Theory" in *Sacred Interconnections: Postmodern Spirituality, Political Economy, and Art,* 123–42. D. R. Griffin, ed. Albany: SUNY Press, 1990.

———. "Two Types of Postmodernism: Deconstruction and Process," *Theology Today* 47, no. 2 (July 1990): 149–64.

Cobb, John B., Jr. and Birch, Charles. *The Liberation of Life: From the Cell to the Community.* Cambridge and New York: Cambridge University Press, 1981.

Cobb, John B., Jr. and Daly, Herman. *For the Common Good: Redirecting the Economy toward Community, the Environment, and a Sustainable Future.* Boston: Beacon, 1989, 1994.

Cohen, Arthur. *The Tremendum: A Theological Interpretation of the Holocaust.* New York: Crossroad, 1981.

Colapietro, Vincent M. "The Integral Self: Systematic Illusion or Inescapable Task?" *Listening* 5:3 (1990) 192–210.

Coleman, John A. "A Common Good Primer," *dialog* 34, no. 4 (fall 1995): 249–54.

Coles, Robert. *Children of Crisis.* Boston: Little, Brown, 1964.

————. *The Moral Intelligence of Children.* New York: Random House, 1997.

"A Collection of Responses from ELCA Academicians and Synodical Bishops to *The Church and Human Sexuality: A Lutheran Perspective.*" Chicago: Division for Church and Society, ELCA, 1994.

Come, Arnold B. *Kierkegaard as Humanist: Discovering My Self.* Montreal and Buffalo, N.Y.: McGill-Queen's University Press, 1995.

Connell, George. *To Be One Thing: Personal Unity in Kierkegaard's Thought.* Macon, Ga.: Mercer University Press, 1985.

Cousins, Norman. *Anatomy of an Illness as Perceived by the Patient.* New York: Norton, 1979.

Cox, Harvey. *Fire from Heaven: The Rise of Pentecostal Spirituality and the Reshaping of Religion in the Twenty-First Century.* Reading, Mass.: Addison-Wesley, 1995.

Creel, Richard. *Divine Impassibility.* Cambridge and New York: Cambridge University Press, 1986.

Csikzentmihalyi, Mihalyi. "Consciousness for the Twenty-first Century," *Zygon* 26, no. 1 (March 1991): 7–25.

————. *Flow: The Psychology of Optimal Experience.* New York: Harper, 1990.

Davidson, Donald. *Inquiries into Truth and Interpretation.* New York: Oxford University Press, 1984.

Dean, William. *The Religious Critic in American Culture.* Albany: SUNY Press, 1994.

De Beauvoir, Simone. *The Ethics of Ambiguity.* B. Frechtman, trans. New York: Philosophical Library, 1948.

Dempsey, Bernard W. *The Functional Economy.* Paramus, N.J.: Prentice Hall, 1958.

Derrida, Jacques. *The Gift of Death.* D. Willis, trans. Chicago: University of Chicago Press, 1995.

————. "How to Avoid Speaking Denials," *Languages of the Unsayable: The Play of Negativity in Literature and Literary Theory*, 3–70. S. Budick and W. Iser, eds. New York: Columbia University Press, 1989.

Descartes, René. "Meditations on First Philosophy," *Descartes: The Philosophical Writings*. 2 vols. J. Cottingham, R. Stoottff, and D. Murdoch, trans. New York: Cambridge University Press, 1984.

Dewey, John. *How We Think*. Boston: Heath, 1910.

Dillistone, Frederick. *The Christian Understanding of the Atonement*. Philadelphia: Westminster, 1968.

Ditmanson, Harold. *Grace in Experience and Theology*. Minneapolis: Augsburg, 1977.

Dols, William L., Jr. "The Church as Crucible for Transformation," *Jung's Challenge to Contemporary Religion*, 127–45. M. Stein and R. L. Moore, eds. Wilmette, Ill.: Chiron, 1987.

Donaldson, Mara. *Holy Places Are Dark Places: C. S. Lewis and Paul Ricoeur on Narrative Transformation*. Lanham, Md.: University Press of America, 1988.

Donne, John. *John Donne: The Complete English Poems*. New York: Knopf, 1991.

Driver, S. R. *The Book of Exodus*. Cambridge: Cambridge University Press, 1911.

Dulles, Avery. *Models of the Church*. Garden City, N.Y.: Doubleday, 1974.

Durning, Alan. *How Much Is Enough? The Consumer Society and the Future of the Earth*. New York: Norton, 1992.

————. *This Place on Earth: Home and the Practice of Permanence*. Seattle: Sasquatch, 1996.

Dykstra, Craig. *Vision and Character: A Christian Educator's Alternative to Kohlberg*. Mahwah, N.J.: Paulist, 1991.

Eigen, Michael. "Winnicott's Area of Freedom: The Uncompromisable," *Liminality and Transitional Phenomena*, 67–88. N. Schwartz-Salant and M. Stein, eds. Wilmette, Ill.: Chiron, 1991.

Eliade, Mircea. *Patterns in Contemporary Religion*. R. Sheed, trans. New York: Sheed and Ward, 1958.

Elshtain, Jean Bethke. *Augustine and the Limits of Politics*. Notre Dame, Ind.: Notre Dame University Press, 1985.

————. *Democracy on Trial*. New York: Basic Books, 1994.

Eslinger, Richard L. *Narrative Imagination: Preaching the Worlds That Shape Us*. Minneapolis: Fortress, 1995.

Farley, Edward. *Good and Evil: Interpreting a Human Condition*. Minneapolis: Fortress, 1991.

Farley, Margaret. *Personal Commitments: Beginning, Keeping, Changing.* San Francisco: Harper, 1986.

Ferreira, M. Jamie. *Transforming Vision: Imagination and Will in Kierkegaardian Faith.* Oxford: Clarendon; New York: Oxford University Press, 1991.

Feyerabend, Paul. *Against Method.* London: Humanities, 1975.

Fiddes, Paul. *The Creative Suffering of God.* Oxford: Clarendon, 1988.

Fiorenza, Elisabeth Schüssler. *In Memory of Her.* New York: Crossroad, 1986.

Fiorenza, Elisabeth Schüssler and Tracy, David, eds. *The Holocaust as Interruption.* Edinburgh: T. and T. Clark, 1984.

Fiorenza, Francis Schüssler. *Foundational Theology: Jesus and the Church.* New York: Crossroad, 1984.

Fisher, Roger and Ury, William. *Getting to Yes: Negotiating Agreement without Giving In.* Boston: Houghton Mifflin, 1981.

Foucault, Michel. *The Use of Pleasure.* R. Hurley, trans. New York: Pantheon, 1985.

Fowler, James. *Faithful Change: The Personal and Public Challenges of Modern Life.* Nashville: Abingdon, 1996.

Fox, Matthew. *Original Blessing: A Primer in Creation Spirituality.* Santa Fe: Bear and Co., 1983.

Fredrickson, David. "Worthily of the Gospel of Christ (Phil. 1:27): The Ecclesiastical Significance of Christ's Political Agency." Unpublished paper.

————. "Christ's Many Friends: The Presence of Jesus in 2 Corinthians 1-7," *Word and World Supplement Series* 3 (1997): 170.

Freedman, David Noel. "The Name of the God of Moses," *The Journal of Biblical Literature* 79 (1960): 151–56.

Fretheim, Terence E. *Exodus.* Louisville: John Knox, 1991.

————. *Genesis, The New Interpreter's Bible.* Nashville: Abingdon, 1994.

————. "The Plagues as Ecological Signs of Historical Disaster," *Journal of Biblical Literature* 110 (1991): 385–96.

————. "The Reclamation of Creation: Redemption and Law in Exodus," *Interpretation* 45 (1991): 354–65.

————. "Salvation in the Bible vs. Salvation in the Church," *Word and World* 13, no. 4 (fall 1993): 363–72.

————. *The Suffering of God: An Old Testament Perspective.* Philadelphia: Fortress, 1984.

Fretheim, Terence E. and Froehlich, Karlfried. *The Bible as Word of God in a Postmodern Age.* Minneapolis: Fortress, 1998.

Frost, Robert. *Robert Frost on Writing.* New Brunswick, N.J.: Rutgers University Press, 1973.

———. "Fire and Ice." *The Poetry of Robert Frost.* E. C. Lathem, ed. New York: Holt, Rinehart, & Winston, 1979.

Fukuyama, Francis. *The End of History and the Last Man.* New York: Free Press, 1992.

———. *Trust: The Social Virtues and the Creation of Prosperity.* New York: Free Press, 1996.

Gates, Bill. *The Road Ahead.* New York: Viking Penguin, 1995.

Gerrish, Brian B. "To the Unknown God," *The Journal of Religion* 53 (July 1973): 263–93.

Gibran, Kahlil. *The Prophet.* New York: Knopf, 1951.

Gilkey, Langdon. *Maker of Heaven and Earth.* Lanham, Md.: Doubleday, 1959, 1965.

———. "Plurality and Its Theological Implications," *The Myth of Christian Uniqueness: Toward a Pluralistic Theology of Religions,* 37–50. J. Hick and P. F. Knitter, eds. Maryknoll, N.Y.: Orbis, 1987.

———. *Reaping the Whirlwind: A Christian Interpretation of History.* New York: Seabury, 1976.

Gilligan, Carol. *In a Different Voice: Psychological Theory and Women's Development.* Cambridge: Harvard University Press, 1982.

Gilligan, Carol, Ward, Janie Victoria and Taylor, Jill McLean, eds. *Mapping the Moral Domain.* Cambridge: Harvard University Press, 1988.

Girard, René. *Deceit, Desire, and the Novel: Self and Other in Literary Structure.* Y. Freccero, trans. Baltimore: Johns Hopkins University Press, 1965, 1976.

Goetz, Ronald. "The Suffering God: The Rise of a New Orthodoxy," *The Christian Century* (April 16, 1986): 385–89.

Gonzalez, Justo. *Mañana: Christian Theology from a Hispanic Perspective.* Nashville: Abingdon, 1990.

Goot, Henry Vander, ed. *Creation and Method: Critical Essays on Christocentric Theology.* Washington, D.C.: University Press of America, 1981.

Gore, Al. *Earth in the Balance.* Boston: Houghton Mifflin, 1992.

Gould, Stephen. *Hen's Teeth and Horse's Toes.* New York: Norton, 1983.

Gouwens, David. *Kierkegaard as Religous Thinker.* Cambridge and New York: Cambridge University Press, 1996.

———. *Kierkegaard's Dialectic of the Imagination.* New York: Peter Lang, 1989.

Green, Garrett. *Imagining God: Theology and the Religious Imagination.* San Francisco: Harper, 1989.

Griffin, David. *Evil Revisited: Responses and Reconsiderations.* Albany: SUNY Press, 1991.

————. *God, Power and Evil: A Process Theodicy.* Philadelphia: Westminster, 1976; Washington, D.C.: University Press of America, 1990.

Griffin, David Ray, ed. *Physics and the Ultimate Significance of Time: Bohm, Prigogine, and Process Philosophy.* Albany: SUNY Press, 1986.

Grundmann, Walter. "The Christ Statements of the New Testament" in *Theological Dictionary of the New Testament,* G. Kittel, ed., G. W. Bromiley, trans. and ed. (Grand Rapids: Eerdmans, 1964–1976), vol. 9.

Guerriere, Daniel. *The Phenomenology of Truth Proper to Religion.* Albany: SUNY Press, 1990.

Gunn, Giles. *Thinking Across the American Grain.* Chicago: University of Chicago Press, 1992.

Gunton, Colin. "Atonement and the Project of Creation," *dialog* 35, no. 1 (winter 1996), 35–41.

Gustafson, James. *Can Ethics Be Christian?* Chicago: University of Chicago Press, 1975.

Gutiérrez, Gustavo. *On Job.* M. J. O'Connell, trans. Maryknoll, N.Y.: Orbis, 1987.

Hall, Douglas John. *God and Human Suffering: An Exercise in the Theology of the Cross.* Minneapolis: Augsburg, 1986.

————. *Imaging God: Dominion as Stewardship.* Grand Rapids: Eerdmans, 1986.

————. *The Steward: A Biblical Symbol Come of Age.* Grand Rapids: Eerdmans, 1990.

Hammarskjold, Dag. *Markings.* New York: Knopf, 1964.

Hammer, Margaret L. *Giving Birth: Reclaiming Biblical Metaphor for Pastoral Practice.* Louisville: Westminster John Knox, 1994.

Hampson, Daphne. "Luther on the Self: A Feminist Critique," *Word and World* 8, no. 4 (fall 1988): 334–42.

————. *Theology and Feminism.* Oxford and Cambridge, Mass.: Blackwell, 1990.

Handlin, Oscar. *The Uprooted.* 2d enl. ed. Boston: Little, Brown, 1951, 1973.

Handwerk, Gary. *Irony and Ethics in Narrative.* New Haven: Yale University Press, 1985.

Harding, Sandra. *The Science Question in Feminism.* Ithaca: Cornell University Press, 1986.

————. *Sex and Scientific Inquiry.* S. Harding and J. O'Barr, eds. Chicago: University of Chicago Press, 1987.

————. *Whose Science, Whose Knowledge: Thinking from Women's Lives.* Ithaca: Cornell University Press, 1991.

Hardy, Lee. *The Fabric of This World.* Grand Rapids: Eerdmans, 1990.

Hart, Ray. *Unfinished Man and the Imagination.* Herder and Herder, 1968.

Hartshorne, Charles. *The Divine Relativity.* New Haven: Yale University Press, 1948.

Hartshorne, Charles and Reese, William, eds. *Philosophers Speak of God.* Chicago: University of Chicago Press, 1953.

Harvey, Van. *Feuerbach and the Interpretation of Religion.* Cambridge: Cambridge University Press, 1995.

Hauerwas, Stanley and Willimon, William. *Resident Aliens: Life in the Christian Colony.* Nashville: Abingdon, 1989.

Havel, Vaclav. *Letters to Olga.* New York: Knopf, 1988.

————. *Foreign Affairs,* March–April, 1994.

Hawken, Paul. *The Ecology of Commerce: A Declaration of Sustainability.* New York: Harper, 1993.

Hawking, Stephen. *A Brief History of Time.* Toronto and New York: Bantam, 1988.

Hefner, Philip. "The Creation" in *Christian Dogmatics,* vol. 1, 265–358. C. E. Braaten and R. W. Jenson, eds. 2 vols. Philadelphia: Fortress, 1984.

————. *The Human Factor: Evolution, Culture, and Religion.* Minneapolis: Fortress, 1993.

Hegel, G. W. F. *The Phenomenology of Mind.* J. B. Baillie, trans. London: Macmillan, 1931.

Heinecken, Martin. "Criticism in the Church," *Certus Sermo,* ed. R. F. Marshall, J. R. Nelson, and R. G. Baker (March–May 1994): 47–49.

Henry, Patrick. "On Teaching Christianity: How to Make the Familiar Surprising," *Bulletin of the Council on the Study of Religion* 16, no. 1 (February 1985): 1–3.

Heschel, Abraham. *The Prophets.* 2 vols. New York: Harper, 1962.

Hill, Samuel S. "Born Again," *Dictionary of Christianity in America.* D. Reid, et al., eds. Downers Grove, Ill.: InterVarsity, 1990.

Hodgson, Peter. *Winds of the Spirit: A Constructive Christian Theology.* Louisville: Westminster John Knox, 1994.

Hofrenning, Daniel. *In Washington, But Not Of It.* Philadelphia: Temple University Press, 1995.

Hopkins, Gerard Manley. *The Oxford Poets: Gerard Manley Hopkins.* Catherine Phillips, ed. New York: Oxford University Press, 1986.

Horgan, John. *The End of Science.* New York: Abrams, 1996.

Hudson, Patricia O'Hanlon and O'Hanlon, William Hudson. *Rewriting Love Stories: Brief Marital Therapy.* New York: Norton, 1991.

Hughes, Robert. *American Visions: The Epic History of Art in America.* New York: Knopf, 1997.

Hultgren, Arland J. *Christ and His Benefits: Christology and Redemption in the New Testament.* Philadelphia: Fortress, 1987.

———. "Expectations of Prayer in the New Testament," 23–35, *A Primer on Prayer.* P. R. Sponheim, ed. Philadelphia: Fortress, 1988.

———. *The Rise of Normative Christianity.* Minneapolis: Fortress, 1994.

Hume, David. *Dialogues Concerning Natural Religion.* H. D. Aiken, ed. New York: Hafner, 1948, 1974.

———. *Inquiry Concerning the Principles of Morals.* Chicago: Open Court, 1953.

Hunsberger, George and Van Gelder, Craig, eds. *The Church between Gospel and Culture: The Emerging Mission in North America.* Grand Rapids: Eerdmans, 1996.

Inbody, Tyron L. *The Transforming God: An Interpretation of Suffering and Evil.* Louisville: Westminster John Knox, 1997.

Jacobson, Diane. "Strengths and Weaknesses of Wisdom/Sophia Talk," *A Reforming Church: Gift and Task,* 107–25. C. P. Lutz, ed. Minneapolis: Kirk House, 1995.

James, William. *Principles of Psychology.* New York: Dover, 1950.

Jenson, Robert. "The Triune God," *Christian Dogmatics,* 83–191. C. E. Braaten and R. W. Jenson, eds. Philadelphia: Fortress, 1984.

Johnson, Elizabeth. *She Who Is: The Mystery of God in Feminist Theological Discourse.* New York: Crossroad, 1992.

Johnson, Mark. *The Body in the Mind: The Bodily Basis of Meaning, Imagination, and Reason.* Chicago: University of Chicago Press, 1987.

———. *Moral Imagination: Implications of Cognitive Science for Ethics.* Chicago: University of Chicago Press, 1993.

Johnson, Mark, and Lakoff, George. *Metaphors We Live By.* Chicago: University of Chicago Press, 1980.

Jones, L. Gregory. *Embodying Forgiveness: A Theological Analysis.* Grand Rapids: Eerdmans, 1995.

Jordan, Judith V., with Kaplan, Alexandra; Miller, Jean Baker; Stiver, Irene P.; and Surrey, Janet L. *Women's Growth in Connection: Writings from the Stone Center.* New York: Guilford, 1991.

Jorstad, Erling. *Popular Religion in America: The Evangelical Voice.* Westport, Conn.: Greenwood, 1993.

Jungel, Eberhard. *God as the Mystery of the World.* D. L. Guder, trans. Grand Rapids: Eerdmans, 1983.

———. "The Truth of Life: Observations on Truth as the Interruption of the Continuity of Life," 231–36, *Creation, Christ and Culture: Studies in Honour of T. F. Torrance.* R. W. A. McKinney, ed. Edinburgh: T. and T. Clark, 1976.

Juntunen, Sammeli. "Luther and Metaphysics: What Is the Structure of Being According to Luther?", *Union with Christ: The New Finnish Interpretation of Luther,* C. E. Braaten and R. W. Jerson, eds. Grand Rapids: Eerdmans, 1998.

Kanpol, Barry. "Critical Pedagogy and Liberation Theology: Borders for a Transformative Agenda," *Educational Theory* 46, no. 1 (winter 1996): 105–17.

Kaplan, Robert D. "The Coming Anarchy," *The Atlantic Monthly* (February 1994): 44–76.

Katz, Jon. *Virtuous Reality.* New York: Random House, 1996.

Kaufman, Gordon. *The Theological Imagination.* Philadelphia: Westminster, 1981.

Kearney, Richard. *The Wake of Imagination: Toward a Postmodern Culture.* Minneapolis: University of Minnesota Press, 1988.

Kegan, Robert. *The Evolving Self: Problem and Process in Human Development.* Cambridge: Harvard University Press, 1987.

———. *In over Our Heads: The Mental Demands of Modern Life.* Cambridge: Harvard University Press, 1994.

Keifert, Patrick. *Welcoming the Stranger: A Public Theology of Worship and Evangelism.* Minneapolis: Fortress, 1991.

Keller, Catherine. *From a Broken Web: Separation, Sexism, and Self.* Boston: Beacon, 1986.

———. "'To Illuminate Your Trace': Self in Late Modern Feminist Theology," *Listening* 5, no. 3 (1990).

Kermode, Frank. *The Sense of an Ending: Studies in the Theory of Fiction.* Oxford: Oxford University Press, 1968.

Kierkegaard, Søren. *Kierkegaard's Writings.* H. V. Hong, ed. Princeton: Princeton University Press.

Christian Discourses, XVII (1994)

The Concept of Anxiety, VIII, trans. R. Thomte (1980)

Concluding Unscientific Postscript to the Philosophical Fragments, XII; 1, 2 (1992)

Either/Or, III and IV, trans. H. V. and E. H. Hong (1987)

Philosophical Fragments, VII (1985)

Practice in Christianity, XX (1985)

The Sickness unto Death, XIX, trans. H. V. and E. H. Hong (1980)

Upbuilding Discourses in Various Spirits, XV (1993)

———. *Søren Kierkegaard's Journals and Papers.* 6 vols. H. V. and E. H. Hong, eds. Bloomington: Indiana University Press, 1970.

———. *Purity of Heart Is to Will One Thing.* D. V. Steere, trans. New York: Harper, 1956.

————. *On Authority and Revelation: The Book on Adler.* W. Lowrie, trans. Princeton: Princeton University Press, 1955.

————. *Concluding Unscientific Postscript to the Philosophical Fragments.* D. F. Swenson and W. Lowrie, eds. Princeton: Princeton University Press, 1944.

————. *Philosophical Fragments or a Fragment of Philosophy.* D. F. Swenson, trans. Princeton: Princeton University Press, 1936.

————. *Søren Kierkegaard's Papirer.* 11 vols. P. A. Heiberg, and V. Kuhr, eds. Copenhagen: Gyldendals, 1909-48.

————. *Samlede Vaerker.* A. B. Drachmann, J. L. Heiberg, and H. O. Lange, eds. Copenhagen: Guldendals, 1901–1936.

King, Martin Luther, Jr. *Strength to Love.* Philadelphia: Fortress, 1963.

Kitamori, Kazoh. *Theology of the Pain of God.* Louisville: John Knox, 1965.

Knutsen, Mary. "The Holocaust in Theology and Philosophy: The Question of Truth," *The Holocaust as Interruption,* 67–74. E. Schussler Fiorenza and D. Tracy, eds. Edinburgh: T. and T. Clark, 1984.

Koenig, John. *New Testament Hospitality: Partnership with Strangers as Promise and Mission.* Philadelphia: Fortress, 1985.

Kolden, Marc. *Called by the Gospel.* Minneapolis: Augsburg, 1983.

Koyama, Kosuke. "How Many Languages Does God Speak?", *Cross Currents* (summer 1996): 178–86.

Kristeva, Julia. *Black Sun.* L. Roudiec, trans. New York: Columbia University Press, 1989.

Kuhn, Thomas. *The Structure of Scientific Revolutions.* 2nd enl. ed. Chicago: University of Chicago Press, 1970.

Kundera, Milan. *The Unbearable Lightness of Being.* M. H. Heim, trans. New York: Harper, 1985.

LaCugna, Catherine. *God for Us: The Trinity and Christian Life.* San Francisco: Harper, 1991.

Land, George T. L. *Grow or Die: The Unifying Principle of Transformation.* New York: New York: Dell, 1973.

Land, George and Jarman, Beth. *Breakpoint and Beyond.* New York: Harper, 1992.

Lasch, Christopher. *The Revolt of the Elites and the Betrayal of Democracy.* New York: Norton, 1995.

Lazareth, William Henry and Rasolondraibe, Peri. *Lutheran Identity and Mission: Evangelical and Evangelistic?* Minneapolis; Fortress, 1994.

Lebeaux, Richard. *Thoreau's Seasons.* Amherst: University of Massachusetts Press, 1984.

Lee, Jung Young. *Marginality: The Key to Multicultural Theology.* Minneapolis: Fortress, 1995.

Leith, Brian. *The Descent of Darwin.* London: Collins, 1982.

Lerner, Harriet. *The Dance of Anger: A Woman's Guide to Changing the Patterns of Intimate Relationships*. New York: Harper, 1985.

Levertov, Denise. *Candles in Babylon*. New York: New Directions, 1982.

———. *The Poet in the World*. New York: New Directions, 1973, 1982.

Levinas, Emmanuel. *Difficult Freedom: Essays on Judaism*. S. Hand, trans. Baltimore: Johns Hopkins University Press, 1990.

———. *Totality and Infinity: An Essay on Exteriority*. A. Linguis, trans. Pittsburgh: Dusquesne University Press, 1969.

Lewis, C. S. *An Experiment in Criticism*. Cambridge: Cambridge University Press, 1961.

———. *Surprised by Joy*. New York: Harcourt, Brace, 1955.

———. *Till We Have Faces*. Grand Rapids: Eerdmans, 1956.

Liddell, Henry George and Scott, Robert. *A Greek-English Lexicon*. Oxford: Clarendon, 1843, 1983.

Lifton, Robert Jay. *The Broken Connection*. New York: Simon & Schuster, 1979.

———. *Death in Life: Survivors of Hiroshima*. New York: Random House, 1967.

———. *The Life of the Self*. New York: Basic Books, 1983.

———. *The Nazi Doctors: Medical Killing and the Psychology of Genocide*. New York: Basic Books, 1986.

Lind, Michael. *The Next American Nation*. New York: Free Press, 1995.

Lindbeck, George A. *The Nature of Doctrine: Religion and Theology in a Postliberal Age*. Philadelphia: Westminster, 1984.

Lindley, David. *The End of Physics*. New York: Basic Books, 1994.

Lippy, Charles H. *Modern American Popular Religion: A Critical Assessment and Annotated Bibliography*. Westport, Conn.: Greenwood, 1996.

Little, David. "Calvin and the Prospects for a Christian Theory of Natural Law," *Norm and Context in Christian Ethics,* 175–98. G. Outka and P. Ramsey, eds. New York: Scribner's, 1968.

Lodahl, Michael E. *Shekhinah Spirit: Divine Presence in Jewish and Christian Religion*. Mawah, N.J.: Paulist, 1992.

Loder, James E. *The Transforming Moment: Understanding Convictional Experiences*. San Francisco: Harper, 1981.

Lonergan, Anne and Richards, Caroline, eds. *Thomas Berry and the New Cosmology*. Mystic, Conn.: Twenty-third Publications, 1987.

Long, Charles H. *Alpha: The Myths of Creation*. New York: Braziller, 1963.

Louw, Johannes P. and Nida, Eugene A. *A Greek-English Lexicon of the New Testament Based on Semantic Domains*. 2 vols. New York: United Bible Societies, 1988.

Lowe, Walter. *Theology and Difference: The Wound of Reason*. Bloomington: Indiana University Press, 1993.

Luther, Martin. *Martin Luther's Basic Theological Writings.* T. F. Lull, ed. Minneapolis: Fortress, 1989.

Theses for the Heidelberg Disputation (1518).

Two Kinds of Righteousness (1519).

—. *Luther's Works.* J. Pelikan and H. T. Lehmann, eds. St. Louis: Concordia; Philadelphia: Fortress, 1958–1972.

The Bondage of the Will (1525). vol. 33. Philadelphia: Fortress, 1972.

John's Gospel (1537). vol. 22. St. Louis: Concordia, 1957.

The Keys (1530) vol. 40. Philadelphia: Fortress, 1958.

The Psalms (1519-21). vol. 14. St. Louis: Concordia, 1958.

Table Talk (1531). vol. 54. Philadelphia: Fortress, 1967.

Lutheran Book of Worship. Minneapolis: Augsburg, 1978.

Lutz, Charles P., ed. *A Reforming Church: Gift and Task.* Minneapolis: Kirk House, 1995.

Lykken, David. "Happiness Is a Stochastic Phenomenon," *Psychological Science* 7, no. 3 (May 1996): 186–89.

MacIntyre, Alasdair. *After Virtue: A Study in Moral Theory.* Notre Dame, Ind.: Notre Dame University Press, 1981.

—. *Three Rival Theories of Moral Inquiry.* Notre Dame, Ind.: Notre Dame University Press, 1990.

Mahn, Jason. "To Dance with Nonbeing: A Study in Alcoholism, Shame, and the Self." Unpublished seminar paper. May, 1996.

Malcolm, Lois. "The Gospel and Feminism: A Proposal for Lutheran Dogmatics," *Word and World* 15, no. 3 (summer 1995): 290–98.

Malony, Newton and Southard, Samuel, ed. *Handbook of Religious Conversion.* Birmingham: Religious Education, 1992.

Marty, Martin E. *The Irony of It All.* Modern American Religion. Chicago: University of Chicago Press, 1986.

—. *Pilgrims in Their Own Land.* Boston: Little, Brown, 1984.

—. *The Public Church.* New York: Crossroad, 1981.

Marty, Martin E. and Appleby, Scott. *Accounting for Fundamentalism: The Dynamic Character of Movements.* The Fundamentalism Project, vol. 4. Chicago: University of Chicago Press, 1994.

—. *The Glory and the Power: The Fundamentalist Challenge to the Modern World.* Boston: Beacon, 1992.

Marx, Karl. "Theses on Feuerbach," *Writings of the Young Marx on Philosophy and Society,* 400–403. L. D. Easton and K. H. Guddat, eds. and trans. Garden City, N.Y.: Doubleday Anchor, 1967.

Matustik, Martin J. and Westphal, Merold. *Kierkegaard in Post/Modernity.* Bloomington: Indiana University Press, 1995.

McKibben, Bill. *The End of Nature.* New York: Random House, 1989.

Mead, Loren B. *The Once and Future Church.* Washington, D.C.: Alban Institute, 1991.

—————. *Transforming Congregations for the Future.* Washington, D.C.: Alban Institute, 1994.

Mead, Sidney E. *The Lively Experiment.* New York: Harper, 1963.

—————. "Reinterpretation in American Church History," *The Lively Experiment Continued.* J. C. Brauer, ed. Macon, Ga.: Mercer University Press, 1987.

Meltzoff, Andrew N. "Infant Imitation and Memory: Nine-Month-Olds in Immediate and Deferred Tests," *Child Development* 59: 217–25.

—————. "Imitation of Televised Models by Infants," *Child Development* 59: 1221–29.

—————. "Infant Imitation after a 1 Week Delay," *Developmental Psychology* 24: 470–76.

Merton, Thomas. *Raids on the Unspeakable.* New York: New Directions, 1966.

Metz, Johannes B. *Faith in History and Society: Toward a Practical Fundamental Theology.* D. Smith, trans. New York: Seabury, 1980.

Middleton, J. Richard. "Is Creation Theology Inherently Conservative? A Dialogue with Walter Brueggemann," *Harvard Theological Review* 87, no. 3 (1994): 257–77.

Miller, Jean Baker. "The Development of Women's Sense of Self," 11–26, in Judith V. Jordan, et al., eds. *Women's Growth in Connection.* New York: Guilford, 1991.

Miller, Perry. *Errand into the Wilderness.* Cambridge: Harvard University Press, 1956.

Minnich, Elizabeth Kamarck. *Transforming Knowledge.* Philadelphia: Temple University Press, 1990.

Moltmann, Jürgen. *The Crucified God.* R. A. Wilson and J. Bowden, trans. New York: Harper, 1974.

—————. *God in Creation: A New Theology of Creation and the Spirit of God.* M. Kohl, trans. Minneapolis: Fortress, 1993.

Mooney, Edward. *Selves in Discord and Resolve.* New York: Routledge, 1996.

Moseley, Romney. *Becoming a Self Before God: Critical Transformations.* Nashville: Abingdon, 1991.

Muhlenberg, Ekkehard. "*Synergia* and Justification by Faith," *Discord, Dialogue, and Concord: Studies in the Lutheran Reformation's Formula of Concord.* 15–37. L. W. Spitz and W. Lohff, eds. Philadelphia: Fortress, 1977.

Muller-Fahrenholz, Geiko. *God's Spirit: Transforming a World in Crisis.* J. Cumming, trans. New York: Continuum, 1995.

Murphy, Nancey. "Divine Action in the Natural Order: Buridan's Ass and Schrodinger's Cat," *Chaos and Complexity: Scientific Perspectives on Divine Action,* 325–58. R. J. Russell, N. Murphy, and A. Peacocke, eds. Berkeley: Vatican Observatory Publications, 1995.

Nagel, Thomas. *The View From Nowhere.* New York: Oxford University Press, 1986.

Neuhaus, Richard John. *The Naked Public Square: Religion and Democracy in America.* Grand Rapids: Eerdmans, 1984.

Neville, Robert Cummings. *Recovery of the Measure: Interpretation and Nature.* Albany: SUNY Press, 1989.

Newbigin, Lesslie. *The Gospel in a Pluralist Society.* Grand Rapids: Eerdmans, 1989.

Niebuhr, Reinhold. *The Nature and Destiny of Man.* 2 vols. New York: Scribner's, 1941, 1964.

Nietzsche, Friedrich. *Beyond Good and Evil: Prelude to a Philosophy of the Future.* W. Kaufmann, trans. New York: Random House, 1966.

Nohrnberg, James. *Like unto Moses: The Constituting of an Interruption.* Bloomington: Indiana University Press, 1995.

Nussbaum, Martha. *The Fragility of Goodness: Luck and Ethics in Greek Tragedy and Philosophy.* Cambridge and New York: Cambridge University Press, 1986.

————. *The Therapy of Desire: Theory and Practice in Hellenistic Ethics.* Princeton: Princeton University Press, 1994.

Ochs, Carol. *Song of the Self: Biblical Spirituality and Human Holiness.* Valley Forge, Pa.: Trinity Press International, 1994.

O'Connor, Daniel and Oakley, Francis. *Creation: The Impact of an Idea.* Cambridge: Cambridge University Press, 1964.

Oden, Thomas C. *The Structure of Awareness.* Nashville: Abingdon, 1969.

Ogletree, Thomas. *Hospitality to the Stranger.* Philadelphia: Fortress, 1985.

O'Leary, Stephen D. "Cyberspace as Sacred Space," *Journal of the American Academy of Religion* 44, no. 4 (winter 1996): 781–808.

Oliver, Mary. *New and Selected Poems.* Boston: Beacon, 1992.

Olson, Dennis. "God the Creator: Bible, Creation, Vocation," *dialog* 36, no. 3 (summer 1997).

Ormerod, Paul. *The Death of Economics.* New York: St. Martin's, 1995.

Otto, Rudolf. *The Idea of the Holy: An Inquiry into the Non-Rational Factor in the Idea of the Divine and its Relation to the Rational.* J. W. Harvey, trans. New York: Oxford University Press, 1958.

Oughourlian, Jean-Michel. *The Puppet of Desire: The Psychology of Hysteria, Possession, and Hypnosis.* E. Webb, trans. Palo Alto: Stanford University Press, 1991.

Outka, Gene. *Agape: An Ethical Analysis.* New Haven: Yale University Press, 1972.

Outler, Albert. *Psychotherapy and the Christian Message.* New York: Harper, 1954.

Owen, H. P. *Concepts of Deity.* New York: Herder and Herder, 1971.

Page, Ruth. *Ambiguity and the Presence of God.* London: SCM, 1985.
Palmer, Parker. *The Company of Strangers.* New York: Crossroad, 1985.
———. *Going Public.* Washington, D.C.: Alban Institute, 1980.
Pannenberg, Wolfhart. *Anthropology in Theological Perspective.* M. J. O'Connell, trans. Philadelphia: Westminster, 1985.
———. *Systematic Theology.* G. Bromiley, trans. 3 vols. Grand Rapids: Eerdmans, 1991–1997.
Parks, Sharon and Parks, Laurent, with Keen, Cheryl and Keen, James. *Common Fire: Lives of Commitment in a Complex World.* Boston: Beacon, 1996.
Pasewark, Kyle A. *A Theology of Power: Being Beyond Domination.* Minneapolis: Fortress, 1993.
Paulson, Steven. "The Wrath of God," *dialog* 33, no. 4 (fall 1994): 245–51.
Peirce, Charles Saunders. "Pragmatism and Pragmaticism." *The Collected Papers of Charles Saunders Peirce.* C. Hartshorne and P. Weiss, eds. Cambridge: Harvard University Press, 1934.
Pelikan, Jaroslav. *Jesus through the Centuries.* New Haven: Yale University Press, 1985.
Peters, Ted. *The Cosmic Self.* San Francisco: Harper, 1991.
———. *God—The World's Future: Systematic Theology for a Postmodern Era.* Minneapolis: Fortress, 1992.
———. "Should We Patent God's Creation?", *dialog* 35, no. 2 (spring 1996): 117–32.
———. "Wholeness in Salvation and Healing," *Lutheran Quarterly* 5 (1991): 297–314.
Peura, Simo. "Christ as Favor and Gift: The Challenge of Luther's Understanding of Justification," *Union with Christ: The New Finnish Interpretation of Luther.* C. E. Braaten and R. W. Jenson, eds. Grand Rapids: Eerdmans, 1998.
Pinnock, Clark H. "God's Sovereignty in Today's World," *Theology Today* 53, no. 1 (April 1996): 15–21.
Placher, William C. *The Domestication of Transcendence: How Modern Thinking about God Went Wrong.* Louisville: Westminster/John Knox, 1996.
———. *A History of Christian Theology.* Philadelphia: Westminster, 1983.
———. *Narratives of a Vulnerable God: Christ, Theology, and Scripture.* Louisville: Westminster/John Knox Press, 1994.
———. *Unapologetic Theology: A Christian Voice in a Pluralistic Conversation.* Louisville: Westminster/John Knox Press, 1989.
Pohl, Christine. "Welcoming Strangers: A Social Ethical Study of Hospitality in Selected Expressions of the Christian Tradition." Unpublished Ph.D. dissertation, Emory University, Atlanta, Georgia, 1993.

Polanyi, Michael. *Personal Knowledge: Towards a Post-Critical Philosophy.* Chicago: University of Chicago Press, 1958.

Porteus, N. "Man, Nature of, in the OT," *The Interpreter's Dictionary of the Bible.* Nashville: Abingdon, 1962.

Prenter, Regin. *Creation and Redemption.* T. I. Jensen, trans. Philadelphia: Fortress, 1967.

Prestige, G. L. *God in Patristic Thought.* London: SPCK, 1964.

Putnam, Hilary. *The Many Faces of Realism.* LaSalle, Ill.: Open Court, 1987.

Putnam, Robert. "Bowling Alone: America's Declining Social Capital," *Journal of Democracy* 6 (1995): 65–78.

Rajchmann, J. and West, C., eds. *Post-Analytic Philosophy.* New York: Columbia University Press, 1985.

Ramsey, Paul. *Basic Christian Ethics.* Chicago: University of Chicago Press, 1950.

Rasmussen Larry. *Moral Fragments and Moral Community: A Proposal for Church in Society.* Minneapolis: Fortress, 1993.

Rice, Mabel and Woodsmall, Linda. "Lessons from Television: Children's Word Learning When Viewing," *Child Development* 59:420–29.

Richardson, Herbert. *Toward an American Theology.* New York: Harper and Row, 1967.

Ricoeur, Paul. *History and Truth.* Chicago: Northwestern University Press, 1965.

———. *Paul Ricoeur on Biblical Hermeneutics.* J. D. Crossan, ed. Semeia 4. Missoula, Mont.: Scholars Press, 1975.

———. *The Symbolism of Evil.* E. Buchanan, trans. Boston: Beacon, 1967.

———. *Time and Narrative.* 3 vols. K. McLaughlin and D. Pellauer, trans. Chicago: University of Chicago Press, 1984–1988.

Ricoeur, Paul and MacIntyre, Alasdair. *The Religious Significance of Atheism.* New York: Columbia University Press, 1969.

Robinson, Jacob. *And the Crooked Shall Be Made Straight: The Eichmann Trial, the Jewish Catastrophe, and Hannah Arendt's Narrative.* New York: Macmillan, 1965.

Rogers, William. "Order and Chaos in Psychopathology and Ontology: A Challenge to Traditional Correlations of Order to Mental Health and Ultimate Reality, and of Chaos to Mental Illness and Alienation," *The Dialogue between Theology and Psychology,* 249–62. P. Homans, ed. Chicago: University of Chicago Press, 1968.

Rorty, Richard. *Contingency, Irony, and Solidarity.* Cambridge and New York: Cambridge University Press, 1989.

———. *Philosophy and the Mirror of Nature.* Princeton: Princeton University Press, 1979.

―――. "The Priority of Democracy to Philosophy," *The Virginia Statute for Religious Freedom*, 257–82. M. D. Peterson and R. C. Vaughan, eds. Cambridge and New York: Cambridge University Press, 1988.

―――. "Solidarity or Objectivity," *Post-Analytic Philosophy*. J. Rajchmann and C. West, eds. New York: Columbia University Press, 1985.

Ruether, Rosemary Radford. "Is Feminism the End of Christianity? A Critique of Daphne Hampson's *Theology and Feminism*," *Scottish Journal of Theology* 43, no. 3.

Russell, Robert John. "Contingency in Physics and Cosmology: A Critique of the Theology of Wolfhart Pannenberg," *Zygon* vol. 23, 23–43.

―――. "Does Creation Have a Beginning?" *dialog* 36, no. 3 (summer 1997): 180–89.

―――. "Does the 'God Who Acts' Really Act? New Approaches to Divine Action in Light of Science," *Theology Today* 54, no. 1 (April 1997): 43–65.

Russell, Robert John; Murphy, Nancey; and Peacocke, Arthur R., eds. *Chaos and Complexity: Scientific Perspectives on Divine Action*. Berkeley: Vatican Observatory, 1995.

Saiving, Valerie. "The Human Situation: A Feminine View," *Womanspirit Rising: A Feminist Reader in Religion*. C. Christ and J. Plaskow, eds. San Francisco: Harper, 1979.

Sandel, Michael. "America's Search for a New Public Philosophy," *The Atlantic Monthly* (March 1996): 57–74.

―――. *Liberalism and the Limits of Justice*. Cambridge: Cambridge University Press, 1982.

Sanders, Cheryl J. *Empowerment Ethics for a Liberated People: A Path to African American Social Transformation*. Minneapolis: Fortress, 1995.

Santmire, H. Paul. "Toward a Christology of Nature," *dialog* 34, no. 4 (fall 1995): 270–80.

―――. *The Travail of Nature: The Ambiguous Ecological Promise of Christian Theology*. Philadelphia: Fortress, 1985.

Sarna, Nahum M. *JPS Commentary: Genesis*. Philadelphia: Jewish Publication Society, 1989.

Schleiermacher, Friedrich. *The Christian Faith*. Eng. trans. of 2d German ed. H. R. Mackintosh and J. S. Stewart, eds. Edinburgh: T. and T. Clark, 1928.

Schmid, Heinrich. *The Doctrinal Theology of the Evangelical Lutheran Church*. 2d English ed. C. A. Hay and H. E. Jacobs, trans. Philadelphia: Lutheran Publication Society, 1899.

Schweiker, William. *Mimetic Reflections*. New York: Fordham University Press, 1990.

Seidler, Victor J. *The Moral Limits of Modernity: Love, Inequality, and Oppression.* New York: St. Martin's, 1991.

Seligmann, Martin, E. P. *What You Can Change and What You Can't.* New York: Knopf, 1994.

Selznick, Philip. *The Moral Commonwealth.* Berkeley: University of California Press, 1992.

Shapiro, Susan. "Hearing the Testimony of Radical Negation," *The Holocaust as Interruption,* 3–10. E. Schussler Fiorenza and D. Tracy, eds. Edinburgh: T. and T. Clark, 1984.

Sherry, Patrick. *Spirit and Beauty: An Introduction to Theological Aesthetics.* Oxford: Clarendon, 1992.

Siirala, Aarne. *Divine Humanness.* T. A. Kantonen, trans. Philadelphia: Fortress, 1970.

Silko, Leslie Marmon. *Ceremony.* New York: Viking, 1977.

Sittler, Joseph. *Gravity and Grace.* Minneapolis: Augsburg, 1986.

Soelle, Dorothee. *Suffering.* E. R. Kalin, trans. Philadelphia: Fortress, 1975.

———. *Revolutionary Patience.* R. and R. Kimber, trans. (Maryknoll, N.Y.: Orbis, 1977.

Solomon, Robert C. *Continental Philosophy since 1750: The Rise and Fall of the Self.* Oxford: Oxford University Press, 1988.

———. *The Passions: The Myth and Nature of Human Emotion.* Notre Dame, Ind.: Notre Dame University Press, 1983.

Solzhenitsyn, Alexandr. *A World Split Apart.* New York: Harper, 1978.

Spector, Janet D. *What This Awl Means: Feminist Archeology at a Wahpeton Dakota Village.* St. Paul: Minnesota Historical Society, 1993.

Spero, Moshe Halevi. *Religious Objects as Psychological Structures: A Critical Integration of Object Relations Theory, Psychotherapy, and Judaism.* Chicago: University of Chicago Press, 1992.

Sponheim, Paul R. "Sin and Evil," *Christian Dogmatics*, vol. 1, 359–464. C. E. Braaten and R. W. Jenson, eds. 2 vols. Philadelphia: Fortress, 1984.

———. *God: The Question and the Quest.* Philadelphia: Fortress, 1985.

———. *Faith and the Other: A Relational Theology.* Minneapolis: Fortress, 1993.

———. "On Being and Becoming before God: A Response to Daphne Hampson," *Word and World* 15, no. 3 (summer 1995): 332–41.

———. "'The Other Is Given': Religion, War and Peace:" *Word and World* 15, no. 4 (fall 1995): 428–42.

———. "To Claim and to Test: Doing Theology in This Time and Place," 74–92, in *A Reforming Church: Gift and Task.* C. P. Lutz, ed. Minneapolis: Kirk House, 1995.

Stafford, William. "Bi-Focal," quoted in Capps, Donald, *The Poet's Gift: Toward the Renewal of Pastoral Care.* Louisville: Westminster/John Knox, 1993.

Stier, Oren Baruch. "Virtual Memories: Mediating the Holocaust at the Simon Wiesenthal Center's *Beit Hashoah* Museum of Tolerance," *Journal of the American Academy of Religion* 64, no. 4 (winter 1996): 831–51.

Stortz, Martha Ellen. "Beyond Justice: Friendship in the City," *Word and World* 14, no. 4 (fall 1994): 409–18.

Strandjord, Jonathan P. "The Politics and Ethics of Beauty: A Theological Reconsideration of Conscience with the Aid of Whitehead and Levinas." Unpublished Ph.D. dissertation, Vanderbilt University, 1996.

Styron, William. *Darkness Visible: A Memoir of Madness.* New York: Random House, 1990.

Suchocki, Marjorie Hewitt. *The Fall to Violence: Original Sin in Relational Theology.* New York: Continuum, 1994.

———. *In God's Presence: Theological Reflections on Prayer.* St. Louis: Chalice, 1996.

Sullivan, Lawrence. "Coming to Our Senses: Religious Studies in the Academy," *Journal of the American Academy of Religion* 66, no. 1 (spring 1998): 1–12.

Tanner, Kathryn. "Creation, the Environmental Crisis, and Ecological Justice," *Reconstructing Christian Theology,* 99–123. R. Chopp and M. L. Taylor, eds. Minneapolis: Fortress, 1994.

Taylor, Charles. "The Politics of Recognition," *Multiculturalism and the Politics of Recognition.* A. Gutman, ed. Princeton: Princeton University Press, 1992.

———. *Sources of the Self: The Making of the Modern Identity.* Cambridge: Harvard University Press, 1989.

Taylor, Daniel. *The Myth of Certainty: The Reflective Christian and the Myth of Commitment.* Waco, Tex.: Jarrell Word, 1986.

Taylor, Mark C. "Denegating God," *Critical Inquiry* (summer 1994): 592–610.

———. *Erring: A Postmodern A/Theology.* Chicago: University of Chicago Press, 1984.

———. *Nots.* Chicago: University of Chicago Press, 1993.

———. *Tears.* Albany: SUNY Press, 1990.

Taylor, Mark Kline. *Remembering Esperanza: A Cultural-Political Theology for North American Praxis.* Maryknoll, N.Y.: Orbis, 1990.

Tellegen, Auke. "Report on Twins Study," *Journal of Personality and Social Psychology* 54, no. 6 (1988): 1–39.

Thiemann, Ronald F. *Religion in Public Life: A Dilemma for Democracy.* Washington, D.C.: Georgetown University Press, 1996.

Thistlethwaite, Susan Brooks and Engel, Mary Potter, eds. *Lift Every Voice: Constructing Christian Theologies from the Underside.* New York: Harper, 1990.

Thomsen, Mark W. *The Word and Way of the Cross: Christian Witness Among Muslim and Buddhist People.* Chicago: Division for Global Mission, ELCA, 1993.

Thoreau, Henry David. "Walden." *Henry David Thoreau.* New York: Library of America, 1985.

Tilby, Angela. *Soul: God, Self and the New Cosmology.* New York: Doubleday, 1992.

Tillich, Paul. *The Shaking of the Foundations.* New York: Scribner's, 1948.

————. *Systematic Theology.* 3 vols. Chicago: University of Chicago Press, 1951–1963.

Toulmin, Stephen. *Cosmopolis: The Hidden Agenda of Modernity.* New York: Free Press, 1990.

————. *The Return to Cosmology: Postmodern Science and the Theology of Nature.* Berkeley: University of California Press, 1982.

Tracy, David. "The Hidden God: The Divine Other of Liberation," *Cross Currents* (spring 1996): 5–15.

————. *Plurality and Ambiguity.* San Francisco: Harper, 1987.

Trigo, Pedro. *Creation and History.* R. R. Barr, trans. Maryknoll, N.Y.: Orbis, 1991.

Ulanov, Ann and Ulanov, Barry. *The Healing Imagination: The Meeting of Psyche and Soul.* New York: Paulist, 1991.

————. *Primary Speech: A Psychology of Prayer.* Louisville: John Knox, 1992.

Ulanov, Ann Belford. "What Do We Think People Are Doing When They Pray?", *Anglican Theological Review* 60 (1978).

von Rad, Gerhard. *Old Testament Theology.* 2 vols. D. M. G. Stalker, trans. New York: Harper, 1965.

Walker, Alice. "Only Justice Can Stop a Curse," *In Search of Our Mothers' Gardens,* 338–42. San Diego: Harcourt Brace, 1983.

Wallis, Jim. *The Soul of Politics.* New York: New Press, 1994.

Walzer, Michael. *Exodus and Revolution.* New York: Basic Books, 1985.

————. *Interpretation and Social Criticism.* Cambridge: Harvard University Press, 1987.

————. *Thick and Thin: Moral Argument at Home and Abroad.* Notre Dame, Ind.: Notre Dame University, 1994.

Ward, Keith. *Rational Theology and the Creativity of God.* New York: Pilgrim, 1982.

Weatherhead, Leslie. *The Will of God.* Nashville: Abingdon, 1944, 1972.

Webb, Stephen H. *The Gifting of God: A Trinitarian Ethics of Excess.* New York: Oxford University Press, 1996.

Wei-Ming, Tu. *Confucian Thought: Selfhood as Creative Transformation.* Albany: SUNY Press, 1985.

Weil, Simone. *On Science, Necessity, and the Love of God.* R. Rees, trans. and ed. New York: Oxford University Press, 1968.

Welch, Sharon. "Dismantling Racism: Strategies for Cultural, Political, and Spiritual Transformation," *Theology and the Interhuman,* 228–43. R. Williams, ed. Valley Forge, Pa.: Trinity Press International, 1995.

———. *A Feminist Ethic of Risk.* Minneapolis: Fortress, 1990.

Welker, Michael. *God the Spirit.* J. F. Hoffmeyer, trans. Minneapolis: Fortress, 1994.

———. "What Is Creation? Rereading Genesis 1 and 2," *Theology Today* 48 (1991–1992): 56–71.

West, Cornel. *Prophetic Fragments.* Grand Rapids: Eerdmans, 1988.

———. *The American Evasion of Philosophy: A Genealogy of Pragmatism.* Madison: University of Wisconsin Press, 1989.

———. *Race Matters.* Boston: Beacon, 1993.

West, Thomas H. *Ultimate Hope without God: The Atheistic Eschatology of Ernst Bloch.* New York: Peter Lang, 1991.

Westermann, Claus. *Blessing in the Bible and in the Life of the Church.* K. Crim, trans. Philadelphia: Fortress, 1978.

———. *Creation.* J. J. Scullion, trans. Philadelphia: Fortress, 1974.

———. *Elements of Old Testament Theology.* Louisville: John Knox, 1982.

Westhelle, Vitor. "Luther and Liberation, or Doing Theology from the Left (Hand of God)." Unpublished paper.

Westphal, Merold. "Nietzsche as a Theological Resource," *Papers of the Nineteenth Century Theological Group,* 164–80. American Academy of Religion, 1995.

———. *Suspicion and Faith: The Religious Uses of Modern Atheism.* Grand Rapids: Eerdmans, 1993.

White, Lynn, "The Historic Roots of Our Ecological Crisis," *Science* 155 (1967): 1203–7.

Whitehead, Alfred North. *Adventures of Ideas.* New York: Macmillan, 1933.

———. *The Concept of Nature.* Cambridge: Cambridge University Press, 1920; Ann Arbor: University of Michigan Press, 1957.

———. *The Function of Reason.* New York: Free Press, 1967.

———. *Modes of Thought.* New York: Free Press, 1938, 1966.

———. *Process and Reality: An Essay in Cosmology.* Corrected ed. by D. R. Griffin and D. Sherburne. New York: Free Press, 1978.

Whyte, David. *The Heart Aroused: Poetry and the Preservation of the Soul in Corporate America.* New York: Doubleday, 1994.

Wicken, Jeffrey. *Evolution, Thermodynamics, and Information: Extending the Darwinian Program.* New York: Oxford University Press, 1987.

――――. "Theology and Science in the Evolving Cosmos: A Need for Dialogue," *Zygon* 23, no. 1 (March 1988): 45–55.

Wiesel, Elie. *Night.* S. Rodway, trans. New York: Bantam, 1960, 1986.

Williamson, Clark. *A Guest in the House of Israel.* Louisville: Westminster/ John Knox, 1993.

Wingren, Gustaf. *Creation and Gospel.* Introduction and bibliography by H. Vander Goot. New York: Edward Mellen, 1979.

――――. *Creation and Law.* R. Mackenzie, trans. Philadelphia: Muhlenberg, 1961.

――――. *Credo: The Christian View of Faith and Life.* E. M. Carlson, trans. Minneapolis: Augsburg, 1981.

――――. *Gospel and Church.* R. Mackenzie, trans. Edinburgh: Oliver & Boyd, 1964.

――――. *Luther on Vocation.* C. C. Rasmussen, trans. Philadelphia: Muhlenberg, 1957.

――――. *Man and the Incarnation.* R. Mackenzie, trans. Philadelphia: Muhlenberg, 1959.

Wink, Walter. *Engaging the Powers: Discernment and Resistance in a World of Domination.* Minneapolis: Fortress, 1992.

Winner, Langdon. *The Whale and the Reactor.* Chicago: University of Chicago Press, 1986.

Winnicott, Donald W. *Home Is Where We Start From.* New York: Norton, 1986.

――――. *The Maturational Processes and the Facilitating Environment.* New York: International Universities Press, 1965.

――――. *Playing and Reality.* New York: Basic Books, 1971.

Winquist, Charles. "Theology, Deconstruction, and Ritual Process," *Zygon* 18, no. 3 (September 1983): 295–309.

Wittgenstein, Ludwig. *Culture and Value.* P. Winch, trans. G. H. von Wright, ed. Chicago: University of Chicago Press, 1980.

Wuthnow, Robert, ed. *"I Come Away Stronger": How Small Groups Are Shaping American Religion.* Grand Rapids: Eerdmans, 1994.

――――. *Sharing the Journey: Support Groups and America's New Quest for Community.* New York: Free Press, 1994.

Wyschogrod, Edith. *Saints and Postmodernism: Revisioning Moral Philosophy.* Chicago: University of Chicago Press, 1990.

Yankelovich, Daniel. "Trends in American Cultural Values," *Criterion* 35, no. 3 (autumn 1996): 2–9.

Yeats, W. B. "The Second Coming." *The Collected Poems of W. B. Yeats.* New York: Macmillan, 1956.

Index

relational constitution
of spacetime, 89–90
scientific revolutions,
85–86
space exploration, 9, 140
technology, 9–10
See also entropy, evolution
self
becoming and being,
42, 67
Cartesian, 4, 6
consciousness, 44
depression, 54–55
dizziness, 43
emergent structure, 71
genes and memes, 44
irritability, 47
memory, 84
openness of, 46
as plant, 46
possibility, 43, 69
relationality, 70, 90–91
saints, 68, 190 n.27
self-definition, 3–4, 135
self-transcendence, 79
self-withdrawal, 76
shame: discretionary;
disgrace, 60, 70, 94
sin and
defiance, 51
denigration, 31
as synthesis, 43
temporality, 43
unification, 69
vulnerability, 47, 52, 94
will, 51, 53
See also human
silence, 62, 131
sin
fall, 20, 50, 99
original, 94
pride, 51–53
rebellion, 51

self-denigration, 53, 74
sins of strength, 53,
74–75
sins of weakness, 53,
74–75
suffering of God,
111–13
violence; origin in vio-
lence, 50
will to harm, 51, 54
Soelle, Dorothee, 125,
131, 144 n.1, 164 n.68,
187 n.115, 194 n.78
soteriology, 124.
See also Christology;
God; Jesus; salvation
Sponheim, Paul R., 151
n.62, 156 n.51, 161
n.41, 165 n.79, 167
n.108, 174 n.72, 176
n.1, 181 n.63, 191,
n.44, 195 n.86
story, 81, 117, 129
Christian story, 87
and meaning, 81
Styron, William, 53, 63,
167 n.98
Suchocki, Marjorie, 156
n.60, 172 n.47, 176
n.86
suffering
denial of, 125
of God; of Christ,
125–26

Taylor, Mark C., 66–67,
128, 146 n.21, 167
n.104, 172 n.50, 186
n.107, 190 n.27, 193
n.63
technology
"device paradigm," 148
n.38
information, 140

"lightness of being," 10,
148 n.37
See also communication,
science
temporality, 6, 78, 108,
120–21, 139
becoming, 42
contingency, 46–47
creativity, 121
God, 95
history, 34, 121
irreversibility, 121
millenium, 120
narrative, story, 81
See also future; middle,
past; present
theodicy, 22–25, 153
n.16
theology
apologetics, dogmatics,
129
claiming and testing
tradition, 123
cross, 75–76, 86, 107
dogma as eschatological
goal, 122–23
and masochism, 74–76
theological speech in
the public square,
136–37
wisdom, 106
Tillich, Paul, 151 n.20,
164 n.73, 193 n.64
time, 40, 81, 128
See also future, past, present, temporality
Tracy, David, 49, 59, 165
n.85, 168 n.1
tradition, 122–23, 130
Trigo, Pedro, 20, 39, 157
n.70
Trinity, 37, 80, 95, 97
See also God
truth, 83–87